Also by Robin Wright

Sacred Rage: The Wrath of Militant Islam
In the Name of God: The Khomeini Decade

Also by Doyle McManus

Landslide: The Unmaking of the President, 1984–1988
(with Jane Mayer)
Free at Last

Flashpoints

FLASHPOINTS
Promise and Peril in a New World

Robin Wright
and Doyle McManus

Fawcett Columbine · New York

A Fawcett Columbine Book
Published by Ballantine Books

Copyright © 1991 by Robin Wright and Doyle McManus

All rights reserved under International and Pan-American Copyright Conventions. Published in the United States by Ballantine Books, a division of Random House, Inc., New York, and simultaneously in Canada by Random House of Canada Limited, Toronto. Originally published in somewhat different form by Alfred A. Knopf, Inc. in 1991.

Library of Congress Catalog Card Number: 92-90391

ISBN: 0-449-90673-6

Cover design by Dale Fiorillo
Cover photograph: Masterfile

Manufactured in the United States of America

First Ballantine Books Edition: January 1993

10 9 8 7 6 5 4 3 2 1

To the next generation:

Alexandra, Cameron,

Johanna, Rosemary and Rachelle

Contents

Flashpoints

Prologue: The Dawn of a New Era

"Change is not made without inconvenience,
even from worse to better."
—RICHARD HOOKER

"I think we are at an historic transition period in world history. The postwar world is collapsing," Brent Scowcroft mused during an interview in the summer of 1989. We were sitting in the national security adviser's White House office for one of those background briefings that anonymous "Administration officials" give journalists before a major event. On this occasion, it was the eve of President Bush's first trip to Eastern Europe— and, as it turned out, the eve of a series of events, then just weeks away, that proved Scowcroft more prescient than any of us realized.

"Our strategy for the world—which has been to build up our allies, help the Third World transition to independence, set in place an international economic and monetary system and hold back the Soviet Union—we've done all those things and done them very well," he continued. "The world is different now. The Soviet Union is changing rapidly. Our allies are now strong. The Third World has massive problems, but they're very different from the problems of coming out of colonialism. So what we're seeing is that now we've got to look ahead . . . and try and figure out how to anticipate what might change."

Scowcroft had proffered a tempting challenge, we reflected as we left the White House and strolled up Pennsylvania Avenue. As foreign correspondents, we had witnessed many of the most dramatic upheavals of the postwar era. But as the Cold War's end shifted the basic factors in world politics like tectonic plates, this round of change was different. The way to understand the full dimensions and impact of the transformation, we decided, was to go out and see what was happening for ourselves.

Two years and six continents later, the result is this book. From Moscow to Johannesburg, from the glass towers of Tokyo to the ancient villages beyond the Hindu Kush, in conversations with presidents and guerrillas, tycoons and laborers, pundits and poets, we journeyed in search of events and people to help explain the larger patterns of the future. When we began, the Soviet Union was still intact, Germany was divided, communism ruled in Eastern Europe, apartheid held sway in South Africa, and Iraq had warm relations with the United States. Like everyone else, we were unprepared for the scope and suddenness of change during our journey through the midst of history.

On our separate travels to corners of the globe both familiar and far-flung, we lit a candle of freedom at Wenceslas Square in Prague, after Czechoslovakia's "velvet revolution." In Berlin, we watched the destruction of the Wall from the once-forbidding eastern side of Checkpoint Charlie, dined in East Germany's parliament in the corner chair reserved for thirteen years for deposed Communist Party chief Erich Honecker, and got lost with an East Berlin taxi driver on his first trip to the West.

In Moscow, we sat in a smoke-filled conference room with a council of brawny Russian coal miners struggling with the newfound challenge of organizing a democratic trade union. In Soviet Central Asia, we found Muslim mullahs and Uzbek folksingers rejoicing in the sudden freedom to revive the centuries-old traditions of their faith and culture. In South Korea and Thailand, at noisy shipyards and bustling construction sites and improbably glittering shopping malls, we saw energetic people lifting whole societies out of poverty through imagination and hard work.

Some of our journeys were to places we had known as foreign correspondents. Going back, we experienced moments of emotion, even awed disbelief. In the Soviet Union and Eastern Europe, we found old friends, who once talked to us furtively, overwhelmed by the new freedoms to talk openly, to express dissent, to join opposition parties—or even to form them. In Soweto, where we had been tear-gassed alongside South African schoolchildren fourteen years earlier, during the first mass black uprising, we witnessed the first stages in the dismantling of apartheid from the lawn of Nelson Mandela's home—a block from where the uprising began. In neighboring Mozambique, where we had covered the birth of one of Africa's most fervently socialist regimes in 1975, we returned in 1990 to find cabinet ministers engrossed in writing a new constitution—this one introducing a multiparty system and ending Marxist rule.

In Latin America, where we had covered the 1973 Chilean coup that brought to power yet another right-wing dictator, General Augusto Pinochet, we sampled the vibrant political life of a continent entirely democratic for the first time. In the Middle East, we tracked the impact of elections bringing pluralism—in some cases slowly, in others almost overnight—to regimes as diverse as the conservative kingdom of Jordan and socialist Algeria.

There was much to celebrate. The end of the Cold War had plunged mankind into a period of change so pervasive that a half-century's assumptions about the shape of the world were suddenly obsolete. Almost overnight, old tyrannies dissolved and new vistas of freedom opened; the threat of a nuclear war that could destroy civilization receded, giving way to hopes of the world's first pervasive peace. But the tumultuous changes represented not only the realization of ideals fostered during four decades of Cold War. They also appeared to ensure fulfillment of two centuries of revolutionary dreams.

First, the most abhorrent ideologies—ranging from military authoritarianism to Marxism and apartheid—were finally succumbing to the universal cry for universal rights from Santiago to Moscow and Cape Town. The premises of the Age of Reason were, at long last, being accepted.

Second, empowerment of the individual, as originally promised by the Enlightenment, was finally making its way down to the common man—and woman—in the poorest and least developed parts of the world. The world's last serfs, at least in principle, were being liberated; the last empires were on the verge of formal collapse.

Third, the progress of the Scientific Era had given mankind unprecedented knowledge and control of everything from space exploration and genetic engineering to the artificial intelligence of computers. Mankind no longer needed to depend on myths for sustenance or answers.

For a few glorious months we, like everyone else, hoped that the world was on a fast track to peace and harmony, that a single universal form of democracy and free enterprise was being embraced on every continent. One prominent American analyst even declared that mankind had reached the "end of history."

For all the promise of a new era, however, the historic evolution seemed, rather abruptly, to take a wrong turn. In many parts of the world, the good news at the end of the 1980s was countered by bad news at the beginning of the 1990s. Signs of hope were matched by unanticipated events, spawning anxiety and fear—often at an astonishing pace. The much-heralded "new world order" was more often than not characterized by new global disorder. Far from a halcyon new dawn, the transition to a new era brought one unexpected nightmare after another.

In our travels, we watched the global dream unravel before our eyes. After an abortive coup, the Soviet empire was dismembered, and its disparate parts went begging for aid. In South Africa, the end of apartheid was stalled by brutal new violence. Worldwide, talk of a peace dividend was stilled by a bloody war in the Persian Gulf.

In Yugoslavia, the one corner of Eastern Europe that managed to keep its borders and its politics open to the West during four decades of communist rule, we witnessed a modern nation-state begin to disintegrate as republics moved to secede. In India, we rose before dawn to watch a military drill by henchmen of a militant Hindu order challenging the secular foundation of the world's largest democracy, then met in secret with Kashmiri Muslim rebels whose insurgency threatened a new war in the subcontinent.

In the capitals of Peru and Mozambique, we spent nights in shanty-towns amidst the crushing poverty and ever-growing populations that, together, threatened the countries' transitions to democracy. In former Soviet Central Asia, we were detained by police who were keeping tabs on leaders of Uzbekistan's democracy movement—and trying desperately to maintain the last bastions of communist rule.

In Zimbabwe, where we had covered the country's struggle to survive years of civil war, international isolation and economic sanctions in the 1970s, we went back in the 1990s to find that the biggest threat of the century is instead going to be a disease—AIDS. And in the developed world—from the United States to Western Europe and Japan, the core of the Cold War alliance—we found pervasive confusion and anxiety about what the new phase of history might bring, as well as the first signs of a new global rivalry.

At every stop, the change we chronicled became as confounding, even frightening, as it was stunning. Part of it was natural. Transitions from one era to another have historically been troubled times, and this one quickly demonstrated that it would be no exception. The final ten years of the second millennium would be just as messy and uncomfortable as earlier periods of rapid change—and maybe even more globally disorienting because of the modern world's interdependency.

But part of it also is a trademark of the new era. Underneath what appeared to be the gathering clouds of chaos, we discovered patterns, even logic—albeit unconventional and even contradictory. Indeed, what most distinguishes the approaching age from the Modern Era is its direction: history is no longer moving on a simple linear course.

The dominant characteristic of the new era—and the transition to it—is likely to be paradox: powerful currents surging in different, even occasionally opposite, directions. The world is simultaneously rushing forward, toward a potential golden age of global unity, and backward, toward a new dark era of fragmentation. At the end of the twentieth century, the hopeful prospects of political integration are countered by the equally potent forces of disintegration over economic rivalries and age-old social differences.

What is going on? Much more than simply the end of the Cold War. "Start with the recognition that something profound has happened," former secretary of state George P. Shultz said as we talked late one afternoon in the sun-dappled quiet of Stanford University's campus. "This is a new epoch. That doesn't mean everything is different—but it means all the important things are different."

By some reckonings, almost five hundred years have passed since mankind experienced anything comparable. The last time was the onset of what historians traditionally call the Modern Era: the ventures of Christopher Columbus and other great geographic explorations, the amalgamation of Europe's parochial fiefdoms into the precursors of modern states and empires, and the first fragile links of communications among distant continents.

From the late fifteenth century until the late twentieth, the quest for power in the Modern Era revolved around the competition among nation-states for territory and markets on new frontiers. Its economics centered on man's race to claim land, exploit resources and extract profit. And its politics culminated in two centuries of struggle between authoritarian rule and democracy in the newly man-centered universe.

For most of that period, Europe dominated. It reached out and colonized on five continents, tying the world together for the first time. Its value system—the Enlightenment's secular creed of rationalism and individualism—was the model for modern ideologies. Its industrialization established the pattern of modern development. Even its languages prevailed. Somewhere between the twentieth century's two world wars, Europe lost the edge to America as its three forces of conquest—territorial, ideological and industrial—petered out. But, still, the West was in control.

How do we know we're approaching a new era? Because the premises of the Modern Age are all either being challenged or replaced.

Five centuries after Columbus, the last earthly frontiers have been erased; if any "new worlds" are to be populated, they will be on other planets. The Industrial Revolution has been replaced by the Technology Revolution; progress now depends far more on science, information and innovation than on iron ore, chemicals or control of land. Even more fundamental, however, are a series of political, economic and social shifts:

Global interdependence and technological prowess have created new equations of power, based more on economic strength than on military muscle or territorial size. As a result, the age of superpowers is over. In its place is a multipolar world in which, for the first time, no single nation or region is sufficiently dominant in all of the four elements—military might, economic superiority, political leadership and social cohesion—required for conquest and long-term domination. The diffusion of power to disparate corners of the world is, in turn, shifting the world's divide to a new set of economic blocs. The end of the East–West conflict is shifting the line of tension to the rich North and a South virtually left behind.

In the realm of ideology, Marxism collapsed almost overnight after decades of aggressive expansion; fascism foundered. But democracy, unable to deliver quickly on its promises of a better life, also faced bracing new challenges in the scarred societies of Eastern Europe, Asia's semifeudal villages and the slums of Latin America. Economic turmoil raised serious questions about whether democracy could survive everywhere, at least in any recognizable form; historically, it has endured mainly in countries where the majority live above the poverty line. In a world no longer dominated exclusively by Europe or America, new ideas and ideologies are instead coming from a dazzling variety of grass-roots groups rather than from Washington or Westminster. Traditional leadership elites are being replaced by unfamiliar faces and political outsiders.

The last great empires of the Modern Age are crumbling, too cumbersome to be viable. Even the nation-state, the most important institution of the past five centuries, is losing its primacy. Modern countries are being pulled in contradictory directions: disintegration into smaller and more homogeneous ethnic or national communities and integration into larger and more economically viable regional blocs.

Warfare, which in the Modern Age usually pitted country against country over ideology or territory, is increasingly erupting within societies over issues of identity and alignment. Traditional powers have diminishing control over either unraveling nation-states or, as their monopolies on technology and advanced armaments are broken, over the path and pace of internal strife.

Cities—for millennia, centers of progress—are becoming overpopulated hubs of poverty and urban migration, reflecting societies' ills rather than their strengths. "Informal" sectors are replacing planned growth with their own unregulated alternatives in housing, employment and social services—and, in the process, creating de facto states-within-states, challenging traditional sources of authority. The mass migration of mankind, both internal and international, is in turn spawning chauvinism and racism in the form of a new "nativism."

The trends are, indeed, sobering. To venture out into the world at the end of the twentieth century is to discover a new crisis every day. Some of the paradoxes are a function of the transition; they represent as much a reaction to modernism as a guide to the future. Mankind may have gone too far in defining life and its goals strictly in terms of reason, secular individualism and science at the expense of primordial values, traditions and needs. The next phase in world history may well be marked by a cathartic backlash against rationalism and secularism.

It will not, however, result in the abandonment of rationalism. Indeed, not all the emerging trends will survive. Some can be countered by policy shifts; the intensity of others may wane with time. In other words, the lessons of history, particularly the Enlightenment's legacy, are not lost. Throughout the tumultuous changes ahead, the ideas of freedom that flowered in the Modern Era will remain the primary sources of inspiration. On the eve of the twenty-first century, Russian coal miners and peasants on Nepalese rice plantations, blacks in South Africa's ghettos and laborers in Peru's barrios understand that they now have—or deserve—rights in controlling their own and their communities' destinies. The message has penetrated to earth's every corner.

The struggles into the twenty-first century will be attempting, under vastly different conditions, to implement those rights, to change systems to equalize and meet expectations while, at the same time, preserving disparate traditions and sources of identity. The transition to a new era will be marked by adaptation, expansion and diversification of modern history's lessons. In many ways, it will represent both the Enlightenment's triumph and its greatest challenge.

The dawn of the postmodern world is the first truly global phase in the first truly global age. Until recently, there was not one world, but many relatively self-contained worlds marked largely by continental and cultural divides: East and West, North or South. Mankind's small planet became one "world" only in the twentieth century, in the scope of two wars as well as the founding of two international bodies to promote peace, in economic interplay and in diseases, in social trends—from music to fashion—as well as in environmental impact. And above all, of course, in communications.

Only a century ago, the map of Africa was still being drawn for the first time by explorers who were "discovering" the interior of what was then called the Dark Continent. In 1871, when American journalist Henry

Morton Stanley traversed unknown lands to find the British missionary and explorer David Livingstone, his dispatches chronicling the land and peoples unknown to the rest of the world took months to reach New York.

Today, in Zambia, where both Livingstone and Stanley explored, the television studios in downtown Lusaka beam images in and out of the central African nation daily by satellite. The outside world is within a second's reach. Among the programs aired weekly, in villages that had no contact with foreign cultures until a few decades ago, are American fantasy-dramas and adventure series like "Beauty and the Beast" and "MacGyver," Australian mini-series and British sports matches.

The world took on literal new meaning, most of all, because of access. The last "lost" tribes have been found; every corner of the earth has been charted. The globe is no longer just a colorized orb spinning on a wooden frame in the classroom or family library; new technology has converted the distant and the abstract into an intimate reality. By 1990, CNN, the first global television network, aired in Prague on televisions suspended from the airport ceiling and in remote Amazon villages with satellite dishes. Video technology, reaching virtually every country, linked up disparate cultures.

Along the way, a new set of images and expectations is uniting the globe. The evolution is as stunning in import as was the signal progress of Mesopotamia, the world's first empire, in bringing together diverse peoples under common laws and culture for the first time during the rule of Sargon, the self-anointed "king of the four corners," three thousand years before Christ.

Yet, in this era of paradox, the greatest contradiction—as well as the single most consistent source of tension—is man's inability, or unwillingness, to act globally, to transcend the narrow loyalties of village, clan or sect. Indeed, as access to other cultures, religions and races increases, the gap among peoples often seems to widen, rather than narrow. Although the same changes are being felt at the same time around the world, thanks to instant communications, mankind's ability to change has outpaced man's ability to understand.

Instead of using the new information technology "to open up communication between men of different ideologies, different colors, different religions," Zambian President Kenneth Kaunda reflected, "we are using this science and technology to bring out a world that is very confrontational. . . . Unless the approach changes from one of confrontation to a genuine desire for peace and not scoring points off each other, then mankind has no chance at all."[1] Rather than bringing diverse peoples together, globalization of communications has only widened the divide by accentuating man's differences.

The "global village" first described in the 1960s is turning out, instead, to be many different villages—some global, others stubbornly parochial. The new era is both the first global age and an age of galloping localism. Indeed, the same communications networks that were supposed to create a single global village now serve the purposes of separatism as well as integration. Immigrants in the United States who once learned English from radio and television can now watch television in Spanish, Chinese, Korean or Persian. Separatists in Yugoslavia and the former Soviet republics gained ground by starting their own radio and television services.

The ultimate paradox of the postmodern era is that man's new ability to link the world's six inhabited continents—to globalize—has outstripped his ability to understand his new global neighbors. Unless that gap is closed, the potential offered by the prospect of new freedoms, recognition of universal human rights, and technological miracles may result in promises wasted, perils ensured.

The past century has been at once the most triumphant and the most destructive in human history—a time of both pitiless wars and unprecedented economic progress. The next century will be no less challenging, if in different ways. Throughout history, man has been buffeted worst by change when he was unable to understand what was before him. When Columbus returned to Spain five centuries ago, he believed that he had found the Indies; he did not understand that he had discovered an entire hemisphere and helped to invent the modern world.

We also may need time to explore before we know exactly where we are. But we have an important advantage over earlier eras: Because of instant communications and worldwide access, we can, if we choose, identify and deal with the issues, challenges and flashpoints of a new era as they emerge. The first generation with the ability to see global change as it occurs now has a unique opportunity to shape and direct the future.

Reshaping World Power

"To complain of the age we live in, to murmur at the present possessors of power, to lament the past, to conceive extravagant hopes of the future, are the common dispositions of the greatest part of mankind."

—EDMUND BURKE

In the autumn of 1990, the American secretary of state, James A. Baker III, set off on an unprecedented mission to ask the king of Saudi Arabia and other foreign leaders for billions of dollars to pay for a U.S.-led military expedition against Iraq. Reporters on Baker's Air Force plane presented him with a tin cup inscribed "Nothing Less Than a Billion, Please," which the secretary of state accepted with the thinnest of smiles. He did not need reminding that the United States, the most powerful nation on earth, was begging for the wherewithal to work its will.

That same month, in the ornate reception room of a glittering new Moscow hotel, Soviet Foreign Minister Eduard A. Shevardnadze signed a treaty promising to withdraw the Red Army from Germany. His signature ended forty-five years of Soviet occupation of Central Europe, the final vestige of World War II. In return, the German government promised to pay ten billion dollars toward the care and feeding of its last Soviet "occupiers," some of whom had been reduced to foraging in garbage dumps and selling their rifles, uniforms and medals for pocket money.

The age of the superpowers is over. For almost half a century, the United States and the Soviet Union had divided the world between them, but by 1990, neither wanted to pay the bills for its own military commitments. The Soviet Union, a disintegrating empire in the throes of revolution, could not house its own army officers, much less launch costly adventures abroad. The Central Intelligence Agency estimated that the Soviet economy would shrink in 1991 by at least 10 percent and perhaps by a staggering 30 percent—numbers that signaled an economic collapse with tragic human consequences. The once-mighty Kremlin was publicly grateful for economic aid from China and food shipments from Germany; some of the food, ironically, came from supplies once stockpiled in West Berlin for fear of a Soviet invasion.[1]

The United States faced a more subtle dilemma. America's combination of military might, economic muscle and political sway was still unmatched. But the crisis in the Persian Gulf revealed a striking paradox: never before in the twentieth century had Washington's leadership been so universally accepted, yet never before had its freedom to flex its muscles been so circumscribed, so dependent on the political and economic support of allies. Earlier American presidents were able to send massive forces into combat at their own discretion. By 1991, George Bush needed international backing—money from Saudi Arabia and Kuwait, troops from Britain, France and Egypt, legal authority from the United Nations—if only to satisfy domestic demands. After the war, when Bush tried to interest his Middle Eastern allies in broader peace negotiations, he found them less interested in American diplomacy than they had been in American protection.

The end of the Cold War, it turned out, meant much more than just a reprieve from the danger of nuclear Armageddon. The sudden collapse of communism that culminated in the 1991 Soviet revolution coincided with a global surge of economic and technological change. Together, those transformations altered the premises of world politics: the shape of the playing field, the number of players and the rules of the game. The result was a global power shift that touched not only the old superpowers but every country on the planet, for it changed not only the distribution of influence among countries but also the ways countries, alliances, trade blocs, corporations and even ethnic groups defined, acquired and used power.

A new, more complicated world system has replaced the old East-West standoff. The new dynamic of power is still evolving, but it centers more on economic prowess than on military muscle. It scatters influence widely instead of concentrating it in the hands of a few. It is changing the reasons nations collide and the kinds of wars they fight.

This changing dynamic of power transformed the United States and Russia from enemies into virtual allies, and the United States and Japan from allies into increasingly bitter adversaries. It made international economic arrangements like the European Community and a proposed U.S.–Mexico trade pact into major, dramatic issues in international affairs, where they once would have been consigned to the obscurity of commercial negotiations. It made the underdeveloped countries of the Third World more vulnerable, more neglected—and, in some ways, more dangerous.

World power has changed in three important ways:

First, economic power has become more important than military power; gross national product has become a better measure of international influence than numbers of tanks, aircraft and troops. The history of the past five centuries has been dominated largely by struggles between nations for military and political superiority; empires from Rome to Britain enriched themselves through conquest. But by 1990, the first priority for every government was that of acquiring customers, not client-states; military conquest became a losing proposition. With almost four million men under arms, the Soviet Union still fielded the largest army on earth, but economic weakness made it unable to control events even within its own borders. By contrast, a growing number of the world's most successful nations boasted of minimal military forces. Japan, the most extreme case, maintained armed forces of only 247,000.

Second, power has become more widely diffused than ever before. Instead of two dominant superpowers, the major political and economic players at the beginning of the 1990s were at least four and possibly five "great" powers—the United States, Russia, the European Community, Japan and perhaps China. The decentralization of power appeared likely to continue; many lesser powers were coming onto the field as full-fledged competitors, from regional military actors, like India, Iraq and Iran, to dynamic new economic powers, like South Korea and Taiwan. Moreover, the diffusion of power has extended beyond national governments; thousands of other institutions have begun to operate on a global scale, from regional trading blocs to multinational corporations.

Third, the redistribution of power has spawned not harmony but a new kind of instability; the diffusion of influence has created a diffusion of threats. The world was safer from the threat of a catastrophic nuclear war, but the end of the Cold War made smaller "hot wars" more likely—and an economic cold war between the United States and its allies quite possible. The elaborate U.S.-Soviet security safeguards of the nuclear age, from the Washington-Moscow "hot line" to formal confidence-building measures, had succeeded at their task of preventing all-out war, but they were of little use in resolving economic disputes between Iraq and Kuwait—or between the United States and Japan. In the world of the nuclear superpowers, as Winston Churchill said at the onset of the Cold War, safety was "the sturdy child of terror." As the terror diminished, so did the safety.[2]

The age of the superpowers ended in part because the kind of power they possessed—the power that made them "super"—gradually became less important. Their huge arsenals of nuclear weapons, the main index of power during the Cold War, turned out to be almost entirely useless, even for generating political pressure. The last time nuclear saber-rattling clearly worked was during the Cuban missile crisis of 1962. Nuclear weapons did not help the Soviet Union in its losing war in Afghanistan in the 1980s, or the United States in Vietnam a decade earlier. The superpowers' large conventional armies were more useful but still constituted a major drain on their economies. Finally, once the Soviet Union abandoned its messianic form of communism, the superpowers' Cold War mission of leading opposing "camps" in a global ideological confrontation was suddenly obsolete.[3]

Even before those events, political leaders and ordinary citizens in both the United States and the Soviet Union began to regard their nations' superpower status as much a burden as an asset. They noticed all too clearly that Japan and Germany, the nations they defeated in World War II, had outstripped them economically, while spending less on defense. During the 1980s the United States spent about 7 percent of its gross national product on defense; the Soviet Union spent 20 percent or more; Germany spent less than 3 percent and Japan spent only 1 percent. The countries that spent least on defense enjoyed the greatest economic growth. Military power, once considered an essential source and guarantor of commercial power, no longer had any clear connection to economic success.[4]

The main reason for this disconnection was the evolution of postindustrial economies. In the Middle Ages, kings and emperors derived their wealth from land, for food and minerals were the essential commodities of the day. In the Modern Era, the great powers' competition for colonies was still driven by the desire for territory and its riches—from the gold Spain sought in Mexico in 1519 to the coal and iron Japan seized in Manchuria in 1931. But in a postindustrial age, coal, iron and steel are no longer critical elements of economic success; technology, information and communications are. Territorial expansion and empire-building have become irrelevant, at best; raw materials and cheap labor can be obtained with less trouble on the open market.

The end of the link between economic power and military power was a major reason Soviet President Mikhail S. Gorbachev meekly withdrew the Red Army from East Germany; what Gorbachev needed was not control of German territory, but German financial aid and investment. Once the Warsaw Pact crumbled, the Soviet Union happily abrogated the deals under which it had sold oil to its satellites at an artificially low price and began selling oil on the world market. By 1991, Gorbachev was negotiating the details of his economic reform program with Western economic powers and publicly pleading for a hundred billion dollars in aid. If catching up with the West required a more open political and economic system at home, he was willing to try—even though it eventually led to his own downfall. Economic necessity superseded ideology.

At the other end of the spectrum, international economic competition also eroded authoritarian rule in capitalist South Africa. The businessmen of Johannesburg could no longer afford the isolation brought on by apartheid (ironically, the Afrikaans word for separateness); they could see that their future lay in linking up with the world economy. In the 1980s, international sanctions and internal instability turned South Africa from a magnet for foreign investment into a country suffering from net capital outflow; billions of dollars were leaving the country in white "flight capital" and in debt repayment to foreign banks. According to one estimate, the South African economy could have grown at least 20 percent larger had it not been for its international isolation.[5]

As the 1990s began, South Africa and the Soviet Union, once fortresses of immutable and opposing ideologies, were frantically making deals with each other. The Soviet government agreed to market its diamonds exclusively through South Africa's De Beers for a credit of a billion dollars, and formal diplomatic relations soon followed the money.

The crucial new fact of economic life, and the force that spurred these changes, was globalization. Money, goods, information and know-how all moved across borders more freely than ever before, often at astonishing speed. The expansion of global trade in goods, from Toyota automobiles to Perrier water, has become a familiar fact of life in only the last generation. Yet far more important was the explosive growth of cross-border capital flows, which were more than three hundred times as large as the trade in goods and services. Twenty-four-hour electronic links transformed national stock markets into a single, unceasing global exchange. By 1989, one of every seven transactions on the world's major stock markets involved foreign investors—not only Japanese or British investors buying equity in America but Americans investing in Europe and Japan as well—and the "foreign" share of transactions was increasing by as much as 20 percent a year.[6]

By the end of 1990, foreign investment in the United States totaled more than two trillion dollars, roughly 40 percent the size of the U.S. gross national product. For the first time in living memory—although not for the first time in history—America's economy was directly and clearly affected by the decisions of foreign investors and bankers at the level of everyday life. Prices of luxury homes in Honolulu and Los Angeles were pushed up by buyers from Tokyo and Hong Kong; interest rates in the Midwest rose and fell on decisions made in Germany's central bank. The sinking sensation of economic vulnerability was new to most Americans, but Europeans and Asians, who had known the feeling for decades, were feeling it more intensely as well. The globalization of the world economy made the impersonal, uncontrollable market a gigantic and unpredictable "world power" in its own right.[7]

Some had hoped that the onset of economic interdependence might bring world harmony, as every country saw its interests intertwine with others'. The result was quite the contrary. Increased trade and financial flows made countries more interdependent, but that new intimacy provoked political and cultural backlashes that were the seeds of serious conflict. The new economic competition even came wrapped in the rhetoric of nineteenth-century military conflict. Americans talked about an "invasion" of Japanese capital. French President François Mitterrand devised a perfect mix of the imperial past and the commercial present: "The French must have a conquering mentality," he told his countrymen. "The French must learn to sell."[8]

By 1990, the most important potential conflicts were no longer between East and West, the old dividing line of the Cold War, but between West and West—between former allies—or between the wealthy North and the impoverished South. The friction between Western countries began over mundane trade issues, like the European Community's barriers to American frozen poultry or Japan's ban on foreign rice, but quickly turned into bitter political arguments over fairness and favoritism. During the Persian Gulf War, Americans asked angrily whether the Japanese and Germans were playing them for fools by leaving the burdens of combat to the United States. The United States, Europe and Japan had argued over such questions before, but during the Cold War the disagreements were often papered over in the interest of the common front against the Soviet Union. Now, much of that restraint was gone, and the first signs of a new cold war—this time over economic issues—were already apparent.

At the same time, as economic competition sharpened, the weakest countries of Africa, Asia and Latin America were left farther and farther behind, widening the bitter political and social divides between the prosperous North and the struggling South. In 1978, the U.S. gross domestic product per person was seven times that of neighboring Mexico; by 1988, the ratio had grown to eleven to one.[9] Even Third World countries that expect strong growth in the 1990s, like Thailand and Malaysia, will remain relatively poor—a harsh reality that, thanks to television and travel, was becoming ever clearer to increasing numbers of their citizens. The United Nations has estimated that by the year 2000 countries accounting for 60 percent of the world's population—some three billion people—will still produce an annual per-capita average of about $840, while Americans will produce almost $18,000. That combination of disappointed expectations and heightened awareness of others' wealth can only create tension.[10]

The increase in economic friction around the world came just as the stabilizing effects of the Cold War were melting away. Even parts of the globe that had been tranquil for thirty years were rediscovering old reasons to fight. In Eastern Europe, ancient feuds dormant for two generations suddenly flared anew, from the status of ethnic minorities in Yugoslavia to the placement of Poland's borders—and the economic benefits of damming the Danube between Czechoslovakia and Hungary. In Asia, the U.S.-protected regional balance that allowed Japan and its neighbors to concentrate on economic progress may not survive the century. Both China and North Korea were heading for political crises—China as provincial leaders battled over the pace of economic reform, North Korea as the aging communist autocrat Kim Il Sung approached his end. The combination of economic friction and political instability produced anxiety almost everywhere. "The control that used to be imposed by the Soviet Union and the United States will disappear," warned General Hiroomi Kurisu, a former chairman of Japan's Joint Chiefs of Staff, in his office overlooking the ancient stone walls of the emperor's palace in Tokyo. "The national interests of all countries will come increasingly into conflict."

At first blush, the American military victory in the Persian Gulf in 1991 suggested that the world had entered an age of breathtaking simplicity: there was only one superpower, the United States, which all other countries would be compelled to follow. The reality was more complicated and less reassuring. However brilliant the triumph of American military skill in the battle against Iraq, the first war of the new era revealed the limits of American power as much as its capabilities. It also demonstrated the new ability of smaller powers to frustrate the will of large ones—even if only temporarily.

The American and allied victory on the battlefield was no surprise. The more remarkable fact was Saddam Hussein's ability to give the great powers pause at all. Iraq, with a population smaller than Canada's and a gross national product smaller than Romania's, tied the world in knots for half a year. And when the United States finally did go to war, *The Economist* noted, the victory "took seventy-five percent of America's tactical aircraft and forty percent of its tanks. Some unipolar gunboat."[11]

Moreover, the world had no guarantee that the next crisis would be so clear-cut—or that the United States would be as capable of mobilizing an equally powerful coalition. "Despite the near-unanimity of U.N. decisions, historians will probably treat the Gulf crisis as an unusual set of circumstances that combined to foster consensus," former Secretary of State Henry A. Kissinger warned. "U.S. preeminence cannot last. Had Kuwait been invaded two years later, the decline of the U.S. defense budget would have precluded a massive overseas deployment. Nor can the U.S. economy indefinitely sustain a policy of essentially unilateral global interventionism; indeed, we had to seek a foreign subsidy of at least fifty billion dollars to sustain the Gulf crisis." With American influence so limited, he concluded, "The new world order cannot possibly fulfill [its] idealistic expectations."[12]

Iraq's defiance reflected a major new factor in the uneasy balance of world power: the increasing leverage of the weak. Small countries are no longer as powerless as were the tribal chiefs of Africa or the caciques of Latin America when European adventurers and colonizers landed on their shores. The gap in usable military power between large and small countries has narrowed; after a global boom in arms sales in the 1970s and 1980s, even countries as poor as Mali and Honduras boast of tanks and jet aircraft.

"The ability of outsiders to influence events is generally declining," said Richard Haass, a White House official who helped direct U.S. policy during the Gulf War. "There are simply too many sources of wealth, technology and arms for either the United States or the Soviet Union to be in a position to dictate local decisions. . . . Denial of military or political support is thus a less credible sanction than it was. So too is the threat to intervene."[13]

In Afghanistan, the last proxy war of the East–West confrontation revealed how the sway of both superpowers has diminished. Afghan guerrillas equipped with U.S. weapons and Muslim zeal humiliated the mighty Soviet Army and forced it to withdraw; they then turned on their American benefactors and rejected Washington's advice on a political settlement. Afghanistan, one of the poorest countries on earth, had eluded the control of both superpowers. "We can't deliver our Afghans," confessed a harried U.S. diplomat in the guerrilla capital of Peshawar, "and they can't deliver theirs." Afghanistan was the rule, not the exception; in other regions torn by conflict over the past decade, from Lebanon to Cambodia, the two old superpowers found it increasingly difficult by 1990 to impose peace settlements, even when they acted in concert.

In the heyday of the Cold War, the superpowers relied on foreign military and economic aid to shape the world, but they have lost their preeminence in that field as well. As recently as 1989, the economically strapped Soviet Union still devoted an estimated $7.1 billion to foreign aid; but by 1992, Russia was a recipient of aid, not a donor. The United States has slipped behind both Japan and Europe as a foreign-aid donor; in 1989, U.S. economic aid totaled $7.7 billion, while Japan gave $9 billion and the twelve member states of the European Community provided more than $10 billion.

The result was a palpable loss of influence for both old superpowers on matters large and small. In a minor example of diminished U.S. clout, Republican Senator Mark O. Hatfield of Oregon, the ranking Republican member of the Senate Appropriations Committee, threatened in 1990 to hold up U.S. aid to Malaysia unless the Kuala Lumpur government admitted more refugees from Indochina. According to a Hatfield aide, a Malaysian diplomat retorted, "We might pay attention to such pressure from Japan"—but not, he implied, from the United States.

The decline of superpower clout also opened the way for the emergence of strong "regional powers" whose interests and demands could not be ignored in their own neighborhoods. In the Middle East, Saddam Hussein used his eight-year-long war with Iran to assert a claim to leadership in the Arab world and built gigantic armed forces to back it up; he failed only because he overreached. In South Asia, India has built the fourth-largest army and seventh-largest navy in the world, including aircraft carriers, submarines and amphibious-assault units to assert influence around the Indian Ocean; Indian "peacekeeping troops" spent three years attempting to end a civil war in neighboring Sri Lanka.* India's growing

---

*Iraq boasted the world's fourth-largest army before the Gulf War, but Baghdad's defeat brought the loss of several thousand tanks—and its place in the standings.

reach has in turn provoked worry not only in Pakistan, her traditional enemy, but among strategists in China and Japan who see the Indian navy athwart their strategic shipping routes.

This new, more diverse diffusion of power is an historic shift. A multipolar world is nothing new; it was the pattern of power in Europe from the end of the sixteenth century until World War II. Over time, the lineup of great powers changed—Spain, Austria and France in the sixteenth century; France, the Netherlands and Sweden in the seventeenth; Britain, France, Austria, Prussia and Russia in the nineteenth—but the principle did not. The bipolar world that lasted forty-four years, from 1945 to 1989, was the exception, not the rule. But the multipolar world that began emerging in the 1980s was markedly different from its predecessors, because it included a non-European great power, Japan, and several non-European regional powers.[14]

Unlike the Cold War line-up, this new multipolar balance of power is not going to be predictable. Without a single, unchanging enemy to serve as the focus of joint efforts and define the division of the world, the 1990s may see a constantly shifting series of ad hoc alliances. If North Korea invades South Korea, if India invades Pakistan, or if Romania invades Hungary, new coalitions will form. But few are likely to be as large or as strong as the coalition that supported the United States in the Persian Gulf War, an exercise in collective security that was based as much on a common need for oil as on a new fraternal spirit. Nor will the new alliances be as reliable or durable as the U.S.–European or U.S.–Japan partnerships that were cemented by the Soviet threat. In a more fluid age, today's allies could be tomorrow's adversaries.

"The Iraqi situation . . . called forth an alliance of a certain configuration," noted France's former president, Valéry Giscard d'Estaing, in a long interview in his Paris office. "But if there's a crisis in Central America, the alliance will be of another configuration, and if China falls apart it'll be another." Thus the strange bedfellows of 1990—the United States embracing once-hostile Syria in alliance against Iraq, Poland appealing to the once-hated Soviet Union for help in fixing its border with Germany—were probably only the first of a long series of international one-night stands.

. . .

When the countries of the European Community quietly signed an agreement in 1986 to create a single, integrated market by 1992, the world
hardly noticed. The enterprise seemed quixotic at first. Three of the
twelve member countries—Denmark, Greece and Italy—initially refused
to sign the pact in hopes of winning more concessions. But as 1992 drew
closer and the Europeans carried out the promises they had made, the rest
of the world finally recognized the impact of their project—the birth of
an economic colossus worthy of both emulation and fear, but also the
triumph of a new model of achieving power.

By the beginning of the 1990s, everybody wanted to be part of a
free-trade bloc. Sweden, Austria, Turkey and most of the former Soviet
satellites asked if they could join the European Community; Italy's foreign
minister, Gianni de Michelis, predicted that the community would double in membership to twenty-four by the end of the century. The United
States and Canada concluded a free-trade pact, and Mexico threw aside
its deep-seated fear of American domination to ask if it, too, could join.
Visionaries and politicians proposed free-trade zones for South America,
South Asia and Southern Africa, and for pieces of Eastern Europe and
bits of the Middle East—everything from a "Black Sea Economic Zone"
to a five-nation European pact, led by Italy, called the "Alpen-Adria
Pentagonal."

Beneath the sudden mania for acronyms and trade promotion lay a
fundamental change: The nation-state, the principal power structure of
the past five centuries, was no longer the only important institution on
the international scene. Until now, modern history had centered on the
struggle of national governments to unite divided peoples and extend their
sovereignty over ever-larger areas as the basis of political, economic and
military competition. Most of American history was the saga of thirteen
colonies that set out to tame a continent and create a new nation. From
the sixteenth century to the beginning of the twentieth, the histories of
Britain and France were chronicles of divided kingdoms, which struggled
first to achieve internal unity, then to acquire far-flung colonies. The
modern histories of Germany, Japan and China all centered on battles
over cohesion, state authority and empire.

By 1990, however, many of the same nations were voluntarily surren-
dering some of their hard-won sovereignty to compete for wealth in the

new global economy. In Europe, the most important centers for economic policy-making were no longer Paris or London but Brussels, the seat of the European Community, and Frankfurt, the headquarters of Germany's largely autonomous central bank. Britons, Frenchmen and Germans—peoples who have long gloried in their distinctive nationalities—carried a uniform burgundy passport marked "European Community." And by 1992 the European Community was scheduled to have a common currency, the Ecu, for transactions from Ireland to Crete, its value upheld by a single monetary policy.

The new economic blocs were only the most prominent of many institutions chipping away at the traditional prerogatives of sovereign states. Power was being diffused not just among countries but among thousands of other entities. Some were larger than nation-states, like the European Community; others were smaller, like Sky Television, a satellite broadcasting firm that helped break Europe's national television monopolies by making dozens of channels available to anyone with an inexpensive dish antenna.

George Shultz called the process "the decline of sovereignty." "Borders don't mean what they used to mean," he explained. "Stuff goes across borders without the permission of governments. It didn't used to do so in such quantity: information, ideas, ballistic missiles, drugs, terrorists, people, goods. The concept of absolute sovereignty is long gone. . . . Sovereignty, statehood and the nation may be becoming disentangled in important ways."

In the early 1990s, supranational institutions like the United Nations have already become more intrusive, moving into a broad variety of areas once preserved for national governments. The United States submitted the terms for Iraq's surrender in the Gulf War to the United Nations Security Council and handed the problem of pacifying Kurdish-populated northern Iraq to a U.N. force. In Europe, the 1990 Paris Treaty on conventional armed forces enabled the continent's major powers to inspect each other's military facilities. Globally, the 1990 protocols on chlorofluorocarbons, chemicals that strip ozone from the atmosphere, bound each nation to phase out production under a supranational monitoring committee—the first time individual nations had agreed jointly to end the use of any nonmilitary commodity.

Some of the most dynamic encroachments on old ideas of national sovereignty have come from the rise of multinational corporations, companies that operate in so many countries they can often assert whatever "nationality" suits their purposes and wield power independently of the country of their origin. In 1988, CBS Records asked U.S. trade negotiator Clayton Yeutter to press Japan for tougher copyright regulations to protect American recording rights. The request would have been entirely normal, except that the man who asked Yeutter's help was Akio Morita, the chairman of Japan's giant Sony Corporation, which had just bought the American record company. "Morita said we could put pressure on Tokyo more easily than he could," recalled an astonished U.S. official. Yeutter agreed to press Sony's case as an "American" firm.[15]

Rupert Murdoch's News International Corporation began as an Australian concern, then shifted the focus of its operations to Britain. But after Murdoch bought the Metromedia and Fox television stations in 1985, he became a U.S. citizen and now lives part of the time in Los Angeles. An Australian press baron has become not only an American television magnate but a global media tycoon whose properties have promoted favorite candidates in all three countries.

In 1988, European investors even formed a "company without a country" to attract customers across national lines. European Silicon Structures, incorporated in Luxembourg and headquartered in Germany, built a factory in France and a laboratory in England.[16] Old, well-established firms were also loosening their allegiances in order to go global. Whirlpool Corporation, which began as a U.S. appliance maker, was operating in forty-five countries and employed more foreigners than Americans by 1990. Ford Motor Company has depended on foreign operations for much of its profit; during most of the 1980s, Ford made more money in Europe than in the United States. "The United States does not have an automatic call on our resources," said Cyrill Siewert, chief financial officer of Colgate-Palmolive Corporation, which sells more products abroad than at home. "There is no mindset that puts this country first."[17]

By 1990, Japan's Honda Motors had sold almost twice as many automobiles in the United States as in its native country and appeared to be on the verge of surpassing Chrysler as the third largest "American" auto firm. In Tokyo, IBM Japan, as one of the country's largest computer manufacturers, has asked to be treated as a Japanese company—and Japanese firms with major stakes in America have asked for entry into U.S. research efforts.

As the world economy has become globalized, national governments have also lost power to the market. When markets were predominantly national or local, governments could attempt to regulate or restrict them. But with a single global market, and with money, goods and services moving more rapidly across borders, the balance of power has swung away from governments in the direction of impersonal economic forces.

Once, the U.S. Federal Reserve Board could react to the first signs of a recession by lowering interest rates to stimulate economic activity. By 1990, the Fed felt less free to push interest down, because lower rates could drive away foreign investors on whom the U.S. economy depended. "The Fed used to move, and the world would follow," said Harald Malmgren, a former U.S. trade negotiator, in Washington. "Today it's paralyzed. If we lower interest rates more than a little, the dollar will fall, we'll have rapid inflation and capital will move out of the country. . . . It's no longer possible to manage the dollar as if it were our national currency; it's been internationalized." The only solace was that every other central bank had the same problem.

Likewise, the force of the global market has confounded attempts by the Organization of Petroleum Exporting Countries (OPEC) to manage the world's oil trade. The cartel succeeded in raising prices and restraining its members' production in the mid-1970s, but its success merely stimulated new drilling in Britain, Texas and elsewhere. As late as 1977, OPEC was producing two-thirds of the free world's crude oil—but by 1982, producers outside OPEC had outstripped the cartel. OPEC spent the 1980s struggling to regain control of the market, without much success. In 1990, the cartel produced 39 percent of the world's oil—a healthy share, but not enough to control prices. One result was a long-term decline in prices from an average of thirty-five dollars a barrel in 1981 to seventeen dollars in 1991.[18]

The power of the global market to defeat the concerted efforts of powerful governments could even be seen in the cocaine boom of the 1980s. In the 1970s, U.S. authorities believed that they had established at least a modicum of control over international drug smuggling, but the rapidly expanding market of the "baby-boom" generation sent the drug trade out of control in the early 1980s. With the street price of cocaine in Miami still many times its wholesale price in Colombia, however, stopping the inflow proved impossible.

All these changes in the possession and use of power have made international relations an infinitely more complicated game. "Nation-states have become less important as political units in the sense of being able to control whatever phenomena—economic, social, environmental or technological—take place in the world," said Francisco Sagasti, the World Bank's chief long-range planner. "This is hard to get accustomed to, for all our political systems are geared to focus on the nation-state as the locus of power [and] decision-making, and as the main unit of political, social and economic analysis. We have not learned as yet to live with the fact that those phenomena transcend national boundaries."

The 1990 economic summit meeting of industrial powers in Houston was supposed to have been a grand celebration of Western unity, held in President George Bush's adopted home town at the height of democracy's triumphs in Europe. But by the time the seven leaders had grumbled through three humid July days to an acrimonious conclusion, their meeting had turned into an unintended demonstration of how old allies were heading down diverging new paths. Germany's Chancellor Helmut Kohl announced bluntly that he was sending aid to the Soviet Union, despite misgivings from the United States and Britain. Japan's Prime Minister Toshiki Kaifu then announced that Tokyo was resuming loans to China, despite the objections of the other six leaders. And when Bush asked for a promise from the Europeans to cut farm subsidies, and for a promise from the Japanese to lower market barriers, actions which would enable the United States to export more American agricultural products, Germany and Japan ducked the request—a standoff that led to the temporary collapse of the Uruguay Round, a four-year-old round of global talks on trade liberalization. At summits in earlier years, Harald Malmgren noted, "The agenda of the [allied] leaders would have included a desire to avoid offending the United States too much, because they needed us as a guard dog. Now they don't need the guard dog any more."

West-West conflict may well be the central problem for U.S. foreign policy in the twenty-first century. The decline of the Soviet Union and the new diffusion of power paradoxically turned the victorious allies of the Cold War against each other, at least in economic affairs. During the 1950s and 1960s, the United States often gave its allies the benefit of the doubt on trade issues; a central goal of U.S. policy was to rebuild their economies as bulwarks against Soviet expansion. During the 1970s and 1980s, Japan and Europe sometimes gave the United States the benefit of the doubt, because they needed American goodwill on political and military questions. By 1990, those reasons for flexibility had evaporated on both sides, making normal tensions over trade and finance more difficult to defuse.

As the world's economy became a single global unit, every move toward integration seemed to touch off a backlash of opposite moves toward political or cultural localism. "Very powerful economic forces compel leaders of the business community to think globally and act globally," noted Sony chairman Akio Morita. "Very powerful electoral pressures force the politicians to think primarily in terms of local constituencies. . . . As the international community has become more integrated, those threatened by internationalism have become more nationalistic."[19]

Protectionism was suddenly no longer a dirty word. As the Uruguay Round trade talks headed toward breakdown in 1990, France's agriculture minister unapologetically declared himself opposed to imports. "I don't want a future of eating cornflakes in a Japanese car," he said. In Japan, newspaper columns and television talk shows bristled with complaints about America's "Japan bashing" and pressure on trade. In the United States, Democrats said they planned to make unfair trade restrictions a central issue in the 1992 presidential campaign. "There is no use hiding any more. . . . I'm a protectionist," Chrysler chairman Lee A. Iacocca wrote. "Those who say that protectionists have their heads buried in the sand have it exactly backwards. The real ostriches are those who believe we can survive economically by simply ignoring those who target our market while protecting their own."[20]

The United States, Europe and Japan, the "Big Three" economic powers, were supposed to be guiding the world toward a new order, but their economic conflicts were leading instead toward acrimony. Initially, the disagreements were polite, carried on in the gentlemanly confines of official trade talks. But leaders in Washington, Tokyo and Berlin already foresaw scenarios that could turn commercial disputes into an economic cold war. The question, Brent Scowcroft reflected, was whether "we are going to have an open trading system, or whether we will break down into giant trading blocs—one with Japan as the center, encompassing East Asia; one with the United States, the Western Hemisphere; one centering on Europe, East and West."

Most Western economists scoffed at the notion that an increasingly global system of trade and finance could reverse direction and seal parts of the world into self-contained blocs. "The economic losses [that would be suffered by] moving to real blocs would be fantastic, and would affect very important political actors within each of these areas," said Harvard's Jeffrey Sachs, a young economist who designed ambitious economic re-form programs for countries from Bolivia to Russia. "There are lots of pressures from very important sources and very important companies against that kind of thing." Still, many of those companies hedged their bets by increasing their direct investment in Europe—thus ensuring that if protectionist walls went up, they would already be inside. AT&T bought a 20 percent stake in Italtel, Italy's state-owned communications equip-ment-maker. Texas Instruments sank some $1.2 billion into calculator and semiconductor plants in Italy. Intel Corp., reacting to stiffened European Community local content requirements, planned a $400 million micro-processor plant in Ireland.

Each major economic power appeared to be shoring up its own trading region—just in case. In the first half of 1991, the United States signed an agreement to link up with the new Southern Cone Common Market of Brazil, Argentina, Uruguay and Paraguay, a key step toward the cre-ation of a single free trade zone for the entire Western Hemisphere. The European Community merged its customs union with that of the neigh-boring European Free Trade Association and worked to integrate the newly capitalistic economies of Poland, Hungary and Czechoslovakia as well. And Japan continued pouring investment into Thailand, Malaysia, Burma, the Philippines and even Vietnam, slowly but inexorably tying their growing economies to Tokyo in a de facto financial bloc.

Even if the world does not divide into rigid blocs, the rise of regional trading alliances could still sharpen the political frictions that fierce economic competition will breed. As a growing number of countries concentrated on banding together with their neighbors, the effect was almost automatically to lock others out—the tendency American businessmen on the continent called "Fortress Europe." "It doesn't mean these will be opposing blocs, but their interest will be inward—not inward nationally, but inward regionally," said Malmgren, the former trade negotiator. "The impulse in Europe is to focus on European integration."

By 1991, the most worrisome tendency, in other words, was not a deliberate course of belligerent conflict but for the Cold War allies, with their political glue dissolved, to move apart unintentionally. "Competing and diverging systems, or blocs, will tend to seek their own 'good' as each conceives it," warned Michael Vlahos, a strategic analyst at the State Department. "The Big Three will surely want to keep things as stable and as open as possible. Yet in the absence of a true global culture, however artificial, by what set of economic values is business to be conducted? The familiar ways American culture does business will no longer be forced on the world. The Big Three will drift."[21]

The most dangerous drift was the souring of the relationship between the world's two largest economic powers: the United States and Japan. The end of the Cold War sharpened attention in both countries on their mounting economic and political disagreements, as if Americans and Japanese had suddenly discovered that the glue which had bound them together for forty years had melted, leaving them with little else in common.

The tension turned up in unusual ways. In the spring of 1990, a series of adult comic books called "The Silent Service" was Tokyo's surprise best-seller of the season. The attraction was its daring story line. "The Silent Service" was the saga of a Japanese Navy submarine crew that seized U.S. nuclear missiles, declared war on the United States, and defeated its slow-witted Navy, establishing "true independence" for Japan. "There is anti-American emotion under the surface here," warned Atsuyuki Sassa, a former adviser to several prime ministers. "If there's a real crisis—an isolation of Japan—then, all of a sudden, a new conservative nationalist party will arise. . . . We have no military capability now. But if we are pushed around, we can't stop the rise of nationalism."

Maseru Yoshitomi, one of the Japanese government's chief economic forecasters, was equally worried. "If this were the time before World War I, we'd be at war already," he mused in a vast office piled high with research papers near the Diet, the Japanese parliament. "The drive for a greater market share by the three big capitalist systems, Germany, France and Britain, led to World War I. Now we have the same situation—but we know the cost of a world war."

Americans and Japanese have long criticized each other's policies, but by 1990 they were also beginning to criticize each other's way of life—a breach of far deeper significance. "I was talking with one of our negotiators the other day," a high-ranking Japanese diplomat confided during one of the endless rounds of U.S.-Japan trade talks in 1990. "He said the people on our side despise the people on your side. They don't have any respect for them." On the other side of the table, U.S. officials were increasingly adopting the views of the foreign Japan scholars known as "revisionists," who charge that Japan's political and social structures are so different from America's that no one from Tokyo will ever play by the same rules as the United States and other countries. "I think it is too early to say what kind of society now exists in Japan . . . whether it is truly a democracy," said a senior official at the White House who, like the Japanese diplomat, spoke anonymously to avoid touching off a public battle. "You can read about the Japanese political system in the 1920s—kind of an oligarchical system, with power groups sharing and arranging things—and it's not all that different [from the system today]. In the past, it led Japan in very dangerous directions." Could there be a rebirth of the kind of U.S.-Japanese hostility that led to World War II? "I don't anticipate it, but"—the White House aide paused—"I don't know."

Part of the problem may be that the two countries share mirror-image anxieties. Americans are distressed by the idea of Japan's surpassing the United States in economic strength and political clout. Surprisingly enough, many Japanese are, too. "We don't want to be Number One," confessed Hideaki Kase, a prominent Japanese nationalist. "We want to stay in the back seat, because it's much more comfortable."

"Both the United States and Japan have been like greyhounds at a dog track chasing a rabbit," said Naohiro Amaya, a former top trade official. "The United States has been chasing the Soviet Union, which has suddenly disappeared. Japan has been chasing the United States, in terms of economic success, and now we have succeeded in that—so our rabbit has disappeared. For both countries, the question is where do you go now? The greyhounds are at a loss."

Japan liked the Cold War, it turns out. The old balance of terror gave the country a secure and stable role as an economic powerhouse that did not have to spend much time—or, until recently, much money—on defense or foreign aid. "The U.S.-Soviet confrontation was in our national interest," explained Sassa, the former national security adviser. "The rapprochement of the two countries makes our position very awkward. . . . All of a sudden, we're the pacesetter, and we don't know how to do it." For traditionally insular Japan, the idea of taking on global leadership may be even more wrenching than the American dilemma of sharing power. "Japan should have a grand design for its world policy—a coordinated economic, diplomatic and defense policy—but we don't," said Sassa. "Japan is a great power without a grand design."

Instead, Japan is still pursuing economic preeminence with the same methods and persistence that produced the successes of the 1960s and 1970s, from automobiles to videocassettes and semiconductors. At the end of the 1980s, Japan's government and industry launched a concerted effort to rise to the top rank of scientific research as well—and leaders in the United States and Europe were beginning to worry about giving knowledge away to the competition. The result was a novel form of conflict over the world's newest source of power: advanced information technology. The phenomenon even spawned a new buzzword, "techno-nationalism"—and by 1991, it had become a regular and sometimes contentious issue in meetings between the president of the United States and the prime minister of Japan.

Administrators at Japan's Ministry for International Trade and Industry (MITI) cheerfully acknowledged that they had targeted basic research as their last frontier in catching up with the United States. Even more striking was the tidal wave of Japanese firms that came to America to buy research expertise from U.S. scientists. The Nippon Electric Company opened a laboratory near Princeton University; Canon and Matsushita planned facilities in Silicon Valley. The Massachusetts Institute of Technology sold a Japanese venture the right to examine and duplicate its innovative Media Lab for ten million dollars. So aggressive were the Japanese that the White House issued a formal warning in 1991 which ordered them to cease contacting U.S. computer researchers directly.[22]

U.S. and European industries complained that far more Western technology was open to their Japanese competitors than the other way around. More than 52,000 Japanese researchers have studied technology in the United States, versus only 4,400 American scientists who have studied in Japan. The United States and Japan also tangled over the control of aerospace technology; Tokyo wanted the blueprints for advanced U.S. fighter planes, but Washington balked. They argued over advanced semiconductors, too; U.S. firms charged that Japanese producers kept their newest chips at home to gain a head start in developing applications.

But the most critical battle over the new weapons of economic power was only beginning: competition over "Computer-Integrated Manufacturing" (C.I.M.), the technology of automated controls and robots which was transforming old assembly lines into high-tech marvels. C.I.M. allowed Japan's Panasonic to build bicycles customized to purchasers' individual body measurements; it allowed Honda to produce a wide variety of cars and trucks in a single factory, changing the mix instantly in response to demand; it allowed Milwaukee's Allen-Bradley Corporation to custom-produce electric motor parts for specialty customers with almost no costly inventory on hand. The technology enabled manufacturers to work at unprecedented levels of efficiency, with almost unlimited flexibility and very little waste.

"The revolution in production technology is going to be a key defining element of the new strategic competition," predicted the State Department's Vlahos. "The old competition over military technology is being replaced by a new competition over production technology. And it is already getting quite fierce." In 1990, Japan's MITI attempted to launch a billion-dollar international consortium for C.I.M. research, presenting it as a prototype for global scientific cooperation. But the United States and the European Community reacted with suspicion, and stalled the plan for fear that it would give Tokyo too much control over the fruits of the research. Some Western officials viewed the Japanese proposal as simply a stratagem for stealing American and European innovations.

Japanese officials protested no such intent. "We want to avoid techno-nationalism," Yukio Honda, director of MITI's technology-policy-planning division, said in the crowded, surprisingly shabby, steel-desk offices from which the ministry's bureaucrats chart Japan's new crusade. "We want techno-globalism, to develop creative technology not only in Japan but in other countries as well." But U.S. officials remained openly skeptical. "When MITI says techno-globalism," a U.S. diplomat in Tokyo said, "that means they already see Japan as Number One."

As such trade and technology frictions increased, Japan's resentment of Western economic policies gave rise to a quiet but steady resurgence of nationalism. In a poll conducted in Japan in 1953, 20 percent of those surveyed said they considered themselves "superior to Westerners"; by 1983, that number had increased to 53 percent and, by all accounts, has continued to grow.[23] Nationalism is only natural in a country that is widely considered to be the world's greatest economic success. But Japan's nationalism has been complicated by two unusual factors: insecurity and fear—both openly expressed. "Deep in our psyche is a deeply seated sense of anxiety that we are weak, that we can be persecuted by the white Christians," Kase said. "U.S. trade pressure, if we begin to suffer economically, will be seen as a threat here."

An increasing number of Americans, in turn, began viewing Japan not only as an economic and technological competitor but as an unscrupulous and unfriendly one. Polls in the late 1980s and early 1990s regularly found that positive views of Japan had declined; some Americans cited Japan, not the Soviet Union, as the principal adversary of the United States.[24] When Japan failed to send troops or ships to the Middle East during the Gulf War, many Americans were furious. Paradoxically, though, some also began to fear Japan as a potential military threat to the United States, half a century after Pearl Harbor. In 1990, the commander of U.S. Marines on Okinawa, Major General Henry C. Stackpole III, indiscreetly described his mission as that of keeping Japan under control. "No one wants a rearmed, resurgent Japan," he said. "So we are a cap in the bottle, if you will."[25]

On a stifling evening in Dhaka, the tattered capital of Bangladesh, the bare electric lights that had lent an air of shabby festivity to the city's

Ramna Park suddenly flickered and went out. Shops rattled down their battered steel gates, bringing the summer evening to an abrupt and premature end. Streets emptied of cars; no one wanted to waste gasoline. It was August 1990; Iraq had invaded Kuwait—and Bangladesh, two thousand miles from the front, was at the mercy of a distant war.

The soaring price of oil was only part of the problem—a small part, in fact, because a poor country like Bangladesh uses much less fuel than a rich, industrialized country. Bangladesh had also lost its income from export sales to Iraq—modest shipments of jute and tea that still made a difference to Dhaka's wheezing economy. The worst part, though, was the sudden loss of income from the 110,000 Bangladeshis who worked in Iraq and Kuwait; their payments home had supported more than a million people, perhaps several million. Some officials estimated that the country's citizens lost $1.4 billion in wages, savings and property in a single month—a crushing calamity to a nation whose annual per capita income hovers around $200. Entire families were plunged into destitution overnight. "They are in a daze," said Animur Rahman Shams-ud-Doha, a former foreign minister. "Saddam Hussein had nothing to do with them."[26]

Bangladesh was far from alone. The economic impact of the Iraqi invasion and the worldwide trade boycott that followed were vivid evidence of how deeply intertwined every country's affairs had become. Turkey, Iraq's northern neighbor, lost an estimated $7 billion in exports, income from tourism and oil pipeline fees from Baghdad. Faraway Uganda suffered a sudden drop in earnings from coffee, the crop that generates 95 percent of the country's export income. Romania saw $1.2 billion in Iraqi contracts and $1.7 billion in Iraqi debt repayments evaporate. Sri Lanka saw one of its largest markets for tea, the island nation's main export, disappear overnight.

Richer countries had fewer problems. Since the first Arab oil embargo, in 1973, most had reduced their dependence on cheap oil so that they could ride out a short crisis. During the 1990 oil crunch, Saudi Arabia also increased its oil production, to make up for most of the lost supply from Iraq and Kuwait, and prices stabilized within two months. Nevertheless, the oil markets initially panicked—in part because they feared an Iraqi attack on Saudi oil facilities could disrupt even the best-designed contingency plans.

The economic jitters of 1990 reflected a world of shared vulnerability that linked countries as different as the United States and Bangladesh in common distress. No country was immune; no power was so strong that it could compel others to make good its losses. Instead, there were only countries of greater or lesser weakness. But the weakest were also the hardest hit. The end of the Cold War and escalating economic competition among industrialized countries had created an unexpected nightmare for much of the developing world: the nightmare of being forgotten.

For decades, underdeveloped countries had extracted aid and favors from the superpowers, whose global rivalry impelled them to compete for influence in the humblest of capitals. But as the U.S.-Soviet rivalry ebbed, the poor countries lost much of their claim on the major powers' interest. "In the past, no matter what kind of leader you were, you could take a chance and count on having one of the superpowers on your side—either the Russians or the Americans," noted Abid Hussain, India's ambassador in Washington. "Now that's gone."

The four billion people in what used to be called the Third World were the most vulnerable players of all in the new economic competition. Entire continents are in danger of dropping out of a competition that hinges less and less on natural resources or on cheap labor—some developing countries' only selling points—and more and more on high technology. The main export of both Zambia and Chile is copper, once the most common metal in electric and telephone wiring, but the North's communications wizards have turned to fiber optics, and much of the copper market has now disappeared, apparently forever. Some pockets of the Third World have benefited from globalization: Peruvian farmers airfreight asparagus to Europe, and Malaysians build computer parts for America and Japan. But most of the South has been left behind. "What is to become of Latin America and Africa?" mourned Arturo O'Connell, a former director of Argentina's central bank. "Are we going to become the shantytowns of the world, while Japan, the United States and the industrialized nations thrive?"

In a desperate attempt to catch up with the global economic express train and retrieve some of the power they see slipping away, poor countries in the South are rushing to emulate the prosperous North by establishing free-trade pacts. By creating larger, integrated markets, they hope to attract new foreign investment and stimulate more production at home.

In 1991, for example, South America's Southern Cone Common Market joined four countries—Brazil, Argentina, Paraguay and Uruguay—with a combined population of 190 million, almost as large as that of the United States. But the most startling proposal for economic integration, although it remained far from a reality, was being discussed in Southern Africa: the five "frontline countries" that had spent years battling South Africa's white minority regime had begun to seek economic integration with it. Mozambique's charismatic rulers were once among Africa's most fervent Marxists, but after fifteen years of famine, war and economic collapse they were ready to try anything. "We count on South Africa," confessed Luis Bernardo Honwana, Mozambique's minister of culture and one of Africa's leading writers. "Unless we succeed in constituting [an economic] bloc, our role in this new century is going to be determined by others."

Once an Indian Ocean paradise, Mozambique has become a terrifying example of how much can go wrong in a newly independent nation. The country's fifteen million people each earn an average of a hundred dollars a year, making them the poorest in the world in the World Bank's official 1990 ranking. Thousands of Mozambicans are without schools, industries have virtually stopped functioning, and highways have deteriorated into rural paths. Even the succulent giant prawns that were once the pride of Maputo have disappeared, decimated by Soviet trawlers.

"The situation is so bad it will go to one of two extremes," said Carlos Cardoso, a prominent Mozambican journalist. "In some areas, people have gone back a century or more. They've gone back to the Stone Age in the way they live: no salt, no sugar, no meat, no fish—roots and wild plants." He scribbled out a little chart on a scrap of paper. On one side, a series of steps joined all of southern Africa's countries, including a post-apartheid South Africa, in a box labeled "Regional Army under Regional Parliament." "In other words, total integration," Cardoso explained. On the other side, he left out the intermediate steps and wrote merely: "Total Disintegration."

In neighboring Zimbabwe, the economy has barely grown in twenty years. At the country's only steel mill, one of the trucks—an ancient Mack—was said, quite seriously, to have entered service with the British Army against Rommel in 1943. "Some people look at our factories and say the last time they saw machines of that sort was in a museum," a Zimbabwean economist, John Robertson, said with a sad smile. "You don't have a place in the future if you don't manage to be competitive, to produce goods the market wants and to make them at prices the market is prepared to pay, and that means keeping up with the technology. But we slip back rather than make progress. Every year that goes by, we don't attract new investment. The whole of Africa south of the Sahara doesn't have a gross domestic product as big as that of Holland," he noted. "If Africa were to disappear beneath the ocean, it would cause a short little bit of mourning, and then the rest of the world would get on with what it's doing and hardly notice the difference."

The last time Robertson was in New York calling on bankers, one of his hosts walked to an office window and pointed across the Hudson River. "I do more business with New Jersey than I do with the whole of Africa," the banker said. "Why do I need Africa? In New Jersey, they speak my language and they pay their bills. In Africa, God knows what will happen next."

Africa is far worse off than any other continent. The Third World no longer exists as a single unit; it is increasingly divided between countries that are competing successfully and those that are not. World Bank figures revealed the new division starkly: During the 1980s, the developing economies of East Asia—including the fast-developing "tigers" of South Korea, Taiwan, Singapore and Hong Kong—grew at an annual rate of 6.7 percent. During the same period, the economies of black Africa shrank, in per capita terms, by an annual rate of 2.2 percent; the economies of Latin America shrank at a rate of 0.6 percent. In short, some of the poor got richer—but millions got seriously poorer. The trend is likely to continue. Investment is pouring into the growing economies of Southeast Asia, which is becoming a new world-manufacturing center. Thailand and Malaysia, for example, are now major producers of appliances, computer components and automobiles, although the companies are Japanese and American. Africa and Latin America, comparatively, have little to offer.

"I'm not sure the stability of the South is really that important to the North," said a worried Domingo Cavallo, Argentina's dapper foreign minister. "Can the North build a new structure of security without us? Or are we going to make enough noise that they can't avoid us?" In fact, some officials and analysts in the industrialized "North" believe exactly that—that the Third World is no longer of much importance.

"We're losing interest in the Third World," said Mark Falcoff of the

American Enterprise Institute in Washington. "Their value as pieces on the strategic and ideological chessboard has depreciated." With the super-powers no longer locked in a global struggle, he reasoned, most local wars in distant parts of the world will no longer interest the United States. "The causes at issue will seem strange and irrelevant," he said. Iraq's invasion of Kuwait was unlikely to set a precedent, he argued; few Third World conflicts involve an outright invasion of one country by another, and fewer still imperil the world's supply of oil. More typical was the case of the Horn of Africa, where the United States and the Soviet Union once jousted for influence in the Cold War game of power. In 1991, when the governments of Ethiopia and Somalia collapsed, neither Washington nor Moscow displayed the slightest concern.

Still, others warn that the globalization of the world's economy is bringing the Third World uncomfortably closer to the First, not pushing it farther away. Los Angeles and every other city of the American South-west have been transformed by a flood of Mexican and Central American immigrants seeking work; one goal of the U.S.-Mexican free-trade agree-ment was to create jobs south of the border to slow the tide northward. Africa's plight is more removed from the United States, but by 1990, the cities of France, Spain and Italy were coping with more refugees from the impoverished continent than ever before.

Even the powerless could still have an impact on the powerful. "The African continent will not remain inert in the face of rising unemploy-ment and a Western Europe in which the standard of living is constantly rising," warned Giscard. "There will be demands for [economic] associa-tion, immigration pressure—phenomena that will be difficult to deal with, because freedom of movement and the speed of travel have put people in closer and closer communication."

"For those of us living in the fortunate, profligate West, there may be an inclination to try and forget the Third World, as though it were an embarrassing romance," added Augustus Richard Norton, a fellow at the International Peace Academy in New York. "But the problems which dog Third World governments will not always respect borders or be quietly resolved. In point of fact, it is a safe bet that the global agenda for the 1990s will be shaped largely by the imperative of responding to Third World crises."

For centuries, the ancient cultures of the South have struggled merely to survive the vagaries of conquest, economic cycles and natural disaster. "But survival is not enough any more," warned Egyptian sociologist Mona Ebeid. "Survival still puts you on the margin of civilization. You need much more. . . . People see that other people live so much better. People see that they have other rights, people see that they have access to better education. It has changed your vision of yourself in the world and your country in the world." She thought for a moment. "The status quo is very dangerous," she said quietly. "Stability and order are more dangerous than anything else, because for the sake of stability and order there is immobilism—and with immobilism, you can get the worst of explosions."

The Rise of Nations

> *"The world has always been inhabited by human beings who have always had the same passions."*
>
> —MACHIAVELLI

On a sultry day in July 1990, Kosovo revolted. After months of mounting tension between Yugoslavia's federal government and the feisty ethnic Albanians in the mountainous southern province, 114 members of Kosovo's parliament arrived at their concrete, pseudo-modern chambers to find the doors locked. Belgrade had exerted its supremacy, sealing off the impoverished province's last official forum and suspending Kosovo's autonomy. The collection of outraged farmers, peasants and local businessmen, all ethnic Albanians, decided to vote in the open air. The ballot was unanimous: Kosovo declared its independence. "Having Yugoslavia was wrong to begin with," said an angry Veton Surroi, a young writer and the president of the Yugoslav Democratic Initiative, a day after the vote. "It was an unnatural country." A purely ethnic force threatened to break up a strategic corner of Eastern Europe after seven decades of unity.

On the other side of the globe six months later, Robert Bourassa, the bespectacled young Quebec premier, stood before the national press and issued an ultimatum: Canada must give Quebec special powers—or the French-speaking province would vote on secession. The long-simmering separatist movement was no longer limited to the political fringe; by early 1991, 70 percent of Quebecois surveyed backed breaking away. An official who helped draft the ultimatum pronounced, "This proposal is the final and decisive test for Canada." After 123 years of union with the English-speaking provinces, Quebec's nationalist resurgence threatened to splinter one of the West's major industrial powers.

In its remote northern hills, India witnessed the worst eruption of violence in a generation when Hindu zealots tried to destroy a Muslim mosque to make room for a Hindu temple. Police detained ninety thousand people to avert trouble and deployed thousands of officers to protect the mosque before the October 1990 showdown. "It's not a question of saving the government but of saving the country," Indian Prime Minister V. P. Singh said in a national address about his crackdown on Hindus in the predominantly Hindu state. "This is the biggest challenge we have faced since the independence of the country." But neither was enough to prevent bloodshed or political backlash. Within days, Singh's government collapsed. Sectarian violence was hardly new to India, but the incident marked the first time a religious issue brought down a secular government in the world's most populous democracy.

Five centuries after the marriage of Ferdinand of Aragon and Isabella of Castile in 1469 created the nucleus of one of the first modern nation-states, the most dominant political institution in the world is under attack. The consolidation of city-states into nation-states as the basic unit of political cohesion and governance has been one of the major feats—and facts—of the Modern Age. But at the end of the twentieth century, in obscure corners of the world as well as in its principal powers, volatile movements spawned by resurgent ethnic, national and religious passions are reemerging in gale-force strength to contest the premises of modern statehood.

In the early 1990s, tensions were highest in heterogeneous states, especially those with limited freedoms. But the challenge was being felt not only in crumbling multiethnic and multinational states like Yugoslavia, Canada, the Soviet Union and Peru, and divisive, multireligious countries such as India, Nigeria and Northern Ireland. In small ways and large, regionalism, racism and religious rivalries were spreading or deepening even in nation-states considered homogeneous. In 1991, Washington, D.C., erupted for the first time in a generation during confrontations between Hispanics and police. In the United Kingdom, 1992 polls showed

75 percent of Scots and almost half of the Welsh favored full independence or devolution of power from London. Bavarians flew their blue-and-white-checked flag more than the German tricolor. In France, the people of Brittany, Corsica and Languedoc displayed "national" emblems on their cars.

The common challenge from diverse movements—each with its own flashpoints, tactics and goals—is the product of multiple phenomena. On one level, many modern nation-states are crumbling because the "melting pot" has failed. Indeed, in several countries, longstanding attempts to assimilate disparate cultures under larger political umbrellas were already visibly, and occasionally violently, disintegrating in the early 1990s. The melting pot's collapse represents the struggle to preserve proud and historic ethnic identities. Ethnic Albanians, Iraqi Kurds, South African Zulus, Peruvian Indians, Spanish Basques, Ethiopia's Eritreans and others are unwilling to have their language, customs or communities erased in the name of progress and modernization or submerged in a world of mass culture and politics.

"What we are facing is the reaction of these groups against oblivion," explained Luis Bernardo Honwana, Mozambique's charismatic minister of culture and one of Africa's great writers, over coffee in his simple book-lined office in Maputo. "In order to be part of an ensemble, of a group, one had to give up something, probably much more than one was prepared to give up. And one had to absorb some foreign, some strange values—normally the values of the stronger part of this ensemble. Now we're trying to make sure that we are not destroyed as a cultural entity. Simply, unity cannot be built at the cost of the existence of some of the elements which are going to be part of this unity."

On a second level, many nation-states are disintegrating because they have, from their inception, been artificial. In contemporary usage, nation and state are often used synonymously because states, in theory, are to be founded in nations. The state was the instrument of government; the nation (or nations) was its people. The Modern Era's dominant ideologies—from liberalism to communism—have, accordingly, required the transfer or surrender of nations' loyalties to the state, either by choice or by force, for the common political good.

That concept has worked in some countries: Japan and France had

common or largely homogeneous cultures. The United States had sufficient flexibility to cater to cultural diversity. But, in practice, many modern states have not reflected or represented the nations under their
authority. For more than four centuries, the more prevalent pattern has
instead been to establish or impose a state—and then try to create a nation
around it. In many countries, however, states and nations have often
turned out to be parts that never coalesced into a common whole. In those
countries, states are no longer seen as the institution to best protect or
provide for their nations.

The trend was most vivid in the former Soviet Union. By 1991, deepening nationalist differences led all fifteen Soviet republics to demand or
declare some form of sovereignty. Then, after the abortive coup attempt
in August, the empire formally collapsed almost overnight. The three
Baltic states—annexed in a secret 1940 pact between Moscow and Nazi
Germany—went their own way. Eleven others formed the Commonwealth of Independent States, although its longevity and collective clout
was tenuous. The dismemberment signaled the formal end of one of the
most ambitious political experiments of the twentieth century: the attempt to weld 104 disparate nationalities into a single nation, to create
a new "Soviet" citizen to support the new Soviet state. The draconian
campaign to suppress languages, cultures and religions—and in effect to
"Russify" millions of non-Russians—had failed.

Yugoslavia's problems were just as stark. Besides the ethnic Albanian
rebellion, four of the six republics demanded a reconfiguration of independent nations in a loose alliance—or a breakup of Yugoslavia altogether.
When Serbia balked, Slovenia, Croatia and Bosnia-Herzegovina seceded.
Of all the "isms" of the twentieth century, nationalism has proven to be
the most enduring.

Modern nation-states are also artificial because their borders were
drawn not by consent but by conquest or imposition. The twentieth
century's two world wars shaped modern Europe: After World War I,
Austria, Hungary, Yugoslavia and Czechoslovakia were molded from the
ruins of the Austro-Hungarian Empire. World War II redrew the borders
of Germany, Italy, Poland, Bulgaria, Romania and the Soviet Union, and
wrenched an independent Korea from Japan. The modern map of Africa
was charted by Europe under the guidance of Belgium's King Leopold

during the 1884 Conference of Berlin with total disregard to tribal lands and divisions—and no African participants. In 1916, much of the Arab world was divided into new nation-states by France and Britain in the Sykes-Picot Agreement, with limited recognition of the region's deep sectarian, communal or religious divisions. At the end of the twentieth century, the consequences are increasingly coming full cycle.

After the collapse of the Ottoman Empire, Iraq's modern borders were outlined by English and French diplomats, who divided the Middle East into spheres of foreign control. Iraq was was formed from the Ottoman provinces of Mosul, Baghdad and Basra—without much concern for the diverse peoples who dwelled within. The new state was held together for seventy-five years, first by British colonial rule, then by a rigid monarchy and, finally, by a series of ruthless dictators. But the three dominant and disparate nations within Iraq never fully coalesced. In the chaotic early days after the 1991 Gulf War, deep ethnic and religious divides rose to the surface; Iraq began to unravel. Both the non-Arab mountain Kurds in the north and the Shi'ite Muslims in the south launched simultaneous uprisings against the Sunni Muslim Arab regime in Baghdad. Although President Saddam Hussein's sophisticated armor and air power managed to quell the rebellions in less than a month, Iraq is still far from a unified nation.

On a third level, the modern nation-state is being challenged because of its secular foundation. In the seventeenth century, one of the major leaps of Western civilization was the shift from a God-centered cosmos to a man-centered world, from a belief in salvation by faith to a belief in human ideologies for temporal deliverance.[1] By the twentieth century, the political spectrum was defined by one superpower that was constitutionally secular and another that was ideologically atheist. Yet, for growing numbers, the logic of the Age of Reason, the universal rights promised by the Enlightenment and the definition of progress in the scientific era have not provided sufficient sustenance or answers.

At the end of the twentieth century, Islamic, Protestant and Jewish fundamentalism, Catholic Liberation Theology, Hindu and Sikh extremism and even political activism in quietist Buddhism are among the most dynamic and energetic idioms of social and political expression—and opposition. In some cases peacefully, in others by taking up arms, vibrant religious movements are reshaping the political spectrum within nation-states as well as challenging the premises on which they have been built. A major theocracy based on religious law and governed by the clergy, the first since the Middle Ages, actually became a viable form of modern government after Iran's 1979 revolution. In 1991, Pakistan's prime minister introduced legislation to make all aspects of life—from school curricula and banking laws to penal codes—conform to Islamic law.

The multiple challenges to the nation-state are, in turn, reshaping the basis of the social contract between the individual and the state. From Plato in the fourth century B.C. and Thomas Aquinas in the Middle Ages to Hobbes, Locke and Rousseau in the seventeenth and eighteenth centuries, various formulations of the social contract concurred that the *polis*—be it the city-state or the nation-state—was the institution best suited to dispense laws, to guarantee justice and rights, and to provide defense. By the end of the twentieth century, however, many states had taken on too much.

Some, such as the Soviet Union, became unwieldy, weighted down by their own internal logic; others, like Yugoslavia, were engrossed in their own survival rather than in serving their nations. The gap between states and nations widened in countries without the flexibility to adapt to shifting agendas or the self-confidence to accommodate growing demands for individual expression. Finally, as the world began to globalize, the state was increasingly perceived more as a constraint on freedoms than a guarantor of rights, a source of vulnerability rather than of protection, the creator of a new elite instead of an equalizer. The result has been a series of revolts with a common message: Survival of the state at the expense of its nations is no longer acceptable.

The erosion of the social contract has, in turn, led to a shift in the primary sources of identity and allegiance from the state in two, seemingly contradictory, directions: to the smaller nuclear community—ethnic, national or religious—and to the world. This shift reflects a fundamental theme of the 1990s and beyond: the paradox of simultaneous disintegration and integration as the world's peoples sort themselves into new groupings and affiliations.

While the Croatian and Slovenian republics moved toward secession from Serbian-dominated Yugoslavia, they were, at the same time, moving toward integration into the European Community; both established offices in Brussels in 1990. The tense relationship between the Czech lands of Bohemia and Moravia and the rival Slovak Republic led both sides to look to Brussels rather than Prague to solve their economic problems.

For the short term, the disintegration of conventional nation-states will be a complicated, emotional, troublesome and sometimes violent factor in the politics of the new era. The trend may also spawn new countries. Among the obvious flashpoints: Central and Eastern Europe are certain to witness large-scale revivals of the same ethnic frictions that sparked World War I. In Western Europe, virulent new political movements will target racial and ethnic groups, from Germany's Turkish "guest workers" to France's North African laborers, who may well respond in kind.

Largest among the disintegrating states were the world's last two great empires, the Soviet Union and China. The Soviet collapse and the potential for China's demise will be the last gasp of the imperial age, which began its decline in the West after World War II with the dismantling of the British, French, Portuguese and other European empires in Africa and Asia. Fifteen countries have already been added to the world roster from the Soviet Union alone; others may also take shape around the world by the end of the century. The deterioration of traditional nation-states may be among the most destabilizing factors in world affairs in the 1990s, especially if states try to repress the will of nations.

But the redefinition of nation-states will not necessarily be destructive over the long term. Governments of nation-states once argued that ethnic or national ministates were not viable, a premise that, in the 1990s, is no longer true. The Asian city-state of Singapore—ironically, an outcast from the multiethnic federation of Malaysia—has proven that bigger is often not better. Luxembourg, once a comic-opera duchy, has become a prosperous banking and corporate center within the European Community. Both have economic strength—and, therefore, legitimacy and power.

The fragments of crumbling nation-states are also seeking integration, some into new wholes more viable in a world increasingly divided into region-states. In the 1960s, the biggest objection to Quebec's demand for autonomy was that the province could become an impoverished French-speaking enclave on a predominantly English-speaking continent. But by

1991, Quebecois were emboldened to seek secession in part because of
confidence that their economy could survive—even thrive—as part of the
larger North American Free Trade Area, including the United States,
Mexico and all the provinces of Canada.

Other fragments may end up in the same configurations, but on different terms. Instead of rigid federal unions, they may form loose confederations, with common defense and foreign-affairs policies, but with
autonomous capitals, multiple languages and even separate financial institutions. After protracted talks, the Czech and Slovak republics headed in
that direction in 1991.

Not all of the new region-states or confederations may yet be visible.
While the three Baltic states looked to the European Community upon
independence, the former Soviet Muslim republics are turning east and
south to form new Asian blocs. In each case, however, the coalescing
foundations are ethnic, national or religious bonds. Indeed, all three
forces promise to be as important in shaping the twenty-first century as
ideology was in the twentieth; all three will be prominent idioms of the
new era.

"The thought that ethnicities and nationalisms and all the other primordial loyalties would disappear as a result of modernization was premature," mused Saad Eddin Ibrahim, a sociologist at the American
University of Cairo, as he stroked his white goatee. "The Marxist paradigm thought class was the most important point of loyalty." By forcibly
creating a single class, old differences would subside; loyalty and identity
would shift to the state. "The capitalist paradigm thought liberalism was
the answer," he added. Open up the system to allow everyone opportunity
and old identities would fade away.

"While coming from different ideological points, they both converged
at predicting that primordial loyalties will disappear. But that was probably one of the big lessons of the twentieth century: Ideology is no substi-
tute for interest or for geography. That's what we are rediscovering."

The day after Kosovo's secession, its border with Serbia was still un-
marked. But antitank mines and small cement pyramids, lined up along
the rough roadsides, underscored the tension. Hanging from shops and

apartment blocks, giant red Albanian flags, emblazoned with a black double-headed eagle, symbolized the political divide. And tall white minarets, rising high among rural Kosovo's small alpine chalets and homes, reflected the deep cultural differences. Once the "cradle" of the Christian Orthodox Serbian state, Kosovo has since become a stronghold of Muslim ethnic Albanians. On the roadside, three Albanian children under the age of seven flashed their fingers in a V, the symbol in Kosovo for independence—and proof of how deep the anti-Serbian animosity had penetrated.

"In Europe, in Yugoslavia, in the Balkans, nations are institutions, different institutions," said Ibrahim Rugova in his tiny flat in one of Pristina's grim cement high-rises. A wiry, long-haired literary critic, Rugova led Kosovo's Democratic Alliance, the largest of five ethnic Albanian opposition movements. The revolt in Pristina, he explained, was not to replace Serbs in their ancient homeland but to secure Albanian political rights in order to protect the cultural identity of what had become Yugoslavia's third largest population group.

"Language, cultural traditions, religious traditions, have been the three pillars of each nation in Europe since the French Revolution. The Albanians, being a small people, want to preserve the traditions they have," he added, almost plaintively.

For Rugova, preserving ethnic identity does not mean rejecting others' or outside values. The symbols of modernity and cross-culturization were widely visible in Kosovo, the most backward Yugoslav region. Underneath the sign of a video rental shop in Pristina was an arrow pointing inside to "Hollywood." In Rugova's apartment, his two sons shared a room decorated with magazine cut-outs of Rambo, Roger Rabbit, Michael Jackson, Madonna and a scantily clad group dancing the lambada. Chuckling as he acknowledged the pin-ups, Rugova said he did not feel threatened by his sons' Western idols. Instead, his concern was that the Albanian langugage and culture may be lost to the next generation—whether by Serbian political domination or Western cultural influence.

To explain what was at stake, he pulled a volume from his crowded bookshelf; it was James Joyce's *Ulysses.* As a literary critic, Rugova said, it was among his favorites. But as an Albanian, he added, one of the great moments in his life was finding more than a hundred words of Albanian origin in the Joyce classic. As obscure as Albanian language and culture are to most of the outside world, they have made a contribution. And, Rugova asserted, they still can.

"Culture is also in development. . . . My son has a small computer with programs and games in English. But he would like also Albanian programs. With the computer, my son wants to preserve his identity." In other words, the ethnic Albanians wanted to use the past to enrich the future and to move into the future within the context of the past—not at its expense.

The problem for Yugoslavia was that the dual passions of nationalism and insecurity ran both ways. The day after Kovoso's parliament voted to become a separate republic, the Serbian government took equally decisive action: It formally scrapped Kosovo's assembly. It fired thousands of Albanians from government jobs, replacing them with Serbs. Its police confronted demonstrating Albanians in clashes that left dozens dead. Although Serbs were only 10 percent of Kosovo's population, Serbia was prepared to take drastic action to prevent losing its historic heartland— and the source of its own identity.

Although the minarets of mosques are more prevalent, famous Serbian monasteries, dating back centuries, are still tucked into Kosovo's craggy mountainsides. Indeed, history haunts this region. Serbs still talk with deep bitterness about the Battle of Kosovo, in 1389, which they lost to the Ottoman Turks. That defeat lasted five centuries, until a new state was carved out of the remains of the Ottoman and Austro-Hungarian empires after World War I. In the new union, Serbia got Kosovo back— only to start losing it again in a demographic war with the ethnic Albanians. And neither side was willing to compromise.

With a shrug of resignation, Surroi, the young Albanian writer, explained, "The melting pot cannot function in Yugoslavia. The Yugoslav people have not found, until now, a consensual way to live together." Instead of unifying diverse nations under a new common banner, bringing them together as parts of the new Yugoslav state—as a kingdom in 1918, as a communist federation in 1945—had instead only made each more aware of its separate identity.

Yugoslavia—a country of six republics and two autonomous provinces patched together from five nationalities, four languages, three religions and two alphabets—is an extreme example of the challenge to the multinational state at the end of the twentieth century. Belgrade's authority was challenged simultaneously by both an ethnic uprising in Kosovo and nationalist rebellions in Croatia and Slovenia. After the two most prosperous republics elected noncommunist governments on nationalist tickets in 1990, both issued ultimatums to the central government: Either decentralize power and transform Yugoslavia into a confederation—with separate treasuries, armies, and foreign policies—or the republics would secede completely.

In response, Serbian nationalism only deepened. The last of the republics to hold free elections after the collapse of communist rule, Serbia overwhelmingly elected a socialist slate. Ironically, the renamed Communist Party won not by preaching socialism but by pledging to protect the largest ethnic group from all of Yugoslavia's other nationalities. Serbia's regional parliament also slapped import duties on products from Croatia and Slovenia, both dependent on the larger Yugoslav market for most of their sales.

Tension quickly turned into open friction; discrimination became rampant against rival nationalities in virtually all republics. "Previously, we had communist Bolshevism. Now we have nationalist Bolshevism," grumbled Predrag Simic, director of the Institute of International Politics and Economics in Belgrade. On a trip to Slovenia from Serbia the previous week, Simic had been stopped by Slovene police six times in two days because his car had Serbian license plates. At local businesses, his Belgrade bank checks were not accepted.

Throughout the country, people began to arm; local police units, supplemented with volunteers, became de facto militias for their respective republics. In Croatia, a crowd of fifteen thousand at a Zagreb rally demanded, "Give us guns." In early 1991, Croatia and Slovenia declared "invalid" all federal laws and formally "dissociated" their republics from the Yugoslav federation. Both refused to pay federal taxes; both ordered designs for their own new currencies. In June, both declared formal independence. The Yugoslav nation-state seemed spent. As Slovenian President Milan Kucan pronounced, Yugoslavia "has ceased to exist." The only outstanding issue was whether the formal divorce would be amicable or bloody.

Yugoslavia's disintegration is, in part, a by-product of the end of socialist dominance in Eastern Europe. For forty-five years, one of Europe's most heterogeneous countries was held—or forced, as many Yugoslavs said in hindsight—together by communism. Once the lid was lifted, long-suppressed divisions reemerged, old conflicts ignited anew. "Post-communism is nothing else but early modern societies in their initial stages," said Dr. Zvonko Letrovic, a political-science professor and member of the Croatian Social-Liberal Alliance.

But the outburst of ethnic and nationality movements worldwide is more than just a reaction to the suppression or the stirring of history's ghosts. Assimilating diverse cultures either by force from the top or by choice from the bottom has failed. "The idea of the melting pot and assimilation was part of the American imagination," said Firuz Kazemzadeh, a Yale historian. "It worked to some extent, imperfectly, in the United States. But it did not work in other parts of the world where assimilation was usually imposed by forces which were not acceptable to the masses of the people."

In his presidential palace in Zagreb, Franjo Tudjman, the burly, white-haired Croatian leader who was twice imprisoned during the communist era, explained how history unraveled in Yugoslavia. "We not only have historically different national individualities. We also have nations who belong to completely different civilizational and cultural spheres—Serbs belonging to the eastern Byzantine civilization, Croats and Slovenians belonging to the western Catholic civilization. It's not by chance that this is the line where the Roman Empire split. Christianity split in the same place into Eastern Orthodox and Western Catholic. The problem really reaches very deep," he sighed. During an election campaign stop in a Serbian stronghold in Croatia, someone tried to shoot him. "So we either have to agree to live as a union of republics or," he concluded, "it's better that each one of us lives on its own."

Throughout Eastern Europe in 1990, similar ethnic or nationality clashes began to undermine the new democratic regimes that had replaced communist dictatorships. After its 1989 "velvet revolution," Czechoslovakia's biggest domestic political crisis was sparked by Slovak nationalism. In the country's first free elections, all fifteen parties vying for Slovak votes in June 1990 advocated greater autonomy from Prague; one promoted secession. Tension was so high that when each chief of state brought a child to New York for celebrations marking the U.N.'s Year of the Child in 1990, President Václav Havel had to bring two—one from the Czech republic and one from Slovakia.

Brought together after World War I, the Slovaks and the Czech peoples of Moravia and Bohemia shared little but a similar language. A largely rural and staunchly Roman Catholic people, Slovaks had been ruled for ten centuries by Hungary; more secular and industrialized, Czechs had been governed by Austria. But what started as a family feud soon turned into an open brawl. In petitions from intellectuals, in public demonstrations and in fiery parliamentary debates after the elections, Slovak nationalists demanded separate banks and currency, an independent foreign policy and even an autonomous army. The Slovak parliament passed a law making Slovak the official language of the republic. During a visit to Slovakia in 1991 to urge continued union, Havel was mobbed, jostled and spit on by separatists. "Go back to Prague, Judas," they chanted.

Throughout the mountainous eastern third of the country, "Enough of Prague" posters, "I ♥ Slovakia" stickers, and the red-and-white Slovak coat of arms proliferated on fences, shop walls and car bumpers. Students adapted the music of "When the Saints Go Marching In" to a separatist ballad called "The Slovak State."[2] "Even though it's a great anachronism, the idea of a national state among the Slovaks is so strong that it will be extremely difficult to fight in any way against it," reflected Alexander Varga, an imposing historian and a member of Slovakia's regional assembly, in his simple office in scenic Bratislava. "You will not find a political force which would be capable of effectively standing up against this very, very strong idea."

In Prague, decisions on badly needed economic reforms were diverted by weeks of debate on a new name for the country and by months of resolving a power-sharing formula for the Czech and Slovak republics. Havel even had to appeal to the federal parliament for emergency powers to prevent the nation from splitting up. Slovak demands for independence, he warned, would signal "the beginning of Czechoslovakia's disintegration as a state . . . and the end of democracy. Our state would fall into the abyss of absolute political chaos."

In Bulgaria, the reform government's first crisis in 1990 flared over the country's 10 percent Turkish population. During communist rule, Turks had been forced to change their Turkish names and abandon their Islamic religious observances. The repressive measures were scrapped after the demise of communism in Sofia—only to trigger a backlash. Bulgarian nationalists took to the streets in mass anti-Turk protests and demanded "Turks to Turkey" and "Bulgaria for Bulgarians." The status of Turks remained as controversial—and volatile—as it had been during the communist era.

In Romania, the worst violence in postwar history erupted in 1990 when demonstrations deteriorated into hand-to-hand combat between Romanian nationalists and Hungarians, Europe's largest national minority spread over several states. The initial flashpoint was separate schools for Hungarians, promised by the reform government, to end the forced-assimilation policy of the communist era. New right-wing nationalist movements protested the special treatment, and the government dropped its promise, triggering an ongoing cycle of violence.

Daniel Kroupa, a political philosopher and a member of Czechoslovakia's new parliament, predicted, "Nationality problems in the upcoming decade will probably be the main subject of our interest—and our anxieties." Nationality issues even helped touch off the 1991 coup attempt against Mikhail Gorbachev, precipitated by a proposed treaty between Moscow and the Soviet Union's fifteen republics to formalize the country's disintegration into new nation-states.

But the dangers are not limited to Eastern Europe. In Latin America, Indians, mestizos and white descendants of European settlers have inhabited the same countries for four centuries yet still live as different nations, with few prospects of unity. Peru has been independent from Spain since 1824, "but we are still not an integrated state," said Luis Bustamante, a Peruvian senator. In Africa, the Ethiopian rebels who ousted Marxist dictator Mengistu Haile Mariam in 1991 passed a charter opening the way for ethnic groups to create their own nations, and the northern province of Eritrea was expected to secede after a referendum scheduled for 1993.

In the Middle East, more than twenty million Kurds constitute the fifth-largest ethnic group in the region. Yet this single nation is spread over five states: Iraq, Iran, Turkey, Syria and Armenia. A promise by the great powers to create an independent Kurdistan from part of the Ottoman Empire after World War I was abruptly abandoned. Since then, not one of the five has allowed autonomy for a proud and well-educated people whose poetry dates back more than a millennium for fear that it could, in turn, lead to a sovereign Kurdistan that would spawn demands for territory from the other four—and a new political powerhouse in Asia.

The Arabs have not wanted a non-Arab people in their midst or, in Iraq's case, have not wanted them claiming rich oilfields in northern Iraq. Turkey and Iran, home to at least 70 percent of the Kurds, have not wanted another group of Indo-Europeans rivaling their states. And the Soviet Union did not want more Muslims in its restive south. The result is that the Kurdish quest for independence has become a disruptive component, in varying degrees, in all five countries.

At the end of the twentieth century, every inhabited continent is touched by ethnic or nationalist challenges. Vast areas of the former Soviet Union and China are torn by conflict among European, Slavic, Turkic, Persian, Armenian factions, and by a host of smaller ones, like the Gagauz* and the Meshketian†, unknown to the outside world. In Belgium, only an uneasy truce curbs the hostility between the Flemish, who speak a Dutch-based language, and French-speaking Walloons. The split has divided the country with such surgical precision that the ancient University of Louvain even divided the books in its library equally between separate Flemish and French universities. Besides Canada's long-simmering French nationalist movement, Mohawk and Cree Indians and Eskimos have repeatedly confronted the government over centuries-old claims to ancestral lands. And Australia has its Aborigine "problem."

The strain on the multinational state has long been evident in a host of other modern border, tribal or communal wars. Most traumatic in the postwar era has been the bloody fragmentation of India into three states—India, Pakistan and Bangladesh. But the strains increasingly turned into crises as political floodgates opened in the late 1980s and empowerment became the cry in the 1990s; nation-states that lacked either popular

*A 150,000-strong minority of Christian Turks, the Gagauz proclaimed independence from the republic of Moldavia in August 1990.
†Predominantly Muslim Turks, the Meshketians were deported from Georgia to Uzbekistan by Stalin's forced migration policy. Because of resentment and harassment by the Uzbeks, many want to return to Georgia.

legitimacy or political viability were seen as a constraint, not as a source of mankind's development or growth. "The state itself has become more and more like a barrier in . . . the evolution of mankind. People can now arrange their own social groupings and organizations without the state," said Valeri Tishkov, the director of the Institute of Ethnography at the Academy of Sciences in Moscow.

Why has the nation-state reached its limits? "Mankind has known itself for eight thousand years, in terms of written history," reflected Croatia's President Tudjman. "During all that time, there have been great univer-salist ideas, civilizational, cosmopolitan efforts to create a unified world— Christian, Islamic, Buddhist, even communist. But all of that is disappearing, and what remains is man and his ethnic national commu-nity. It still exists today when the world is turning into a global village. And still the smallest national individualities claim a place in that world."

The challenge well into the twenty-first century will be to avert civil strife by adapting old formulas or by finding new ones that accommodate nationalities, ethnic groups and other primordial sources of human iden-tity. "There is a great task ahead to clarify what exactly a nation is, what its role is in modern liberal civilization, whether it has, in fact, meaning," said Kroupa, the Czech political philosopher.

During the transition to a new era, fragments of many traditional nation-states may try to strike out on their own; some may succeed. "All great powers and big states are now experiencing very hard times. It seems that, at the contemporary stage of mankind's evolution, small states are doing better at providing for the social existence of their citizens," said Tishkov, the Soviet ethnographer.

The sorting-out process may be messy. In several countries, tension is not limited to whether nations should stay together or separate. Modern man's mobility, combined with history's shifting borders, have left prov-inces or republics with a heterogeneous—and combustible—mosaic of peoples. Yugoslavia had five nationalities—but also twenty-four ethnic groups spread throughout the country. Croatia's population is at least 10 percent Serbian. After Croatia demanded separation from Serbia, the Serbian stronghold of Krajina and other enclaves within Croatia declared their own secession. Clashes between Serbs and Croats in 1991 touched off a full-scale civil war among Serbs, Croats and Bosnians in 1992—the worst eruption of violence in Europe since World War II.

The same trouble made the new Commonwealth of Independent States vulnerable after its birth: ethnic Russians still accounted for about 40 percent of the populations in Estonia and Kazakhstan and almost half of Latvia's residents. Not one of the new states has a purely homogeneous society. And in each, the new minorities are adamant about not being abandoned—to the point of taking up arms. As each sorts out its identity, from new laws to new languages, the worst-case scenario is serious unrest among polyglot populations, even a host of civil wars.

The transition may also be accompanied by demands for redrawing borders, not always by consent. "Conflicts within Yugoslavia would certainly imply conflicts on a larger scale in Europe," predicted Mladen Plese, a Croatian journalist. "Croatia has unresolved problems with Italy, Slovenia with Austria, Serbia with Romania, Macedonia with Greece and Bulgaria—all questions of borders. So any kind of conflict on one front would quite logically inspire tensions with all those countries, maybe conflicts with them."

But disintegration is only half of the future. What may mark the beginning of the new era will be the settling-down process, a political evolution during which ethnic or nationalist fragments will seek attachment to a larger entity or a new power base to survive economically.

"The next stage, they are liberated, they feel free. They will be able to make their choice," predicted Helmut Wagner, a political scientist at the Free University of Berlin. "They will long for, they will pray for, becoming part of a bigger union which they can accept freely and which gives them their autonomy in special areas, especially in language, culture and their own ways. This is as strong as the disintegration effort, to become a member of a bigger union. If you don't do that, you have to pay a price, and the price is economic misery, and that means weakness."

Some "unions" may look like loose political confederations, some more like trade alliances. Others may take new, still-unshaped forms. Among the possibilities is an old idea being revived in a new form: unifying under one independent political and cultural umbrella the millions of Muslims who speak languages in the "Turkic" family of tongues and who occupy the landmass stretching from Europe into China. A region historically referred to as "Turkestan," it represents the accumulated legacies of

Genghis Khan, Tamerlane and the Ottoman Empire.

Turkestan is not, however, just an idea. Both the Soviet Union and China began experiencing political tremors with new import in April of 1990. In the Chinese province of Xinjiang, a Muslim separatist uprising near Kashgar, an oasis on the ancient Silk Road in the northwest's forbidding mountains and rolling deserts, was the bloodiest challenge to the central government since the 1989 Tiananmen Square rebellion. Thousands of troops had to be airlifted to remote Xinjiang before the April uprising was crushed.

Four months later, three thousand delegates from the Soviet Union's five volatile southern republics assembled in Uzbekistan to declare an Islamic "revolution" against the Soviet state and to demand imposition of Islamic law in all Muslim areas. The meeting marked the birth of the Islamic Democratic Party—and a daring assertion of political and cultural independence from communist rule and the Christian Orthodox tradition that had shaped Russian identity for centuries. Its intent was as potentially explosive as the uprising in neighboring Xinjiang.

Although long divided and widely scattered, the Turkic communities had begun tapping into the ancient roots of a common identity to claim a more prominent—and distinctive—place for their peoples. While Islamic in religion, their movement was unlike the fundamentalism of Iran or the Arab Middle East. The attempt to recreate Turkestan marked an effort to preserve, or reassert, the values and customs of a culture submerged in the secular materialism of the modern state.

The idea of Turkestan is not new, nor are Turkic uprisings in Central Asia. But in the past, Turkestan was merely the pipedream of individual communities seeking autonomy within their respective countries. This time around, disparate but determined separatist movements have sought independence in order to lay the groundwork for a single alliance, crossing traditional—and powerful—borders.

"Central Asian republics will find rapprochement and cooperation in their own union because we have too close cultural, economic and ecological problems for us not to find a kind of cooperation between us. We are already close to the people of Pakistan, Iran, Afghanistan and Turkey, and we should cooperate more closely," boasted Abdul Rahim Pulatov, the bearded and ebullient Uzbek chairman of an organization known as Birlik., which is the Turkish word for "Unity."

Birlik is just one of a handful of new pan-Turkic or Islamic groups in Soviet Central Asia espousing the cause. Formed in 1989, it called for Uzbekistan's independence from Moscow, a pan-Turkic alliance among Soviet Muslims and an Islamic revival. But Birlik's longer-term hopes were visible on the faded blue walls of its headquarters, an old mud-brick house with uneven wood floors and high ceilings in the ancient center of Tashkent, the Uzbek capital. Most prominent among the posters and charts tacked up in a meeting room was a crisp new wall map. Beneath the map, hand-lettered in Arabic script in the Uzbek language, was a simple inscription: "United Turkestan." Outlined above it was an entity stretching across nine countries on two continents.

Although initially limited to intellectuals and Muslim activists, the vision of a new Turkestan is not necessarily a quixotic fantasy. First, it would bring together peoples drifting on the periphery of several countries who fit the criteria of a viable nation-state: a common language, culture and religious heritage. "In the West, they speak too much about the common European home," said Mohammed Salikh, a member of the Uzbek Supreme Soviet and the author of the bill declaring Uzbekistan independence. "Why not speak about a common Asian home?"

Second, Turkestan could build a world powerhouse in terms of numbers and resources. While Xinjiang's population of fourteen million is comparatively sparse, its landmass—four times the size of California—is one-sixth of China. Underneath its barren land lies a third of China's coal reserves. And the discovery of massive oil deposits in 1989—heralded by some as the last region in the world to find major new deposits—has led to claims that the province will be the next Kuwait in terms of oil reserves.

And the five Muslim republics in former Soviet Central Asia, which all gained independence in 1991, offer some of the richest pastures and agricultural fields in the region, as well as vital oil, gold, uranium and other mineral resources. The landmass of the new states with exotic, tongue-twisting names—Kazakhstan, Uzbekistan, Kyrgyzstan, Turkmenistan and Tajikistan—is roughly two-thirds the size of the United States; the population exceeds fifty million people. In total, the fifteen Turkic groups of Europe and Central Asia—which also include parts of Afghanistan, Iran, Bulgaria and other smaller communities—account for some 135 million people.

As far away from their roots as they are in time and distance, most have not forgotten their ancient ways. The Muslim Uighurs of China's Xin-jiang province still use the Arabic script of their Islamic faith. The Muslim prohibition on alcohol and pork is still widely observed, as is Ramadan, the Islamic holy month of fasting and reflection. By custom and by language, separatists feel closer to their ethnic brethren in distant Turkey than to the Chinese among whom they have lived for centuries.

Despite common bonds, Turkestan may never become a nation-state, at least as traditionally defined. Many of the Turkic groups have their own, often rival, identities that have led to clashes; each also has its own particular version of Turkestan. The idea of Turkestan is more likely to draw together Turkic Muslim fragments from the world's last two great empires—and perhaps elsewhere—into a new kind of entity: a "brother-hood" of cultural, religious, legal and economic ties that hold sway across traditional borders and are beyond the reach of any central government. But the idea offers a taste of how the world's political spectrum may be redefined—and possibly the world map redrawn—as the powerful pas-sions of ethnicity and nationality assert their primacy.

On a broader level, Turkestan also reflects how the paradox between disintegration and integration—the simultaneous race toward villagiza-tion and globalization—will require new approaches in both domestic affairs and international relations. The 1992 world roster of 190 countries will, by the end of the century, almost certainly have new members, many also formed along unfamiliar lines, with fluid structures and unconven-tional identities. The challenge ahead, according to Ibrahim, the Egyptian sociologist, will be learning to live with "diversity within unity."

"We see localization, villagization of the globe. But you also see an internationalization of the globe. The two trends are emerging side by side. At one time, we thought it was globalization alone [that would work]. Now we see that it doesn't work. I don't think it will disappear. The world is becoming so interdependent that the smallest, humblest peasant in my village is affected in his daily life by what happened in Iowa or Texas, in Western Europe and in Japan, both in terms of products and ideas.

"But within that globalization of interdependence," he added, "there is also the assertion of local identities, whether it's religious, ethnic or subnational or national. The challenge for everybody is how to reconcile these two trends—not stop either one, because they are nonstoppable—

but how to harmonize them. How could I assert my local identity in food, in lifestyle, in dress, in feelings and so on and yet not be isolated or insulated or enclaved or marginalized or forgotten. That is the challenge now and it will continue to be the challenge in the first two or three decades of the twenty-first century."

Blowing rams' horns and strumming ancient Jewish harps, the little band from the Temple Mount Faithful set out October 8, 1990, on what was supposed to be a symbolic march. A court order barred the three hundred Israelis from bringing a three-ton cornerstone for a new Jewish temple anywhere near Jerusalem's most sacred square; for thirteen centuries, the Temple Mount has been the preserve of two of Islam's holiest shrines. But, as advertised in a widely distributed leaflet, the Faithful were determined to show that "the Temple Mount will not be silent until it is again the religious and national center of our people."

By the end of the day, Jerusalem had witnessed its worst violence since the 1967 War: twenty-one Palestinians killed and hundreds of Arabs and Israelis injured.

Twenty-two days later and 2,800 miles away, a similar tragedy erupted in India. In Ayodhya, Hindus massed on the holy city to lay the foundation for a new temple at the birthplace of the god Rama. For months, villages throughout the country had baked individual bricks inscribed with the lord Rama's name for the ceremony which, astrologers ordained, would be most auspicious between 9:44 a.m. and 11:48 a.m. on October 30. The only problem was that, for the past four centuries, the site had been occupied by a mosque.

As in Israel, the government tried to preempt trouble. The ceremony was banned, and ninety thousand were detained. A curfew confined all residents to their homes. And thousands of police set up barricades around the simple, single-story mosque with three graying domes. But, by the end of the day, twenty were dead and hundreds wounded in violence that swept six Indian states.

The tale of two temples reflects one of the most striking trends at the end of the twentieth century: In the world's most secular age, religion has reemerged as a formidable political force worldwide. "With few exceptions, not since before the Age of Enlightenment has religion been so globally vital, energetic and ambitious," said Ehud Sprinzak, a political scientist at Jerusalem's Hebrew University, during an interview on the Mount Scopus campus.

The politicization of religion has less to do with changes among the world's major faiths than with the contemporary political environment. "It's not a theological revolution—that suddenly some philosopher came and demonstrated the existence of God that wasn't available before," said Rabbi David Hartman, a philosopher and the director of Israel's Hartman Institute. Indeed, it is more often an effect, not a cause; a reaction, rather than an initiative, related less to renewed piety than to the themes of the Modern Age. In growing numbers, men and women are unsatisfied by the sterility of modern institutions, which have met neither their material nor deeper psychological needs. Three prominent voices from three prominent religions echoed similar thoughts:

"After we try to shed in this century all those things which have nothing to do with pure reasons, we found that pure reasons are something very sad, very empty," reflected Eliyakum Haetzmi, a member of Israel's Knesset, on a windy afternoon at Kiryat Arba, the early West Bank settlement he helped establish.

Added Gustavo Gutierrez, the reclusive Peruvian founder of Catholicism's Liberation Theology, "Modernity was born with the affirmation of the individual as the beginning, as the basis of the social contract." But, he suggested, a mentality which has the individual as the absolute principle does not fulfill man's basic need to believe that life is something more than just a process of survival.

And Rachid Ghannouchi, the soft-spoken philosopher and founder of Tunisia's Islamic Tendency Movement, offered, "Western thought is based on the principle that society can build a civilization without God. The slogans of development and nationalism and science were represented as substitutes for God. But this new God did not give happiness or stability to people. Science acknowledges that the human is so high and so wide, but it does not take into account man's depth."

Indeed, virtually all the ideologies of the Modern Era, both major and minor, relegated faith to a separate realm. Communism simply erased religion. Democracy privatized it. Even Zionism originally separated synagogue from state. Among ideologies designed for countries with strong single religious traditions—such as Peronism in Catholic Argentina and Kemalism in Islamic Turkey—most either ignored or gave lip service to those traditions. Even apartheid, justified by South Africa's white Calvinist leaders with Old Testament quotations, was secular.

For substantial numbers of people around the world, secular ideologies have failed, in varying degrees, to meet expectations or to provide fulfillment. "The promises of modernity in its various forms—whether an industrial consumer society or a classless society—don't seem to have worked out," said Harvey Cox, a Harvard Divinity School theologian.

Despite the democratic wave sweeping the world, secular liberalism has also not always provided a panacea, as reflected in the resurgence of religious and moral issues in American politics. In 1988, for the first time in U.S. history, both major parties had clergymen as serious contenders for the presidency, while abortion and prayer in the classroom were hot political issues. "Even in countries where national identity is not on the agenda, religion is growing," said Sprinzak, the Israeli political scientist. As a result of disillusionment or malaise, "more people today are leaving ideology on the road to theology in search of political solutions to the miseries of our times."

The reaction against failed ideologies has spawned some of the world's most vibrant—and most successful—religion-based opposition movements. When most of South Africa's black leaders were still exiled or imprisoned, Desmond Tutu, now the Anglican archbishop of Cape Town, led the anti-apartheid campaign; he won the 1984 Nobel Peace Prize. Buddhist monks have spearheaded opposition to Chinese communist control of Tibet; the Dalai Lama won the 1989 Nobel Peace Prize.

Romania's 1989 political upheaval originally exploded over the arrest of Lazlo Tokes, a Calvinist minister in Timişoara outspoken on minority rights. Mobs who took to the streets to demand his release eventually ousted the entire government of Nicolae Ceauçescu. In East Berlin, the Lutheran Gethsemane Church was the command center for public vigils and the pro-democracy movement before the fall of the Berlin Wall. "The [opposition] movement came out from the churches. I think it is quite impossible that [the revolution] would happen without the church," reflected Konrad Vekel, a member of New Forum, after Sunday services at the nineteenth-century red-brick church.

In some cases, religion is a refuge of last resort; in countries where opposition is outlawed, the church, mosque, synagogue or temple provides an alternative infrastructure and network through which to mobilize dissent. In totalitarian Iraq, the tightknit infrastructure of Shi'ite Islam provided the lone means for opposition to Saddam Hussein, who banned all but his own political party. Unlike the Kurds, the Shi'a did not want autonomy or a separate state—only representation in government, equal job opportunities and a proportionate share of the country's wealth.

The goals of many politicized religious movements are thus often similar to the goals of secular interest groups and parties. In other movements, religion serves as an anchor during times of turmoil. "We are so insecure," mused Shimon Peres, the former Israeli prime minister and leader of the Labor Party. "We need something to hang on to, to believe in. To believe is like to love, you must be a little blind."

In many corners of the globe, religion has already redefined politics. And the results are not always as clear-cut as the end of apartheid or the collapse of communism. Indeed, politicized religions are adding complex new dimensions to the world's political spectrum—as demonstrated most vividly in the 1979 Iranian revolution. Since then, Islam has become a powerful new player throughout the Middle East, challenging all forms of government and often by democratic means.

In socialist Algeria, in mid-1990, the Islamic Salvation Front swept the first multiparty elections in the country's independent history. It swept aside a party that had captured the hearts and minds of struggling liberation movements worldwide during the National Liberation Front's guerrilla war against French colonialism and that had ruled the country since its independence in 1962. In the Kingdom of Jordan, Islamists won thirty-three of the eighty parliamentary seats in the 1989 elections—the first poll in twenty-two years. In pro-Western Egypt, the Muslim Brotherhood has been the largest opposition force in the national assembly since 1987.

As the only major monotheistic religion with a set of laws by which to govern a state as well as a set of spiritual beliefs, Islam is more adaptable—and more legitimate—as a political alternative. But Islam is not the only religion challenging the secular premise of the modern nation-state.

Nowhere is the challenge of politicized religion more visible—in scope or complexity—than in India, the world's most populous democracy. In 1990, India was on the brink of war with Pakistan over the idyllic valley of Kashmir, where Muslims were fighting to secede. And in Punjab, violence over the Sikhs' demand for autonomy—or, among extremists, secession—resulted in an average of six hundred deaths a month.

But the issue that determined the fate of two governments was the hilly Ayodhya site where Hindus sought to replace a Muslim mosque with a temple to the Hindu god Rama. When former Prime Minister Rajiv Gandhi allowed fundamentalist Hindus to lay a foundation stone for the temple in 1989, Muslims withdrew their support from his Congress Party. In 1989 elections, Gandhi—whose family dynasty and Congress Party had ruled India for all but four years since independence in 1947—lost.

The same election marked the stunning emergence of a Hindu fundamentalist party as a major political player. With the temple as the centerpiece of its campaign in a country 82 percent Hindu, the Bharatiya Janata Party (B.J.P.)—or Indian People's Party—suddenly became the third-largest party in India. Its representation in parliament soared from two seats to eighty-six—and made it pivotal to the coalition formed to succeed Gandhi.

Unlike Islam, Hinduism is a highly individualistic religion, which incorporates thousands of sects loyal to different gods; its loose structure and hierarchy made it an improbable political mobilizing force. And Hindu nationalism is hardly new. Its modern focus and goals, however, have traditionally been secular—driving out British colonists, building a powerful and industrialized Asian state and maintaining democratic rule despite mass poverty. But with the B.J.P.'s ascension to the political mainstream, Hindu nationalism took on a religious agenda—shattering India's traditionally secular political spectrum.

"The overall growth of the party can be attributed to the people's disillusionment that the other ideologies are not moving up to the mark. They are not able to deliver," explained B.J.P. leader Lal Krishan Advani, a bespectacled figure who acted more like a soft-spoken grandfather than a fanatic during an interview at his bustling party headquarters in New Delhi. Advani claimed that the B.J.P. was a "Hindu renaissance movement rather than a fundamentalist or revivalist movement." And he insisted that he was not "a ritualistic person" and only "occasionally" went to temple. But in a matter-of-fact tone, he added, "I am against secularism. It has become a euphemism for minoritism, or a euphemism for covering up your allergy to Hinduism. This has made the Hindu react. Here's a party that does not shy away from the word Hindu."

Advani was also the mastermind of the 1990 Ayodhya temple campaign, orchestrating the village brick-making and leading a month-long, 6,200-mile "chariot journey" across northern India to mobilize Hindu support. Ignoring government orders to stop, he warned of "a mass upsurge the likes of which this country has never seen" if police moved to stop him. But, a week before the scheduled temple ceremony, Advani was among tens of thousands of fundamentalists detained.

"Religious fanaticism is the first step toward the foundation for a theocratic state. It will be the death of India as a secular state," warned Prime Minister Singh in a nationally televised address to urge Hindus not to march on Ayodhya. It was not an overstatement. At least three groups more extreme than the B.J.P. were already advocating the creation of a Hindu Raj or Hindutva, a Hindu nation-state. During the crisis, *The Hindu,* a secular paper despite its name, concluded, "However dismaying it may be to those committed to a vision of this country as conceptualized by Mahatma Gandhi or Jawaharlal Nehru, there is now a distinct phenomenon of Hindu fundamentalism to contend with in political terms."

After Advani's arrest, the reaction was, as promised, massive. Despite a ban on the temple ceremony, thousands of youths, wearing saffron headbands and shouting "Hail the Lord Rama," broke through police barricades. Defying tear gas and rifle fire, they planted three saffron flags—the color of the Hindu faith—on the mosque's domes and pummeled the building before being chased away. The worst single outburst of violence since independence from Britain raged for weeks. With its leadership under arrest, militant B.J.P. Hindus withdrew their support from the coalition. As India verged on chaos, Singh's government collapsed.

Ironically, historians and archeologists seriously doubt that the site now occupied by the Babri Masjid—or the Mosque of Babar, named after the mogul emperor—really was the "birthplace" of the warrior-god Rama. "Can you prove this is the birthplace of Rama?" Advani said. "No, you can't. No one can prove it. The issue is not whether it is the birthplace of Rama. The issue is whether it is *believed* to be the birthplace of Rama. This," he pronounced, "is a belief."

And a deep belief. After his release, Advani won support for the B.J.P.'s platform from six thousand Hindu religious leaders; many openly declared that politics should conform to faith.[3] The B.J.P. leader then summoned the faithful. The April 1991 rally, devoted to new plans to promote a temple in Ayodhya, turned out to be was the biggest in Indian history. In mid-1991 elections, the B.J.P. won at least 125 seats in parliament—officially making it the second largest party and the second most powerful force in Indian politics. As a result, the long-dominant Congress Party failed to win the clear majority needed to lead the country without coalition support. Even the assassination of Congress Party leader Rajiv Gandhi, one of an estimated three hundred to die during the most violent campaign in India's forty-four-year history, failed to elicit a sympathy vote strong enough to counter the B.J.P.'s growing appeal.

Religious fanaticism and conflicts are not unusual—especially in India and the Middle East. The words thug, zealot and assassin are derived from ancient extremist movements within Hinduism, Judaism and Islam. But, during the Modern Era, religious issues have rarely, if ever, had such grassroots influence or impact on political agenda—and never such global repercussions.

In Jerusalem, a religious march by three hundred members of the Temple Mount Faithful resulted in two U.N. resolutions; it even briefly threatened to shift world attention away from Iraq's invasion of Kuwait. The dispute, however, did not center just on whether a small band of Jews could gain access to the Temple Mount, the scenic thirty-five-acre plateau that dominates old Jerusalem's skyline. The historic center of Judaism, the Temple Mount's two Islamic shrines have been under Muslim control for centuries—and forbidden to Jews.* The dispute instead centered on rival religious missions: The devout of both Judaism and Islam believed that

---

*The Temple Mount—where King Solomon's temple was destroyed by Babylonians in 586 B.C. and Herod's temple was destroyed by the Romans in 70 A.D.—has been off-limits to Jews for almost two millennia. Although Israel conquered East Jerusalem in the 1967 war, the government allowed Muslim religious authorities to maintain control of the Temple Mount and its two seventh-century Islamic shrines—and to continue their prohibition on Jewish worship on the site.

control of the sacred area was a God-given right; allowing other faiths to have it amounted to betrayal.

For the Temple Mount Faithful, regaining Jewish access to the site of the First and Second Temples would be a major step toward man's salvation. "We live now in an age which uses words like 'redemption,' and it is a little ashamed to do so because it is a very logical age," said Gershon Solomon, the Faithful's leader, in his West Jerusalem home. "My struggle is not just for the physical site but for the broader mission. We must make the Temple Mount as it was in the past—the religious, spiritual and national center of all the Israeli and Jewish people."

Like Advani, Solomon, a white-haired anthropologist who walked with a limp from a war injury, did not consider himself a fundamentalist. He also only "occasionally" went to synagogue. "Our movement is nationalist," he insisted, adding in the same breath, "Our coming back to the Temple Mount is the will of God."

Religious nationalism, however, has explosive political import. Jewish absorption of the Temple Mount might fulfill "God's mission" by restoring ancient claims to the site. But taking over its mosque and the famous Dome of the Rock—or the site where Muslims believe the prophet Mohammed ascended into heaven in the seventh century to hear the word of God—would spark passions among Arabs as well as millions of other Muslims in the seventy-nation "House of Islam." The potential was visible when, on the morning Gershon Solomon and his little band marched into the old city, hundreds of Palestinians turned out and threw a barrage of rocks and stones against any Jew praying at the Wailing Wall next to the Temple Mount. Israeli police, in turn, opened fire; a bloody melee ensued.

In the early 1990s, the Temple Mount Faithful accounted for only a tiny fringe of Israeli society; it had the lone objective of building the third Jewish Temple on an ancient religious site. But many of its members belonged to a growing roster of Jewish religious parties with disproportionate political clout—and more ambitious and controversial goals. Among them: Jewish absorption of the Biblical lands of Judea and Samaria to create Greater Israel, as part of the covenant made between Abraham and God five millennia ago, to pave the way for the Messiah. Judea and Samaria are better known today as the Palestinian West Bank.

Formally annexing the West Bank would also effectively void the premise of a land-for-peace swap between Israel and its Arab neighbors to end
the world's longest modern conflict. While Israel's religious parties are
still a long way from their goal, they have, since 1984, gained sufficient
seats in the Knesset to determine which of the country's two major parties
will form a coalition. In exchange for its swing votes, each party has made
growing demands, ranging from bans on El Al flights on the sabbath and
public movies on the sabbath eve to control of key government portfolios.
The total effect has been, as in India, to erode Israel's identity as a strictly
secular state.

Just as stunning, however, has been the emergence of religious parties
among Palestinian Muslims.* After the outbreak of the *intifada*, or uprising, in 1987, a fervently Muslim faction called Hamas and the smaller
Islamic Jihad issued the most serious challenge ever to the Palestine
Liberation Organization (P.L.O.). Hamas, an underground movement,
attracted a new generation of Palestinians frustrated with the secular
P.L.O.'s failure after twenty years to gain ground, politically or physically.

"It is easier and more familiar for people to go with the ones who are,
like them, Muslims," explained Sheikh Saleh Amera, a bearded young
West Bank clergyman, about the growing Islamic fundamentalism in the
Arab world's traditionally most secular community. "People now think
[the one] who can liberate them is God. And [the movement] which is
closer to God is the Islamic movement."

But in a sharp split with the P.L.O.'s goals, the two Islamic fundamentalist parties also began to redefine the Palestinian conflict with Israel.
"The Islamic Resistance Movement considers that Palestine is inalienable
Islamic land, assigned to Muslims until the end of time," the forty-page
Hamas manifesto declared. "Renouncing any part of Palestine is equivalent to renouncing part of the religion. There is no solution to the Palestinian problem except through *jihad,*" or holy war. For Hamas, a
land-for-peace swap was also out. And, as the movement grew, the secular
focus of the Palestinian nationalist movement also eroded.

"We are witnessing a turning point," conceded Ziad Abu Amr, a

---

*Not all Palestinians are Muslims. Up to 20 percent are Christians. Most of the Palestinians
in the West Bank town of Bethlehem, for example, are Christian.

Palestinian political scientist at the West Bank's Bir Zeit University. "If the P.L.O. stumbles and falls, people who are now disaffected will go and seek something more simple, more authentic, more appealing, more comfortable . . . one that is more powerful than everybody. And that is God."

In 1991, both Jewish and Islamic groups espousing religious nationalism were distinct minorities. But, in the absence of a settlement, their appeal seemed certain to grow. "Jerusalem, eventually, will only be divided on religious lines: conflict between Arabs and Jews and between Jews and Christians," predicted Teddy Kollek, Jerusalem's legendary mayor. "I think nationalism will fade out, and it will remain a religious conflict." Echoed Ziad Abu Ghaneimeh, the spokesman for Jordan's Muslim Brotherhood in Amman, "Now, many of our Muslims all over the world are believing that the battle is a religious battle and not a nationalist battle." Even with a settlement, the strength of both Jewish and Islamic fundamentalist groups was already sufficient for either side to play spoiler.

The deadly skirmish at the Temple Mount in October 1990 reflected how longstanding secular conflicts can ascend to a higher—and more threatening—plane when a religious component is added. The entire political environment around it can be transformed. Should the appeal of either or both movements widen, the conflict between Israelis and Arabs over land and security could effectively be elevated to a crusade between Judaism and Islam. The flashpoint would no longer be Israeli security versus a Palestinian homeland, but the fundamental tenets and goals of the two faiths—a potentially insoluble conflict.

"Toward the end of the century, we find out that religious movements do not just want to participate in politics; they are fighting for ascendency, to take over," explained Sprinzak, the Israeli political scientist. "They're not going to make it, but they will change the agenda. They've already changed the agenda, and they will change it more."

The long-term impact from politicized religions and religious nationalism will indeed vary dramatically. Despite international isolation, economic sanctions and a devastating war, Iran's Islamic revolution surprised the world by surviving into the 1990s. Others may also succeed at reshaping nations, reconfiguring states or redefining conflicts. The influence and growth of individual movements, however, may depend more on the depth of the issues and problems that spawned them than on the faiths themselves.

The interim period of tumultuous change, Max Hernandez, a Peruvian psychiatrist and historian, reflected on a steamy day in Lima, "is like a violent tornado. When there's a tornado, what do people do? They go to the basement and cling to the pillars. It's the same with the current political transition in the world. As the tornado sweeps through, people go to the basements of their soul and cling to the pillars—things that have survived other political tornados, things like religion and ethnic roots."

The impact may be deep, but the results not necessarily destructive. "After the tornado passes," Hernandez added with a smile and a nod, "they come up and start to rebuild."

Democracy and Its Discontents

> *"Democracy is on trial in the world on a more colossal scale than ever before."*
>
> —CHARLES FLETCHER DOLE

On a dazzling August day in 1991, Moscow celebrated a victory over generations of fear. The evening before, an attempted coup d'état by hard-line communists collapsed in the face of popular resistance. As the army's tanks rolled back to the garrisons, thousands of people flooded to the headquarters of Russian President Boris N. Yeltsin to hear him proclaim the arrival of democracy in a land whose history had been dominated by tyrants. "The people of Russia saved democracy, saved the Union and saved the world!" Yeltsin declared. *"Svo-bo-da!"* the crowd replied—"Freedom!"

That evening, as fireworks lit the sky over the Kremlin, Muscovites strolled along tree-lined boulevards and laughed in front of the shuttered doors of Communist Party buildings, seized by the democratic authorities. As a crowd cheered, a pair of tall construction cranes completed the day's transformation by wrenching the twelve-ton statue of Felix Dzerzhinsky, the founder of the Bolshevik secret police, from its pedestal before the headquarters of the once-omnipotent K.G.B.

"We feel joy," exclaimed Alexandra Sunyakova, a forty-year-old nurse, as she walked arm-in-arm with a girlfriend. "It's the first time that we feel we really want to live."

But the morning after came all too quickly. Only a block away from the celebration, at the huge Tsum department store, doleful shoppers still waited for hours to file past shelves that were nearly bare of goods. "It is a holiday, yes, but with tears," a fifty-four-year-old bureaucrat complained. "All the problems we face will still be there tomorrow." Outside the Russian Federation parliament, where the demonstrators had cheered, an old woman in rags picked among the debris—and looked pleased when she found a paper bag of discarded carrots. Inside the building, Russia's new democratic rulers struggled to master the chaotic and desperate country they inherited.

"Very soon, people will begin judging the new democratic leaders by the way they cope in new conditions with the extremely serious problems facing the country," warned former foreign minister Eduard A. Shevardnadze, a Yeltsin ally. "The harvest is bad, production is in a free-fall and inflation is going to grow. . . . If these problems are not resolved, I am afraid that people may take to the streets."

Within months, communists and ultra-nationalists were demanding Yeltsin's resignation. "I have faith in our reforms," the Russian president said in 1992. "But if they fail, I can already feel the breath of the redshirts and the brownshirts on our necks."[1]

The dilemma of Russia's new democrats was more dramatic than most, but it was far from unique. Around the world, from Prague's Hradcany Castle to the Royal Palace of Katmandu, the end of the 1980s and the first years of the 1990s saw an extraordinary uprising of popular will sweep authoritarian governments from power. But on almost every continent, newly democratic regimes also found themselves mired in economic distress and under pressure from impatient constituents. Instead of a Golden Age of stable, humane politics, democracy brought new forms of anxiety and insecurity. "We have all become somewhat neurotic from the burden of freedom," said Václav Havel, the playwright who led Czechoslovakia's "velvet revolution" in 1989 and was elected its first democratic president. "Our hopes for a better future are increasingly mixed with a feeling of the opposite kind: fear of the future. . . . The old system has collapsed, the new one is not yet built and our life together is marked by a subconscious uncertainty about what kind of system we want, how to build it, and whether we have the know-how to build it in the first place."[2]

Every political system in the world, democratic and nondemocratic alike, faced a common crisis in the 1990s: the crisis of legitimacy. Ordinary people, increasingly knowledgeable about their own societies and informed by television about how other nations live, placed escalating demands on their rulers for prosperity, justice and honesty. "We are seeing the awakening of the citizen, where he begins to be conscious of his place and role in society," observed Andrei Shumaikhin of the Soviet Institute on the U.S.A. and Canada. "He becomes very assertive, sometimes in a negative way. He becomes politically conscious in a different sense, not just in an ideological sense. People are in search of their identity in society, in a huge and diverse society. It's like people coming out of slumber."[3]

During the 1980s, a new impatience in ordinary people challenged or toppled authoritarian regimes in dozens of countries, from the military dictatorships of Latin America to the entrenched communist systems of the Soviet Union and Eastern Europe.* But in the 1990s those fallen regimes' new democratic successors faced the same demands—and not all were equipped to meet them. In Argentina, a collapsing economy produced popular despair and a round of coup attempts from a new generation of colonels. In Dresden, the same East Germans who marched against communism in 1989 went back into the streets in 1991 to riot over unemployment under democratic rule. Even in the long-established democracies of North America and Europe, popular confidence in government declined, disenchantment with politics grew and small but troubling outbursts of extremism reappeared, from France's xenophobic National Front to America's Ku Klux Klan.

As a result, the 1990s promised new challenges to the world's remaining authoritarian regimes—and, paradoxically, new tests for its democracies

---

*From 1980 through early 1992, according to the private monitoring organization Freedom House, twenty-six countries attained full democracy: Bangladesh, Benin, Bolivia, Brazil, Bulgaria, Cape Verde, Chile, Cyprus, Czechoslovakia, East Germany, Estonia, Gambia, Grenada, Honduras, Hungary, Latvia, Lithuania, Mongolia, Namibia, Nepal, Poland, Sao Tome and Principe, South Korea, Uruguay, Western Samoa and Zambia. Thirty-two countries also made progress toward democracy: Albania, Algeria, Angola, Armenia, Azerbaijan, Belarus, Ethiopia, Gabon, Ivory Coast, Jordan, Kazakhstan, Kyrgyzstan, Lebanon, Mali, Moldavia, Mozambique, Nicaragua, Nigeria, Pakistan, Paraguay, Peru, Philippines, Romania, Russia, South Africa, Sri Lanka, Suriname, Taiwan, Tajikistan, Turkmenistan, Ukraine and Uzbekistan.

as well. Never, since its invention by the revolutionaries of America and France, has modern democracy been attempted in so many places and so many cultures, but its chances for success were not uniformly good. Just as the 1980s will be remembered for the unraveling of the communist faith, so the 1990s may well see the unraveling of the opposite idea—the notion of Western democracy as a universally applicable model. Democracy will almost certainly remain a universal touchstone. But after its adaptation to different cultures and political traditions, some of its new forms may be scarcely recognizable; in other societies, it will likely fail altogether. "The tide is coming in now; I think the tide will go out," predicted Brent Scowcroft. "A lot of them will not survive the strains of societies trying to cope with very difficult problems."

Democracy's crisis is taking three basic forms. First, where prosperity seemed beyond reach, as in Eastern Europe and Latin America, citizens frequently despaired of newly elected governments and sometimes turned back toward authoritarian rule. Empty grocery shelves and high unemployment tempted some to trade freedom for promises of order and security. In Romania, Bulgaria and Albania, remnants of the old communist regimes won the first "postcommunist" elections because people opted for safety before freedom. In Peru and Argentina, voters demanded economic salvation and democracy at the same time—but whether democracy could survive without prosperity became the central question of national life. "It's the first time democracy and poverty have been combined," Argentina's former foreign minister Dante Caputo claimed, with a measure of exaggeration. "We have a new kind of animal, with the legs of an elephant, the head of a dog and the eyes of a cat."

Second, in countries outside the Western cultural tradition, American and European ideas of pluralism and diversity sometimes collided with unfamiliar social and political doctrines. In the Arab world, the central political struggle was not between left and right, but between politicized Islam and secularism; in Egypt, Jordan and Algeria, the Arab world's first steps toward democracy produced victories not for Western-style liberals, but for Muslim fundamentalists.* In East Asia, the struggle was between

*Lebanon once claimed the title of the Arab world's only democracy, but lost that distinction during its long civil war.

the Confucian tradition of hierarchical authority and newer, more populist challenges. In Africa, it was between tribal and nationalistic forms of
political life. Even European Russia seemed headed down a tortuous path
toward a Slavic combination of democracy and authoritarianism. New
forms of democracy did not always produce identical views; despite the
end of the left-right confrontation of the Cold War, ideological friction
between democratic governments was still possible—such as the tension
between the Islamic world and the West.

Third, even in the stable and prosperous West, there was a consensus
among politicians and citizens that democracy needed renewal, but little
agreement on how to go about it. In parts of Western Europe, the radical
right and the radical left showed worrisome bursts of strength; traditional
conservative and social democratic parties seemed exhausted. In the
United States, polls found Americans deeply troubled by the chronic
shortcomings of their own political system, its empty campaigns and
paralyzed governments; in 1992's primary elections, "none of the above"
ran strongly. On both continents, new movements and pressure groups
were seeking to make government more responsive.

Still, those convolutions were merely products of an historic shift toward democracy. Two centuries ago, the world had only two democracies,
the small United States and France—and France's first republic fell to a
military dictator after only ten years. By the beginning of the twentieth
century, the number of democratic governments had risen to exactly ten,
eight in Western Europe and two in North America. In the 1930s, the
rise of fascism so threatened democracy's survival in Europe that the
British historian Arnold Toynbee wondered "whether this political plant
can really strike permanent root anywhere except in its native soil."[5] Only
after World War II did the democratic idea spread more widely—if only
slowly at first—to scattered countries like India, Japan and Costa Rica.

As recently as 1980, Freedom House, a private organization that moni-
tors civil liberties worldwide, counted only fifty-six democracies among the
world's 160-odd countries. By 1992, the number had jumped to eighty-
nine, and thirty-two more were in transition toward freedom—the first
time in history that democracies constituted a majority among the nations
of the earth.[6]

The roll of new democracies is impressive. In Latin America, Argentina, Bolivia, Brazil, Chile, El Salvador, Guatemala, Panama, Paraguay and Uruguay all turned away from dictatorship in the 1980s. In Asia, the Philippines, South Korea and Taiwan shed authoritarian rule. In the communist world, the Solidarity revolt in Poland, liberal experiments in Hungary and Gorbachev's reforms in the Soviet Union created a slowly building tidal wave, which broke with the revolutions of 1989: Poland in August, Hungary in September, East Germany and Czechoslovakia in November, Bulgaria and Romania in December. The aftershocks rippled as far as Mongolia, where a parliament called the Great Hural was elected in 1990, and Albania, where Europe's last Stalinist rulers submitted to elections in early 1991. The wave crested again in Moscow's August 1991 revolution, when Russia's democrats defeated a rear-guard authoritarian coup and banished communism from the Kremlin itself.

The democratic trend rolled across Africa, too, where in 1991 Benin's president, Mathieu Kérekou, became the first strongman on the continent ever voted out of office. By then, Cape Verde, São Tomé and Príncipe, Ivory Coast and Gabon had all held elections; Nigeria and Mozambique were promising elections; spirited campaigns for democracy arose in Cameroon, the Congo, Ghana, Guinea, Kenya, Madagascar, Mali, Togo, Zaire and Zambia. Even the Arab world, the last great undemocratic swath of earth, felt some ripples at last: Jordan held elections in 1989, Algeria in 1990, and the emir of Kuwait, his legitimacy tattered by his regime's incompetence during and after the Gulf War, promised a vote in 1992.

The sweeping trend found democracy struggling to take root in sometimes arid ground, and a dizzying new diversity of democratic forms as well. The old left-to-right political spectrum that had defined politics during most of the twentieth century—with authoritarian communism at one end, authoritarian fascism at the other and a more-or-less uniform model of Western democracy in the center—had disintegrated. In its place was not a single, linear spectrum, based on European or American political institutions, but a wild proliferation of competing democratic models and ideologies, which reflected the traditions of many cultures: the hierarchical authority networks of Japan, the tribal social structures of Africa, the ineradicable caste system of India, the Koranic strictures of the Muslim world. In the United States, Christian activists sought to promote their own religious agenda, Germany's Greens made harmony with nature a political goal, and a new Soviet party called the Blues even looked to other planets. Each reflected a search for solutions to economic and social problems which the Modern Age had failed to provide; each pulled the political spectrum into new and unfamiliar shapes.

A few months before the collapse of the Berlin Wall in 1989, an audacious scholar named Francis Fukuyama suggested that the coming triumph of democracy could mean that humanity had reached its final, highest stage of development—or, as he titled his provocative essay, "The End of History?" He wrote, "What we may be witnessing is not just the end of the Cold War, or the passing of a particular period of postwar history, but the end of history as such: that is, the end point of mankind's ideological evolution and the universalization of Western liberal democracy as the final form of human government." The culmination of civilization, he suggested puckishly, had turned out to be "liberal democracy in the political sphere, combined with easy access to VCRs and stereos in the economic."[7]

But even Fukuyama soon admitted to misgivings about his venturesome thesis. Democracy and capitalism appeared triumphant at the beginning of the decade—but would they remain so? "Is life in liberal democracies going to be satisfying?" he mused. "If not, then history is going to continue."

The worldwide wave of revolution and renewal in the 1980s was unprecedented precisely because it was so widespread. In sophisticated Prague and remote Katmandu, in Catholic Chile and Buddhist Burma, newly mobilized populations linked for the first time by global communications asked for the same things: political empowerment and economic survival. The 1990s would test the limits of both of those aspirations.

"As long as people are people, democracy, in the full sense of the word, will always be no more than an ideal," Czechoslovakia's Havel said in a speech to the U.S. Congress. "One can approach it as one would the horizon, in ways that may be better or worse, but it can never be fully attained. In this sense, you, too, are merely approaching democracy."

With luck, Daman Dhungane, a middle-aged lawyer from Katmandu, may some day be remembered as the James Madison of the Himalayas.

A member of the commission to draft the first democratic constitution for Nepal's twelve-hundred-year-old monarchy, Dhungane trekked from the slopes of Mount Everest down to jungle valleys in 1990 to ask his countrymen what their charter should say. He got responses Madison never imagined.

"All they say is 'airplanes,' " Dhungane recounted with a sigh. "Everyone wants an airfield and an airplane, plus seeds and fertilizer. How can we write that into the constitution?"[8]

The dilemma of the lawyer from Katmandu reflected a predicament facing many of the world's new democracies: From Asia to the Andes, citizens want fundamental political liberties. But they often judge a government first on how well it delivers material goods—airplanes and fertilizer, jobs and prosperity. Throughout the twentieth century, when economic troubles hit countries with weak democratic institutions, democracy frequently collapsed. The regimes that followed were authoritarian and sometimes bellicose—from Germany's Hitler to Latin America's generals.

Nowhere was the problem starker or more heartbreaking in the early 1990s than in Poland and Argentina, where people struggled bravely to escape from tyranny only to bog down in a legacy of economic misrule. In both countries, the old political struggle between the left and the right was transformed into the question of whether citizens would maintain their faith in democracy or surrender to the siren promises of authoritarian demagogues.

Poland opened the way for democracy in Eastern Europe with the epic, decade-long struggle of the Solidarity trade union movement. But little more than a year after Solidarity's 1989 triumph, economic hardship stripped democracy of its initial luster and allure. An economic-austerity program stunned Poles with its severity; in 1990, more than a million found themselves suddenly unemployed, and the price of bread more than tripled. In Gdansk, at the very shipyard where an electrician named Lech Walesa had launched Solidarity, workers staged a wildcat strike over hardships under President Walesa. Almost overnight, the language of politics changed from celebration to recrimination.

"We have freedom, but we still have not achieved the democratic order," warned Adam Michnik, one of Solidarity's leading intellectuals.

"Even as we are conscious of our victory, we feel that we are, in a strange way, losing." Political life in Poland, he predicted, would not follow the classic path of "a Western European state, with division into left and right. It will be a conflict of two political cultures: on one side, the culture of European liberalism, and the other, nationalist, authoritarian and conservative."[9]

Indeed, Solidarity split in two along the lines Michnik predicted. The movement's charismatic leader, Walesa, ran for president in 1990 on a populist platform tinged with authoritarian zeal. "Today, when we are changing the system, we need a president with an axe: decisive, tough, straightforward," the blunt-spoken Walesa declared. The president, he said, should be able to issue decrees, without waiting for parliament to act: "I would save half of Poland if I had such powers." His main rival, the Polish-Canadian entrepreneur Stanislaw Tyminski, campaigned for "a democracy of money," a free-market economic policy that he promised would make every Pole wealthy within a month of his inauguration. Only one candidate, Prime Minister Tadeusz Mazowiecki, called for both scrupulous adherence to the democratic process and perseverance with the austerity plan—and the voters rejected him decisively.

Hungary and Czechoslovakia, which had enjoyed some experience with democracy before World War II, suffered the same ills as Poland; Bulgaria, Romania and Yugoslavia, with a more meager democratic heritage, did even worse. A 1991 poll found that only 22 percent of Poles said they were satisfied with democracy; in more prosperous Hungary, only 30 percent were satisfied.[10]

Part of the problem was that the transition to prosperous democratic capitalism proved much longer and more difficult than almost anyone had imagined. Instead of growing, Eastern Europe's economies initially declined; the World Bank forecast that they would need the entire decade of the 1990s merely to recover to their 1989 levels of production.

But part of the problem, as well, was that many East Europeans were ill-prepared for the risks that capitalism imposed. Even where the transition should have been easiest, in the East German lands that were absorbed into the ready-made structure of West Germany, the change was wrenching. "Maybe it's all gone too fast," fretted Hans-Joachim Rockstroh, who was trying to turn his East Berlin typewriter-repair shop into a business that could compete in the new Germany. A few doors down, he noted, the neighborhood handyman had tried to turn his knife-sharpening shop into a Western-style retail outlet, and had failed. "He didn't have any business for four weeks. He tried to hang himself," Rockstroh said, adding, "The rope broke." The syndrome was widespread: in 1991, psychologists in Leipzig, the former East Germany's second largest city, reported that suicides had more than doubled since the country's unification.

South America also had to struggle to hold the gains of its democratic revolutions. A continent once run by so many generals that military rule was dubbed "the Latin model" boasted an unbroken string of elected civilian governments by 1990. And after a long period of economic disaster, most governments proclaimed that protectionism and state management of the economy were wrong.

"We in South America are enacting a true epic," said Argentina's former president Raul Alfonsin, who restored democracy after seven years of brutal military rule. "This has occurred in the framework of the worst [economic] crisis we have suffered in this century. This thoroughly gives the lie to those who suggest that democracy is not viable in countries that don't have a given level of well-being or economic growth."

But while Alfonsin's words at the rundown headquarters of his political party were hopeful, his tone was melancholy; the democracy he had restored was in danger of collapsing amid economic chaos. In 1989, inflation soared to more than 3,000 percent, hungry mobs looted supermarkets, and Alfonsin decided not to run for reelection. His populist successor, Carlos Saul Menem, launched economic reforms so stringent that they shocked his own followers. Menem's program drove inflation down to an estimated 30 percent in 1992, but the achievement was painful for many citizens. By the early 1990s, thousands of Argentines were so disillusioned that they applied to emigrate back to Spain and Italy, the countries their grandparents had left almost a century before in search of a better life.

"There is a danger that with this disenchantment could come a pre-Nazi climate, a climate that would allow all the authoritarian sectors to move us backwards," Alfonsin warned.

Political scientist Atilio Boron was blunter. "You can save democracy only when you can show that democracy matters and that democracy works," he said. "Alfonsin said that with democracy people would eat, people would find their [kidnapped] children and people would be cured. None of that came true. . . . Democracy for us has been nothing. If democracy does not work in Latin America, then the way is open for . . . an ultra-nationalist right-wing movement," he concluded.

Estebal Lijalad, the director of a Buenos Aires polling organization, confirmed that a kind of selective despair had begun to take hold—and that popular faith in democracy was one of its victims. "We are polarized between two options: people who want democracy and people who want order; people who want privatization and people who think the state is important for social services," he said. "The economic and social decay has diminished support for democracy. There has been a deterioration of liberal values. In 1983, democratic values were supported by ninety percent of Argentines; today, that number is smaller."

In 1981, after Argentina's generals led the country into a disastrous war with Great Britain over the Falkland Islands, the nation rejected military dictatorship. But by the end of the decade, the military was restive again, and the cafés of Buenos Aires buzzed with speculation about the next coup attempt. The country's fastest-growing party was the Republican Force, a rightist group led by retired General Antonio Domingo Bussi. In 1984, Bussi was charged with ordering the summary execution of political prisoners during the military dictatorship; he was never tried. In 1989, his party won ten of twenty contested seats in the legislative assembly of the province of Tucumán in northwest Argentina.

"This battered society has said enough is enough," the general proclaimed. "There is no stopping us now."

Jordan's 1989 parliamentary election was its first open vote in twenty-two years and one of the most democratic ever held in the Arab world. The campaigning was spirited; for the first time, women were allowed to vote; and the count was scrupulously honest. And the winner of a clear plurality in this exemplary contest was an alliance of "Islamists"—Muslim fundamentalists—who held democracy legitimate only as long as it obeyed the dictates of the Koran. "Islam is the solution," the winning campaign slogan had promised. Many of the new legislators openly rejected the secular Western values that most Americans and Europeans think of as part and parcel of democracy. In a telling moment in the Persian Gulf War of 1991, most of Jordan's democratically elected parliamentarians stood in fervent support of Iraq's dictatorial Saddam Hussein.

"We accept democracy," said Laith Shubeilat, a soft-spoken civil engineer who was one of the newly elected Islamists. But in the next breath he added, "We do not accept *liberal* democracy. . . . The values of society should be Islamic." One of the basic goals of Islamic democracy, he said, was to make Muslim values the moral standards of Jordanian society and Muslim religious law the basis of civil jurisprudence. Otherwise, he complained, "We are Muslim hardware being reprogrammed to carry Western software."

In the decade ahead, the banner of democracy may unfurl over forms of government the West will find hard to accept or even understand. "The American model is a model that will not function in certain countries," noted Valéry Giscard d'Estaing. "The universal values will be values of liberty. But the organization of power can be on very different models."

In China, the students who occupied Beijing's Tiananmen Square in 1989 erected a homemade version of the Statue of Liberty. But their vision of democracy was not at all identical to what demonstrators in Prague and Berlin wanted. "I believe the form of pluralism most suited to stable change [in China] is not the multiparty system of the West, but, rather, a 'regional pluralism' that would evolve along ethnic and regional lines," wrote Li Xianglu, one of the Beijing reformers.[11]

In Africa, leaders of one-party autocracies, from Zaire's Mobutu on the right to Mozambique's Joaquim Chissano on the left, moved haltingly toward multiparty systems. But in some countries, the target was a distinctly African hybrid relying on an autocratic president to balance rival ethnic and tribal groups. In Kenya, when the government moved reluctantly toward a popular vote, leaders of the minority Luo tribe declared that they did not want democracy if it meant domination by the majority Kikuyu. In Nigeria, the continent's largest proto-democracy, two parties contested elections in 1991, but both had been established by the military; one was strong in the Muslim north, the other in the Christian and animist south. "The idea of the nation [in Africa] still will need time to consolidate," explained Luis Bernardo Honwana, Mozambique's minister of culture.

"The trend in Africa is less a drive toward democracy per se than a popular turn against established governments," explained Pauline Baker of the Carnegie Endowment for International Peace. "They want good government as much as they want open government. In some countries, it may lapse into benevolent dictatorship, if that seems to be the quickest way to get good government."

What was happening in each country was a new marriage of modern democracy and traditional culture. As government and opposition groups sought legitimacy in the eyes of an increasingly demanding public, the most successful candidates made a triple promise: political empowerment, preservation of traditional values and economic betterment. Even Iraq's defeated Saddam Hussein, who came to power as an explicitly secular strongman, tried to assuage his people after the catastrophic defeat of the Gulf War by pledging to institute multiparty democracy, redouble his faith in Islam and devote himself to rebuilding the country. His sincerity may have been suspect, but his need for legitimacy was not.

In the Muslim world, democracy and political Islam developed hand-in-hand; many of the new religious-oriented parties advertised themselves as democratic precisely because they appealed to the values of the devout man in the street rather than the secularized elite. In 1989 and 1990, Islamist movements won a majority in Pakistan and an apparent majority in Algeria, where the government annulled the election. Islamists also commanded significant minority support in Egypt and Turkey. In Tunisia, an Islamic party led the democratic challenge to an autocratic regime.

To citizens of the West whose image of Islam has been formed largely by the actions of terrorists or the excesses of Iran's revolution, Islam and democracy may seem incompatible. But Muslim scholars say their faith admits more diversity and tolerance than most outsiders realize. "There is no single Islam: there is regressive Islam, reactionary Islam, progressive Islam—all sorts of Islam," said Essam Montasser, an economist at the American University of Cairo and the former director of the United

Nations Africa Institute. Likewise, he added, "There isn't one single democracy: there is regressive democracy, corrupt democracy, progressive democracy, efficient democracy. . . . Democracy has many shapes."

In Iran, the followers of Ayatollah Ruhollah Khomeini have instituted a limited democracy that holds competitive elections and extends the vote to women, but requires that all laws pass the scrutiny of Shi'ite theologians and severely restricts women's conduct. In Tunisia, on the other hand, the leader of the Islamic Renaissance Party, Rachid Ghannouchi, has espoused a more moderate Muslim democracy that would take religious law only as an inspiration and would guarantee equal rights to women in the workplace and the right to initiate divorce.

The experience of power has had a moderating effect on some Islamists. In Pakistan, Prime Minister Nawaz Sharif won office in 1990 on a Muslim religious platform and declared the Koran to be the supreme law of the land—but carefully deferred most specific questions of how its principles might be enforced.[12] In Jordan, after the Muslim Brotherhood and its allies won thirty-three of eighty seats in parliament, King Hussein also gave them a third of the cabinet seats, including the important ministries of education and health. They soon discovered the frustrations of governing, especially in a country that had lost most of its foreign aid and much of its trade by siding with Iraq in the Gulf War. "The present government inherited a huge burden, a huge foreign debt," explained Ghassan Tamimi, a spokesman for the Islamists, in what sounded like a rather conventional, nonrevolutionary excuse. "The Muslim Brotherhood never promised that within a certain span of time they'd be able to correct the damage."[13]

Of all the globe's cultures, the Arab world has been slowest to take up the challenge of empowerment. The twenty-one Arabic-speaking countries sprawling from the Persian Gulf to the Atlantic Ocean make up the world's largest sanctuary of old-fashioned absolute rule—by kings, sultans, emirs and one-party "presidents." The result is festering public frustration and cynicism. "The Arab countries have neither a stable political logic nor an identifiable political creed," the Egyptian columnist Mahmoud Saadani complained during the Gulf War. "They are more like a circus with no manager in charge. Sometimes they are moved by regional interests, sometimes class interests or clan interests. In the end, it is all a matter of crass interests, and nothing else."[14] To many Arab scholars and politicians, a political and social explosion—many explosions—seemed inevitable.

But the test of democracy in which the world held the greatest and most immediate stake was in Russia and the other republics of the former Soviet Union. A millennium of Russian history produced nothing resembling democracy, save nine chaotic months in 1917, an interlude that was cut off by Gorbachev's Bolshevik predecessors. Insulated from the rationalistic and humanitarian precepts of the Enlightenment, Moscow's sprawling empire became an ironbound collection of authoritarian cultures, from czarist Leningrad to the Mongol steppes. Even this generation's drive toward democracy was initially ordered from above, in good Russian fashion, by Gorbachev.

Ultimately, of course, Gorbachev's reforms far outraced their author's intentions. The general secretary launched his program of *perestroika* in 1985 as a measured attempt to perfect communism; instead, in only seven years, he presided over the destruction of his faith and the disintegration of his empire. In the place of the Soviet Union at the dawn of 1992 stood fifteen independent republics, each struggling to nurture its own home-grown democracy, each with a free parliament, angry protesters, robust debates—and deep economic problems.

The new freedom was exhilarating, but it brought nearly 300 million former Soviet citizens only halfway toward a stable democratic political system. Many were deeply skeptical of pluralism, worried about a general breakdown of order and angry about the empty shelves of their grocery stores. In 1990, pollster Nikolai Popov found that almost two-thirds of ordinary Russians were cool to the idea of political pluralism; only 27 percent said they wanted a multiparty system. During the aborted coup d'etat in August 1991, when Yeltsin appealed for a general strike, there was little immediate response from the Moscow public; only after the coup began to collapse did large crowds rally to his side. Within half a year, the initial thrill was decisively gone; a Gallup poll found that only 15 percent were satisfied with democracy, and only a third said they believed the country was going in the right direction.[15]

The central problem, said Vyacheslav N. Shostakovsky, the leader of a reformist group of former communists, was that Soviet citizens did not know what democracy was. "We do not have a democratic tradition," he said, as he cleaned out his cavernous office at the Moscow Higher Party School, a training academy for communists which he directed until he publicly abandoned the party in 1990. "The Soviet people do not know what a multiparty system is. We had a period in February 1917 with literally thousands of parties, but the Bolsheviks exterminated both their opponents and their allies. In Eastern Europe, as soon as there was no threat of Soviet tanks, you had a rapid destruction of the communist structures. Our situation is different. All this grew on our own soil.

"Soviet society is turning its back on Marxism-Leninism, but at the same time it needs a new religion, a civil religion," he went on. "No wonder. There has been an ideological brainwashing which has affected millions of people over decades. Take a value like collectivism. Soviet man is not ready for individual risk. He views the collective as the basis of life. He would like to believe that his leaders are virtuous, but he can see that isn't true. . . . Everybody here wants a party to lead him by the hand."

On the extreme right, Shostakovsky noted, democratization had an unforeseen side effect: the resurrection of fascist, anti-Semitic and extreme nationalist groups. "They can exploit sentiment toward minorities and Jews—and the old Russian idea of empire is still alive," he said.

Even democrats like Yeltsin sometimes showed an authoritarian streak. The Russian president issued peremptory decrees, ran his parliament of his Russian Republic like an old-fashioned boss, and gathered control of the republic's media in his own hands. One of his new outlets, a weekly called *Democratic Russia*, even had a censor with the Orwellian title of "Editor for Democracy," who made sure that nothing was published that might harm the cause. Yeltsin's courage was undeniable, but his own supporters worried that his devotion to civil liberties might prove thin.

Some forecast a form of rough democracy tied to traditional Russian nationalism, with the Russian Orthodox Church playing a major role. Alexander I. Solzhenitsyn, the exiled novelist, proposed a revival of the "Zemstvos," local councils that existed in czarist times, as the core of a partly democratic, partly aristocratic system. Russia "does need democracy and needs it badly," Solzhenitsyn wrote in a 1990 essay. "But given our lack of preparation for the complications of democratic life, it should be built little by little, from the bottom up."[16]

What finally emerges, French social historian Emmanuel Todd suggested, may be a kind of hybrid: "a liberal facade on an authoritarian population." He said, "I don't think [Gorbachev's reforms] mean that the traditional authoritarian aspect of Russian culture has dissipated. I'm quite sure they are going to produce something intermediate. I think their conversion to democracy is sort of instrumental; they are converting to liberal democracy because it works, not because they love it."

In an old five-story apartment building at 122 Weitlingstrasse in what was once the communist half of Berlin, the leaders of Germany's newest political movement met in 1990 behind reinforced doors. Their headquarters' narrow entryway was filled with shiny new rolls of barbed wire; steel grates leaned against a wall, ready for use as instant barricades.

Officially, the members called their movement the "National Alternative." But almost everyone in the neighborhood called them by their old name: Nazis. Its members were young and disaffected, like the Nazis of an earlier era. And while no one in the new, unified Germany expected the National Alternative to win any elections, few expected them to disappear soon either.

"The potential in [the former] East Germany today for people on the right and people who think in terms of nationalism is very big," declared Andreas Richard, a twenty-year-old, fatigue-clad machinist and a member of National Alternative's ruling council.

Within a year of its unification, Berlin was already showing signs of the vicious political polarization that had divided it in the 1920s. For every neo-Nazi cell, the city harbored an equally eccentric leftist faction, from anarchists to radical Greens. Rightists and leftists regularly traded punches in the streets, in a dim echo of the political brawls of their grandfathers' days. On Hitler's 101st birthday in 1990, small mobs of rightists smashed shop windows, stormed a homosexual bar and harassed foreign tourists; a few weeks later, leftists attacked the National Alternative's headquarters on Weitlingstrasse.

On paper, at least, the Germans seemed to have everything: general prosperity, a stable democracy and, now, reunification. So why were so many unhappy with the new order? Spokesmen for the neo-Nazis, the anarchists and radical Greens offered vaguely similar answers, despite enormous differences in their ideologies: Somehow, parliamentary democracy failed to satisfy all the vast hungers of people caught up in a confusing, changing world. Some Europeans still yearned for causes and ideologies more transcendent than smoothly functioning market capitalism.

"I am convinced that this capitalist market economy is going to disappoint people," said Baerbel Bohley, one of the leaders of New Forum, a popular movement that helped topple East Germany's communist regime. "A market economy has no vision of society. It's a very hard reality." She reflected, "We're going to have to think completely anew again. One of the problems with the world economy now is that it places so much emphasis on growth. . . . The world ecological system isn't going to be able to support all this growth.

"The fall of communism was actually very simple; millions of people went to the streets and they just said no," Bohley added. "I think people are going also to have to say no to capitalism. That will be our task—to think how we should say no to capitalism. The task isn't just to topple the system; it's also to change humanity. . . . The most important task now for New Forum is not to sit in parliament, but to try to restructure society from underneath."

That kind of utopian vision worries even some of the Greens, who are divided between radical fundamentalists ("Fundis") and more moderate realists ("Realos"). Some of the Realos, who have espoused cooperation with the mainstream Social Democratic Party, have warned that German nationalism and romantic environmentalism could merge into a movement some have dubbed "eco-fascism."

Rudolf Bahro, one of the Greens' founders, has even warned that Germany might turn to a "Green Adolf," an environmentalist authoritarian. "Empty men full of fear, as we Germans know, are the raw material of authoritarianism," he said. "If someone comes to the German people and says, 'I am the man who will make the pine needles green again,' he will be given a chance. In the deep crises of humanity, charisma always plays a role. The deeper the crisis, the darker the charismatic figure who will emerge."[17]

Of course, in any society, someone is always unhappy; and the Germans, with their tradition of romanticism in politics and philosophy, as well as art, have developed more elaborate forms of unhappiness than most. "I think ten years from now we will need to have gone through a real reevaluation of our current values," said Vera Wollenberger, a leader of the Green movement in the former East Germany. Eventually, she said, "I think we will experience a similar collapse of the capitalist system."

There was little sign of that in the short run. Still, in Germany's 1992 state elections, the "fringe" parties scored their highest votes in postwar history. In normally conservative Baden-Wuerttemberg, the rightist Republican Party won 11 percent of the vote; on the left, the Greens won almost 10 percent.

The upsurge of extremist politics was not confined to Germany. In France, the rightist National Front won 14 percent of the vote in local elections in 1992, largely by stirring hatred for non-European immigrants. In Austria, Belgium, Italy, Sweden and Switzerland, rightist parties advanced at the expense of the center. Even in the United States, former Ku Klux Klan leader David Duke won a startling 44 percent of the vote in 1990 for a U.S. Senate seat from Louisiana.

There was more going on than simple racism or xenophobia. The fringe movements of the 1990s were similar, in a sense, to the unorthodox parties that sprang up during the Industrial Revolution of the nineteenth century and at similar times of serious social stress. They were responses to larger strains of adjustment. Paradoxically, as traditional quarrels between left and right died down, fringe movements gained more support. Both the new European right and the Greens arose in part to provide those disoriented by economic and social change "a chance to express their anguish," as historian Todd put it.[18]

But there was yet a deeper question, a philosophical one: Is democracy satisfying to the soul?

The two totalitarian ideologies of the twentieth century, communism and fascism, were both utopian creeds, born of dissatisfaction with democracy abetted by economic distress. Even amid the triumphal celebrations of 1989 and 1990, there were some who suggested that the same bleak mood could arise again.

"Liberalism has won, but it may be decisively unsatisfactory," wrote Allan Bloom, the conservative social philosopher at the University of

Chicago. "It appears that the world has been made safe for reason, as understood by the market, and we are moving toward a global common market, the only goal of which is to minister to man's bodily needs and whims," he wrote. And in such a future, he argued, a rebirth of fascism could not be counted out. "If an alternative is sought, there is nowhere else to seek it," Bloom wrote. "I would suggest that fascism has a future, if not *the* future."[19]

Bloom's gloom was prompted, paradoxically, by Francis Fukuyama's ebullient suggestion that history had reached its apogee with the universal acceptance of liberal democracy. Few agreed with him that totalitarianism was likely to resurge in any significant way. Yet even Fukuyama admitted that his venturesome theory might stumble on a philosophical question.

"The question is this: Is perfect security and material prosperity sufficient for people? Those have been fragile enough goals for all of human history thus far. The philosophical question will be: Is that what makes people happy? Or is it the struggle to get there that makes people happy?"

In a sense, the collapse of communism, the end of the Cold War and the surge of democracy during the last years of the 1980s may only have been the first wave of an even broader transformation—a wholesale reinvention of the political spectrum.

"Behind all those changes there is a changed world—and I think the world has changed before our mind is changing," reflected Israel's Shimon Peres. "Actually, there are more changes in reality than changes in ideology. Ideology is a latecomer." Of the major currents in modern politics, Peres argued, "All three have passed away: communism, socialism and capitalism. Nothing is left. The capitalists are loaded with social responsibilities . . . communism is a total failure . . . socialism was wavering in between."

Political thinking, in short, has yet to catch up with events. "Things are changing faster on the ground than we have been able to revise our conceptual categories," said Egypt's Saad Eddin Ibrahim. "It used to be that intellectuals were ahead of changes on the ground. Now, all of a sudden, we find that the changes are running faster than our ability to generate new schemes to understand things."

That has left a vacuum in both fledgling new democracies and stable old ones. Public opinion in almost every country reflects deep disaffection with political institutions. In a 1990 poll of Americans, 57 percent complained that ordinary people had no say in what the government did; 53 percent felt that elected officials did not care what the people thought.[20]

Such findings have driven some Western politicians to adopt an ambitious but as yet ill-defined goal: the revitalization of democracy itself. Amid sweeping changes in economic activity, social structures and technology, they argued, political systems will be forced to evolve—either by design or by necessity.

"Democracy will have to be reinvented," predicted Gianni de Michelis, the foreign minister of Italy. "We will have to move from what I call Newtonian democracy, based on a mechanistic understanding of science and culture, to democracy based on systems theory, interaction and flexible feedback—with no fixed flow of information and power [moving] from top to bottom or bottom to top."[21] In the 1992 U.S. presidential campaign, Ross Perot proposed much the same thing, in the form of "national town meetings" that would help him make decisions in the White House.

"When you see this process of change, the only way you can basically keep in touch with what is going on is by having an open society and a democratic regime," said the World Bank's Sagasti. "Are we going to be able to evolve sufficiently quickly over the next two to three decades to make this transition to whatever comes next? What we need to do is to move in terms of our concepts. I think the ultimate frontier is going to be that of empowerment. This means how do you empower people to think for themselves, and then to act?"

In the absence of ideologies, individual issues were the crucibles of political and social change. One such issue with unexpected political impact was the environment. Environmental protection was the unforeseen rallying point that helped spark 1989's revolutions in Eastern Europe; Bulgaria's opposition front was even called "Eco-Glasnost." The 1986 explosion at the Chernobyl nuclear power plant in the Ukraine, which scattered a plume of radioactive fallout across half of Europe before Soviet authorities even acknowledged the problem, was a watershed event that convinced many Soviet citizens that their government's promises had been lies. "Chernobyl helped us to understand that we are a colony," said Sergei Odarich, secretary general of the Ukrainian nationalist movement Rukh. Soon the most effective grassroots organizations in the Soviet Union were environmental groups, from committees to protect Leningrad's eighteenth-century canals, to the campaign to save Lake Baikal in Siberia. A 1990 poll by the Soviet Institute of Sociology found that more Soviet citizens cited pollution as a pressing issue than any other—more than either the future of *perestroika* or the lack of food in the shops.[22]

By 1990, environmental issues had become surprisingly potent in poor countries as well as rich ones. In India, impoverished peasants joined a campaign to stop the construction of dams on the Narmada River because of the damage they would do. In Brazil, after decades of promoting slash-and-burn clearing in the Amazon basin, the government moved under both domestic and international pressure to stop the destruction.

"This I would consider a major change, a fundamental change: We have realized that we cannot act with impunity on the environment," said Sagasti. "We have become as human beings too large in terms of the scale of our activities to treat the environment in the way we did in the past. That is a fundamental economic, political and value shift. And it happened in twenty years."

The shift could have at least one broad ideological consequence: a demand for bigger government. Environmental protection often requires action on a gigantic scale, from the U.S. Superfund program to clean up toxic wastes to the international restraints on the release of chlorofluorocarbons and other harmful chemicals into the atmosphere. By nature, most of these are government actions, so public demands for environmental protection become demands for government activism.

One last factor affected Western politics at the start of the 1990s: the simple swing of the pendulum. Despite the triumph of free market capitalism around the world, the conservative crusades of Ronald Reagan in the United States and Margaret Thatcher in Great Britain appeared to have run their course. In the United States, the Republicans' national coalition was "rooted mainly in the distant psychologies of the 1960s and 1970s," Republican analyst Kevin Phillips wrote. "Historical patterns suggesting that a new U.S. political cycle might begin in the 1990s took on a new plausibility."[23]

The new cycle did not begin right away; neither a rejuvenated socialism nor a Green crusade nor the old extremisms rose to pick up the pieces. The political systems of the West seemed afflicted with a kind of conceptual exhaustion. The fringe parties were little more than symptoms of disaffection; the "mainstream" parties produced few challenging new thinkers. "If there is a positive side in the early 1990s, it is that even ideologues are growing impatient with ideological conflict," wrote the *Washington Post*'s political guru, E. J. Dionne, Jr.[24] But rather than a new centrist synthesis, the exhaustion of the old struggle instead left a vacuum.

The end of history, it appeared, would take a while yet to arrive; the transition from one political era to another was only beginning. But one signal lesson should have been clear: the citizens of every country retained the right to surprise their rulers—not only in Beijing and Leipzig but in the West as well. It was a good time for insurgents, whether right or left.

On September 6, 1990, the voters of Ontario, Canada's largest province, elected a new government. Disaffected with two major parties, which seemed to have run out of ideas, they turned, for the first time in their history, to a third party, the socialist New Democrats. The old-line parties, the Liberals and Conservatives, were stunned. But then, so was Bob Rae, the leader of the New Democrats, who suddenly found himself the province's new premier.

"If I believed in forecasts," he said. "I wouldn't be here."[25]

Empowering the People

"Men make history and not the other way around."

—HARRY S. TRUMAN

On the eve of the twenty-first century, the world is feeling the power of the individual more than at any time in history—often in novel ways. On January 1, 1990, Tres Arroyos, a sleepy Argentine farming village, erupted. Hundreds of unarmed villagers stormed the local police station, overturning police cars, smashing their windows, then setting the cars alight. Police trapped inside the station opened fire, wounding more than twenty. But the chanting crowd refused to disperse. The siege at Three Little Rivers, as the town three hundred fifty miles south of Buenos Aires translates from Spanish, had begun.

The unprecedented display of popular rage was sparked by the disappearance of nine-year-old Nair Mustafa on New Year's Eve. The police had rebuffed repeated family appeals for a search; in desperation, the little girl's frantic mother had gone to the local radio station. On the air, she pleaded with the public to provide the help that the police had refused. Dozens of farmers in Three Little Rivers responded. On New Year's Day, they found Nair near the railway tracks. The little girl had been raped and strangled. Infuriated, the villagers turned on the police.

"These were only farmers, with no traditional local leadership, a peaceful people," reflected Martin Granovsky, a bearded young Argentine political analyst, a few days later. "In the 1970s, these people would have turned to the military. No longer. They no longer believe in anybody— civil, political or military. They felt exhausted with no solutions, so they set out to resolve this problem themselves." And they did. To end the siege at Three Little Rivers, the provincial government was forced to replace the entire police force; the villagers were allowed to choose the new chief.

The Age of Enlightenment, born in eighteenth-century Europe upon the principles of liberty, equality and justice for all, has finally begun to penetrate down to the lowest strata of society in the most remote corners of the globe. Old frustrations and new awareness among people once on the political fringe have combined, with potent impact: Just as nations have begun to balk at subjugation in the name of the state's interests, so too have individuals begun to reject authority that excludes them—sometimes by violence, sometimes by creating their own alternatives and increasingly by finding new faces or new forms of leadership. Demands for empowerment, participation and accountability have become among the most energetic forces of change.

The result is a redistribution of internal power, the reallocation of authority. By the early 1990s, longstanding elites—ancient clan chieftains as well as modern dynasties, local officials as well as national politicos— were being challenged or swept aside. The power to lead was, in turn, no longer beyond the reach of everyman. A novelist, a priest and a village of angry farmers, actors, housewives and talk-show hosts, even a beekeeper and a plumber—the leaders emerging in politics around the world were as striking as the changes in ideologies.

The transformation marks the evolution of the very concept of empowerment. After the French and American revolutions of the eighteenth century, "empowering the people" meant giving white men equality and the vote. Excluding women and blacks, the franchise was hardly universal, elected officials rarely a fair representation. American blacks had to wait until the late nineteenth century, and women in both countries until the twentieth—1945 and 1920, respectively—to gain access to the polling booth as well as to public office.

Citizens in more than ninety countries—almost half the world's total— were not enfranchised until they gained independence in the twentieth century. Even then, however, the end of colonialism did not guarantee empowerment. France waited until 1977 to transfer power to Djibouti, its northeast African colony. But Djibouti is still a one-party state and has been ruled without interruption by one man since independence. Brunei, an oil-rich British colony in southeast Asia, did not become independent until 1984—and the sultan has still never allowed elections. Indeed, the island kingdom resisted independence in part because the sultan refused to give up absolute rule. Elsewhere, states have waited until the end of this century, and then only under duress, to truly empower. Still others are yet to move.

The struggle to fulfill the Enlightenment's promise will be the trademark of the 1990s and beyond—not only among the last holdouts and even in democratic countries. In the twentieth century, hundreds of grass-roots movements have bubbled up from the bottom to challenge the status quo, but the uprising at Three Little Rivers was especially striking because it did not target a totalitarian regime of either the right or the left—as did the 1986 "people power" revolt against dictator Ferdinand Marcos in Manila and Beijing's 1989 mass pro-democracy sit-in at Tiananmen Square. Indeed, it happened at a time when South America's governments were, for the first time, all democratic.

Nor did it arise from a new doctrine of social activism, such as Liberation Theology, which has spawned thousands of self-help "base communities" among the impoverished or oppressed, from Peru to the Philippines, from Hungary to Haiti, since first espoused by Father Gustavo Gutierrez in the early 1970s. The Argentine mutiny was, instead, a spontaneous popular outcry. It came out of nowhere, involved no dogma or institution, and had no leader.

Demands to make empowerment real through active inclusion of all segments of society and to make authority accountable will be at the center of changes to come. "In Peru, it is true that we now have democracy. But all that allows us to do is elect a new king every five years," lamented a young Peruvian journalist during a walk through Lima's teeming barrios on the eve of the 1990 democratic presidential election, the third in a decade. "In between, we have no rights, no one to hold responsible. Legislators pass thousands of laws, but the laws just sit there. No one does anything with them. The population is basically ignored.

"That," he said, smiling, "will be the next change." Hardly novel in the First World of industrialized democracies, accountability and participation have revolutionary portent throughout the Second and Third Worlds. Even within countries deep into democratization by 1992, people were no longer blithely accepting what they were being given. Individuals and local communities were reaching for greater control over the sources of authority and types of laws that regulated their lives—a phenomenon that was vividly visible in the resistance to the abortive 1991 Soviet coup. The push is now to decentralize, to further disperse power from the top and bring it down to the bottom.

The new participants were also giving the process a new twist. The push for empowerment worldwide has traditionally been led by oppressed communities' most educated or experienced elites: the Reverend Martin Luther King, Jr., among American blacks; Mohandas Gandhi, a lawyer, among Indian nationalists; Nelson Mandela and Oliver Tambo, both lawyers, among South African blacks. Most populist movements of both the left and the right have middle-class origins: James Weaver, an Iowa lawyer, was the first populist U.S. presidential candidate from the People's Party in 1892; the Italian dictator Benito Mussolini was a journalist and editor; Argentina's Juan Perón was a career military officer.

Even insurgencies have historically been led by elites: Yasir Arafat, an engineer, was one of five middle-class Palestinians who formed the P.L.O.; Abimael Guzman, a philosophy professor, founded Peru's Shining Path insurgency; Jonas Savimbi of Angola's UNITA guerrilla movement was educated in Switzerland.

In stark contrast, many of the new faces and forms of leadership were giving populism new meaning in the early 1990s. They sprang spontaneously from the bottom instead of from the middle or the top.

The Argentine uprising represented the first and most unconventional of three new types of leadership emerging as empowerment spread. Not just a standard grass-roots movement, it was also, in the traditional sense, leaderless. It had a body but no head. The uprising was empowerment in its purest form. Everyman *was* a leader. And it was not an isolated incident. Working-class populations in three other small Argentine towns—San Vicente, Medanos and General Alvear—launched impromptu mass protests the same month against official abuses, bribery and corruption. In San Vicente, hundreds took to the streets day after day until the police chief and two ranking aides were sacked for failing to investigate crime.

Among Bulgarian artists and teachers, Sri Lanka mothers and Turkish bazaar merchants, other ad hoc forces emerged to empower themselves and hold officialdom accountable on issues ranging from government misdeeds and missing persons to unexplained price hikes of Coca-Cola.

"Because leadership is a social function, if the existing leaders do not respond to the needs of the grass roots, then the marginals, the un-privileged, the disfranchised, will generate their own leaders," explained Saad Eddin Ibrahim, the Egyptian sociologist. As empowerment spreads, "we'll see more of it everywhere."

Empowerment gained momentum in the 1990s because the tools of political action were available to more people than ever before. Changes in leadership were produced in no small part because of knowledge; people worldwide increasingly became aware of how much more was possible—and of what they had a right to demand.

The media revolution in the second half of the twentieth century stimulated the drive for empowerment, participation and accountability more than any single factor over the previous two centuries. In the 1960s and 1970s, the transistor radio hooked up remote villages with limited electricity to the rest of their countries, and then the world. By the end of the 1970s and into the 1980s, affordable and portable short-waves offered uncensored accounts of what was happening elsewhere, videos and international television news services a regular look at the rest of the world.

By the end of the 1980s, CNN provided the first truly global medium. In the 1990s, most countries had access to live CNN coverage of Eastern Europe's revolutions against communist dictators, a Kurdish uprising against Saddam Hussein, Nelson Mandela's release from the jails of apartheid, and the minute-by-minute unraveling of a three-day coup attempt in Moscow. The evolution of empowerment and participation worldwide was played out in living rooms thousands of miles away.

Media technology, by accident as much as intent, also helped to standardize the definition of "rights," "freedoms" and "power" worldwide—and, in turn, to diminish public tolerance for official promises or duties unfulfilled. It also gave everyman a means of being heard when leaders refused to listen. Finally, it provided a channel of alternative action or recourse. Even where communications were government-controlled, technology has so proliferated that people have gained access to the tools— tape recorders, photocopiers, computers, fax machines and video cameras—needed to empower themselves.

The media have also contributed to a second category of new leaders: the nonpolitical politician with no independent base of support or experience. The actress-mayor of Istanbul, two former-housewife presidents of the Philippines and of Nicaragua, and the housewife–prime minister of Bangladesh were but a few. Some filled a vacuum left after the demise of communist or authoritarian rule. Some drew support merely for being untainted by politics or for being relatives of bygone heroes. Others had the sole credential of public exposure—and acceptance.

Candidates in India's 1991 elections were a microcosm of each category. Among the contenders for parliament in the world's most populous democracy were a movie star, a bordello owner, three former members of the national cricket team, a rifle-toting ex-bandit who claimed credit for almost a hundred and fifty deaths before he gave up a life of crime, a former king and his mother (on different tickets), and a seventy-eight-year-old former world body-building champion. Even the Hindu fundamentalist party put forward a movie actor who had played a leading role in *A Passage to India,* as well as two local television stars.[1] Indian politics were no longer the preserve of traditional politicians who, polls showed, were losing credibility and respectability among voters.

"People are now experimenting more and looking for new faces," said Granovsky, the Argentine analyst. "Democratic values are not going down, but they are deeply frustrated by traditional parties and politicians." The media, from radio to movies, helped to create visible alternatives.

The search for men and women who will share power rather than construct new dynasties or ideologies named after them has often focused less on ideological positions than on credibility, public trust and fresh approaches to governance. In a reversal of the old axiom, electorates often appeared to prefer the devil they did not know politically than the devil they did; novelty attracted more votes than experience.

The change in criteria contributed to the rise in the early 1990s of a third group of new faces: the fringe politicians and "outsiders within the system" who had not had the backing of party bosses—and often not even the parties. Among them were a rebel K.G.B. general who won a Soviet congressional seat, only to start calling for the dismantling of the Soviet Union, and the presidents of Peru, Brazil and Argentina. Like a host of others, they mixed promises of something different with a tinge of legitimacy. They also attracted electorates who increasingly used their votes to reject traditional political elites.

"People are beginning to use democracy very well," Armando Cavalieri, leader of a major Argentine union, said, chuckling, during a meeting in his plush Buenos Aires office. "They are using their rights as a way to punish politicians." Constituents are also less bonded to the traditional political spectrum and are willing to take risks in selecting leaders. "They are no longer linked to one party or one politician," he added.

But as with all the stunning shifts during the transition to a new era, the search for new and more representative leaders holds both promise and frustrating paradox. Empowerment is requisite to genuine pluralism and democracy; from it, in principle, springs consensus and therefore stability. But empowerment, particularly the abrupt overhauls in Eastern Europe and Latin America, can also combine inexperienced constituents with unconventional candidates which, together, can create greater instability or even undermine democratic trends.

On the extreme edge of the fringe politicians by the early 1990s were the new charismatic and messianic leaders. In countries plagued with deepening economic problems and social divisions, they played to or exploited public desperation with sweeping pledges of decisive action delivered in fiery orations. Seeking the moral high ground, they often played off deep religious, national or ethnic passions and problems of social decay. Among the new charismatics were the priest who was elected president of Haiti, the protestant evangelist who was elected president of Guatemala and a charismatic former general who was elected governor of an Argentine state.

"Economies are increasingly subsistence, so people limit themselves to worrying about survival," reflected Raul Carignano, Latin American Affairs secretary at the Argentine foreign ministry. "It's the rule of the jungle. Saving yourself is the prime goal, and so there's indifference to ideology. That is when the danger of messianic leaders emerges."

Indeed, the single common denominator among all three categories of new leaders was the diminished role of ideology in the pursuit of empowerment. Disillusioned or exhausted with the gamut of political creeds, societies were looking instead for more tangible or practical formulas and faces for solutions. Shifts in the premises of power—from ideological dominance and military might to economic strength—further changed the criteria by which leaders were judged. Challenges to traditional nation-states—from both larger regional blocs and smaller ethnic, national or religious communities—also altered the constituencies around which people grouped and the type of leaders they selected.

Even in democracies, electorates were demanding a greater say in shaping political agendas; leaders, in turn, had less freedom in choosing the issues their governments addressed. The bottom line: Domestic balances of power, especially in newly empowered communities, could change as much as the international balance of power.

"The new politicians do not mean a negative reaction to politics. They express a renovation of politics from the point of view that the masses discover," asserted Enrique Bernales, a tall, imposing Peruvian senator who was reelected in 1990. "The masses are looking to become protagonists. They want to be in a position where *their* imput determines the future."

In May 1990, Turkey went on strike. No one organized it; no one was even sure quite how it started. But everyone—from Istanbul's legendary bazaaris and shop managers in the Aegean seaport of Izmir to café owners in rural villages—participated. With unusual fanfare, the nation's press made the first "people's strike" a cause célèbre. The issue that galvanized the nation: the price of cola.

When the price soared, overnight, by more than 60 percent, "it became more expensive than in Europe," recounted an angry Erol Kazanci, a middle-aged mustachioed carpet dealer who owns a little stall in Istanbul's famous bazaar. "And we do not make the wages they do in Europe.

"So everybody voluntarily latched on and stopped buying it. Turkey is suffering terrible inflation—up to seventy, eighty percent. Everything is going up—margarine, detergents. Meat is the worst. Turks are generally very patient people, but now they've been pushed to the point they are exploding. This was our way of saying 'no.' " Within a week, Coke and Pepsi were down to just a fraction above their original price.

"In my lifetime, I haven't seen anything like it," Kazanci recounted, shaking his head in amused amazement. Since the military transferred power to civilian rule, Turkey has witnessed several formal strikes called by unions over wage disputes and working conditions. But the raw surge of people mobilizing themselves—without an initiative from a union or a party or the summons of a leader—was a new political phenomenon.

The "people's strike" reflected the progress of pluralism in the twentieth century—and a new direction as it comes to a close. For centuries concentrated in formal institutions emanating from central authority or operating at its grace, power has slowly but consistently devolved. Governments have increasingly had to share power with autonomous trade unions and political-action committees, giant corporations and private interest groups, social associations and even the press. The twentieth century has been marked by the growth of diverse and often rival power centers.[2] In the postwar era, grass-roots movements added a further component, vying for power or building alternative social and political blocs. In the 1990s, power is devolving even further. Indeed, the central authority of the state is being challenged as much by devolution of power within as it is by the globalization of power worldwide.

In Sri Lanka, the challenge within took the form of twenty-five thousand members of the "Mothers' Front," which first took to the streets in February 1991 to demand that the government account for up to sixty thousand Sinhalese men and boys who had disappeared since 1988. Most were believed to have been executed by death squads.[3] The same month, in Brazil, truckloads of teachers, farmers and police stormed the steel-and-glass governor's palace in the southern state of Mato Grosso do Sul, forcing the governor to flee. A statewide strike had failed to restore salary payments, stopped when the province ran out of funds, so a group of strikers decided among themselves to take over the palace.[4]

"One thing that is different from where we were forty years ago: We thought if we had an elected president in power, then people had control of the state," commented Felipe Ortiz de Zevallos, a Peruvian sociologist at Lima's Pacífico University. But even in countries where democracy has been restored—Turkey in 1983 and Brazil in 1985—electorates want more. "Now people are saying that getting [democratic] power is not sufficient to solve things."

The most energetic political dynamic as empowerment spreads is the informal consensus that awakens or arouses communities once resigned to political acquiescence. Usually leaderless, it grows up around an issue rather than an ideological dispute; many are even apolitical. Although its form of mobilization is grass roots, informal consensus can bring together disparate economic groups, as it did in Turkey; diverse races, as in Brazil; or different classes, as in Sri Lanka. Its impact, however, can be as powerful as the vote in changing society as well as the state.

Community consensus galvanized peasant farmers in Peru. Since 1980, hundreds of villages in the lush mountainous interior have been trapped in a war between the army and Shining Path, a Maoist group waging South America's most serious insurgency. Guerrillas have killed village farmers who refused support, leaving their mutilated bodies as a warning to the rest of the villagers. But thousands of mestizos, people of mixed Spanish and Indian blood, and Indians have also been tortured or executed by the army for suspected aid to Shining Path. By 1990, an estimated twenty thousand Peruvians, mainly civilians caught in the middle, had been killed since the insurgency began in 1980—the same year democracy was restored in Peru.

So in February 1990, the untrained peasants of Andamarca, a farming hamlet a hundred and sixty miles east of Lima, took matters into their own hands. Armed only with machetes, sticks and slingshots, they took on a guerrilla band trying to wrest control of the area. Eight Shining Path guerrillas were hacked to death; the rest were scared away.[5]

"Something new is growing," explained Luis Pasara, a Peruvian sociologist and lawyer. "It's a kind of popular privatization, where one small part of society takes its own way and substitutes for the state organization." Added Ortiz, "There's a failure of the intellectual class to interpret events right now. The ideas come from the grass roots, from the poor, who are not long-term or intellectually oriented. Through these new communities, people start learning"—and acting.

The ragtag group in Andamarca was one of dozens—some said hundreds—of *rondas campesinas,* or informal peasant patrols. They first appeared in Peru's rural areas in the 1980s in response to the exclusion of Indians and mestizos from the political mainstream; a minority of Spanish whites have dominated Peru, even in a democratic era. As former apathy turned to anger, and then action, the *rondas* began offering an alternative. In some areas, they were vigilantes who took on cattle rustlers and petty criminals and, once captured, enacted their own, often crude justice. Elsewhere, they substituted for Peru's unwieldy court system, adjudicating conflicts among neighbors, and even issuing divorce decrees. By the early 1990s, the *rondas* had become so powerful that the government mobilized and armed several as formal militias—and the first line of defense against Shining Path.

"We may be creating democracy in Latin America that fits formal standards," said Diego Garcia Sayan, a young lawyer who heads both the Andean Jurists Commission and Peru's Human Rights Association. "But the process so far is still not enough because these governments do not allow participation of people in the daily events of government. As a result, people are creating new mechanisms to empower themselves." By creating viable alternatives, power is being, de facto, decentralized.

The most novel expression of informal collective empowerment was the "City of Truth," a camp of pup tents that sprang up overnight in central Sofia, next to the office of the Bulgarian president, in July 1990. The thousand residents represented a cross-section of students and teachers, artists and housewives. Leadership was shared; each day, they elected a new "mayor."

The eyesore "city" was erected to demand accountability from the reformed communist government, elected just a month earlier. It worked. After a videotape exposed President Petar Mladenov calling for the use of tanks against demonstrators during the 1989 uprising, the protesters demanded that he resign. He did; his replacement was the first noncommunist Bulgarian president in four decades. On grounds that deposed communist leader Todor Zhivkov should publicly account for the political and economic disasters of his thirty-five-year rule, the city demanded an investigation. Zhivkov was formally charged with corruption and misappropriating funds, and then tried. Charging continued communist bias in the media, the group called for the resignation of the chief of Bulgarian television. He was forced to comply. And to remove the most conspicuous symbol of former communist rule, the street politicians pressured the government to remove the embalmed body of Georgi Dimitrov, the father of Bulgarian communism, from a Sofia shrine. The embattled Socialist Party leadership succumbed. Dimitrov was cremated. Afterwards, the City of Truth inhabitants hung a none-too-subtle sign on the empty crypt: "It stinks."[6]

Within a month, the City of Truth, which had by then spawned thirteen other tent cities across Bulgaria with an estimated quarter of a million supporters, began dismantling. Its main demands—inconceivable just a few weeks earlier—had been met. The street politicians had irrevocably changed the political atmosphere in Bulgaria, as well as the system; the primary residual leaders and symbols of communism had been eliminated. Like the Turkish consumers, the Brazilian civil servants and the Sri Lanka mothers, they had also established important precedents for the future: Small communities have since been emboldened, politicians cowed.

A new populist consensus even cracked through the largest and most powerful authoritarian government on earth—ironically, based on collective will, in theory at least—and forced the Soviet Union to surrender power. Once again, the challenge was sparked spontaneously when a handful of coal miners launched a protest over food supplies in the small Siberian town of Mezhdurechensk. Within two weeks, half a million workers—from western Ukraine to eastern Siberia, from southern Russia to the Arctic Circle—had joined in; the demands expanded to include better working and living conditions across the board. The industry-wide strike, unprecedented in the Soviet Union, almost paralyzed the nation in mid-1989.

"Nobody organized it ahead of time," recalled Anatoly Malykhin, a hulking Siberian miner in his thirties who has since become the recognized leader of the new Russian labor movement. Nor was there a counterpart to Poland's Lech Walesa to spearhead the initial challenge. Instead, "It was like nature. It was a storm," he said. Throughout the night, laborers elsewhere commandeered trucks from their own mines to go see what was happening at Mezhdurechensk. They were impressed. "We decided to go around to all the mines in our city, explain the situation to them, and ask their support," Malykhin recounted. "At first, people were afraid to support us, but within twenty-four hours the entire region was on strike."

As remarkable as the strike was the discipline and calm that prevailed in the miners' tense standoff with the government and its own tightly controlled unions, from which the strikers were breaking away. During the crucial two weeks, laborers in both Siberia and the Ukraine organized patrols to prevent trouble, women set up outdoor cafeterias, liquor stores were closed.[7] A viable alternative was born, and the framework for the nation's first independent trade union established.

By the end of 1990, the grass-roots coal miners' movement had formally organized nationwide. Along the way, they brought in Soviet railway workers, a combination so powerful that the two groups could shut down the entire country. The nation's oil and gas workers subsequently signed on, creating a body capable of cutting off the nation's only major source of foreign exchange.

For the first time since the 1917 revolution, the Soviet Union had a genuine workers' movement that had grown from the bottom rather than been imposed from the top. The episode set a vital precedent in the country's transformation. Long term, the collective clout of workers—reinforced with repeated strikes and sweeping political demands for officials' resignations—posed a challenge to state and Communist Party power as serious as the republics' demand to secede from the Soviet empire. A new group of worker-politicians, who once had no say in the system, suddenly had the power to determine its future—an experience of critical importance in the demise of the Soviet empire.

"Suddenly everybody realizes that the secret word is participation at the grass-roots level," concluded Emre Kongar, a Turkish political analyst and pollster. "The changes in the communist world have nothing to do with whether Marx was right or whether Lenin was wrong. It has to do with whether people are taking part in the government apparatus or not"—and in the decisions affecting their lives.

Since 1976, Ricardo Belmont Cassinelli, an athletic, curly-haired former boxing promoter, has been a fixture on Peruvian television. From game shows, he went on to host a national talk show. He likes to refer to himself as the Johnny Carson of Peru. Belmont's popularity was such that, in 1988, a hundred thousand viewers contributed enough money for him to buy a television station. He named it RBC, which are also his initials.

In January 1990, Belmont was inaugurated mayor of Lima. "My victory was an electoral earthquake. The traditional politicians were surprised, but I wasn't," he reflected in the cavernous mayor's office at city hall, erected by Spanish conquistadors in 1662. After years of interviewing politicians, he said, "I realized I could do a better job. If you have credibility and know how to speak the language of the people, you can easily be a leader. People don't care anymore about having leaders explain things to them. They want to have politicians speak to their hearts."

With the theme from *Rocky* as his campaign song, Belmont won 46 percent in a field of nine candidates. "During the campaign," he flashed a wide television smile, "many people called me and said, 'This is the first time I'm going to vote because I've known you since I was five.' When you're on TV you're part of the family. You're in their bedrooms."

Peruvian politicos scoffed at Belmont. But the talk-show host was not a fluke. He was among a growing number of nonpolitical politicians filling city halls, parliament seats and even presidential palaces. The reasons varied: In some places, the wave of democratic changes in the 1980s offered freedom of choice—but often not much to choose from. In others, old parties resurrected had failed before, while new parties were not yet sufficiently well-rooted to sway voters. And virtually anywhere, political transitions produced transitional politicians—and wild cards. But the common denominator was that the new faces in politics were all people perceived by electorates as accountable—to them, not just to party bosses.

Distinct from Belmont, but selected for similar reasons, were relatives of past politicians elected to office: Corazon Aquino, the widow of an assassinated opposition leader, replaced dictator Ferdinand Marcos as president of the Philippines in 1986. Benazir Bhutto, the daughter of an executed former prime minister, was elected premier of Pakistan in 1989, after the death of General Zia ul-Haq. In 1990, Violeta Chamorro, the widow of another assassinated opposition leader and press baron, replaced the Sandinista president in Nicaragua. In 1991, Khaleda Zia, the widow of an assassinated former president, was elected prime minister of Bangladesh after a popular uprising forced her predecessor, a general, to resign. The day after former Prime Minister Rajiv Gandhi's 1991 assassination, his Italian-born widow Sonia was elected head of India's Congress Party.* Each offered a different form of celebrity or familiarity reinforced by past political bonds. Whatever their qualifications, each initially was a symbol of a commitment to empower.

Belmont's election represented a combination of frustration with the old, the unknowns among the new, and the vacuum in between, with one other factor. His election fell at a time when expanding pluralism and the absence of popular alternatives was mixed with the growing influence of the media. "Experience" had taken on a whole new meaning. To a plurality of voters, Belmont had credibility merely because of his accessibility. After his election, he still hosted a talk show every Saturday morning on RBC, fielding questions from his constituents.

During one show, a woman called in. "Mayor," she began.

Belmont quickly interrupted, "Please, call me Ricardo."

The caller then explained a complicated problem she had with municipal officials over paperwork and asked why the city did not have computers.

"Do you have kids?" the mayor responded.

"Yes, ten," she said.

Belmont then offered, "So what do you do when the kids ask for toys? Sure, they're in the shops, but you can't afford them. So your children have to do without them. Me, too." Although Lima's mayor had no specific new solutions, his unprecedented visibility gave him the appearance of bonding with his constituents, the illusion of being accountable.

The celebrity-politician has had particular appeal in developing countries, where the gap between politicians and the newly empowered was still wide. For thirty-two years, Fatma Girik was best known as an actress who, in 170 films, played roles that ranged from the Turkish version of Norma Rae to a female Hamlet. In 1990, she still looked—and acted—the star. "In the films, I was always a very respectable hero," she said, spraying a tissue from a bottle of Giorgio, one of several colognes on her desk, and wiping her forehead, neck and wrists. "No one would ever believe that Fatma Girik could do something bad—in the same way that people would

*She declined to accept the post.

never believe that John Wayne couldn't shoot straight." The image was convincing. In 1989, voters in Sisli, an historic district of Istanbul, elected the aging actress mayor.

"I'm not a leader," she conceded. "I didn't have anything to do with municipal affairs before." Nor, by her own admission, did she have any interest in running for office, until Turkey's Social Democrat Party approached her. The odds were also against her: Female politicians were still a rarity in Islamic Turkey and, in Sisli, the country's ruling Motherhood Party had a longstanding hold.

Because of limited campaign funds, "We didn't hire halls. We didn't hire secretaries. We couldn't use radio or television," Girik recounted. "Instead, we went knocking door to door. I told people, 'I'm Fatma Girik. I'm a candidate from the Social Democrat Party. I don't know anything about being a mayoress. But together we'll make it.' "

In a five-way contest, she won 45 percent of the local vote, overwhelming the opposition. How? "I think I have goodwill," she said, smiling, her blue-green eyes dazzling. "Today, that is enough." For growing numbers, the appearance of bonding between voters and new politicians and the ability to communicate to constituents has been enough to win votes—regardless of the quality of the candidate or the content of the message conveyed.

"People have become disappointed with the so-called traditional parties," said Eric Rouleau, a widely respected French commentator and ambassador to Turkey. "They've tried them all. They're not over, they're not dead, let's be clear about it. But when you are disappointed, you look elsewhere."

The nonpoliticians have not, however, been just celebrities, relatives or political lightweights. With the demise of communism in 1989 and 1990, Eastern Europe underwent a leadership overhaul to fill the vacuums at the top. Electorates consistently turned to writers, artists, scholars and scientists as men and women trusted to tell the truth: Dissident playwright Václav Havel in Czechoslovakia. Writer and translator Arpad Goncz in Hungary. Philosopher Zhelyu Zhelev in Bulgaria. They and others surfaced in leadership roles as the strongest symbols of opposition.

The emergence of most nonpolitical politicians appeared, in part, to be a function of the transition; the longevity of each was precarious. Mayors

Belmont and Girik can sustain public trust only as long as the technocrats they brought with them come up with solutions. Among the relatives, Bhutto was out of office within eleven months. Aquino survived six military coup attempts, but even her vice-president opposed her. Chamorro could do little to restore economic order; the political climate in Managua remained divisive. Zia was educated only through the equivalent of the tenth grade.

While Eastern Europe's intelligentsia were clearly capable, committed and eloquent, they will probably also end up as transition figures as the formerly united opposition divides into new political parties. Each category appeared to be filling a gap until a new generation of leaders emerges and a new political spectrum is defined.

Far less exotic than Girik and less exalted than Havel was a distinct group of political novices linked to specific, and usually populist, issues. Until 1983, Vera Wollenberger and her husband both worked at East Germany's Academy of Sciences. She was a philosopher, he a mathematician. Then both were expelled, the reasons never explained. For the next six years, until the Berlin Wall came down, the Wollenbergers and their three children were forced to survive off beekeeping.

In March 1990, Wollenberger, a tall, blond, winsome woman, was elected to East Germany's first noncommunist parliament. One of eight successful Green Party candidates, she was representative of the kinds of nonpoliticians who emerge as changing ideologies shift the political focus. Wollenberger emerged from nowhere to gain leadership credentials simply because of her connection to the issue most critical or most emotional among a constituency.

"The environmental issue played a very important role in all the changes of 1989 because we live in a country whose environmental status is really alarming. It was so bad that we had a law which made environmental data top secret," she explained over lunch at the table in parliament once reserved for East Germany's former Communist Party chief. "Now it turns out that the environmental status was far worse than we had expected. There are some industrial areas that are so bad that they are no longer usable even for industries."

The issue-oriented nonpoliticians were not, however, limited to new elites. Until March, 1990, Hans Zimmerman was a plumber in Bitterfeld, the most notoriously polluted industrial city in East Germany. During the communist era, he was also a closet environmentalist. A rotund and jolly figure, Zimmerman's life changed after he gave an impromptu talk on poison toxins, deforestation and energy policy after the Wall came down. He also ended up in East Germany's first and only democratic parliament.

"I had no political intentions. I was, as you say, drafted by the Christian Democratic Union," he explained. "Besides the economy, ecology is our biggest problem. It will determine many of the people who are selected to lead in the future." The new leaders East Germany will contribute to a united Germany, he speculated, will be the "watchdogs," who will ensure mistakes of the past are not repeated.

"The kind of leadership the world had before the explosion of peace will be different from the leadership of the next phase," predicted Dante Caputo, the former president of the U.N. General Assembly and Argentine foreign minister. "Leadership is no longer related to the issue of global security and trying to ensure there is no domination—political or military—by one of the superpowers." The leaders who will attract support during the next stage of history, he added, will be less ideological. Those who emerge during the transition—and survive it—will instead be those who acknowledge and act on the demand for empowerment, those who are in touch with the people and, most of all, those who survive the populist accounting.

In March 1990, Alberto Fujimori was an obscure agronomist, the son of Japanese immigrants who had settled in Lima during World War II. In what was widely considered one of the most bizarre twists in Peruvian political history, the shy, fifty-one-year-old academic decided to run for the presidency, a position held for centuries by descendants of Spanish settlers.

No one gave him much of a chance. Fujimori had been one of those who had lost, rather badly, to Ricardo Belmont for the mayor's job just a few months earlier; his quest for the presidency was initially ridiculed by the press. Fujimori's new party—Cambio ["Change"] 90—had almost no organization and an undefined platform. Local polls showed that he was drawing less than 1 percent of public support. Backing was so limited that in an overwhelmingly Catholic country, the only vice-presidential running mates he could find were a Baptist minister and a bakery-equipment manufacturer.

Within a month, however, Fujimori's support had miraculously risen to more than 30 percent. His come-from-behind campaign forced a runoff against the powerfully handsome and well-financed novelist Mario Vargas Llosa, long considered a shoo-in. In June 1990, Fujimori defied all Peruvian predictions and history. He won the presidency.

The outcome in Peru cemented a trend toward the election of "outsiders within the system" over old-line politicos throughout South America and in a host of other regions. Electorates consistently rejected the legacies of past failures as the path to the future.

Fernando Collor de Mello also rose from relative obscurity. The former governor of Alagoas, Brazil's second-smallest state, came from the National Reconstruction Party, which controlled only 5 percent of the national congress. But in March 1990, Collor became Brazil's first freely elected president in three decades*—and the first ever to win without the support of a major party. In Argentina, Carlos Saul Menem, the son of Syrian immigrants and a Catholic convert from Islam, did not even have the backing of his own Peronist party when he made a run for the presidency. But in May 1989, he defied the Peronists as well as the incumbent Radical Civic Union, and won.

The common denominators in Peru, Brazil and Argentina were economic disaster, social turmoil and political erosion. All three candidates offered fresh faces with limited or no political past but enough credentials to make them legitimate alternatives. Each campaigned against traditional oligarchs and local party apparatuses. All three were middle-of-the-road candidates promising comfortable, albeit vague, solutions. That was enough. In all three newly democratic nations, voters were sufficiently disgruntled to vote for the dark horses.

"The world changes faster than its leaders. When the traditional leaders don't lead the changes, the people seek others—those who anticipate the tendencies, not just those who swim with the current," explained

---

*Although Brazil's military transferred power to civilian rule in 1985, the first president was elected by parliament.

Argentine pollster Manuel Mora y Araujo.[8] Apparently, just swimming against the current was enough to win.

Peru's contest was the most telling. Both the leading contenders were outsiders. Neither had ever before held public office. What may have cost novelist Vargas Llosa the election, ironically, was that during his compara- tively long and well-formulated campaign, he built a coalition with two conventional parties and hooked up with old-time analysts, pollsters and political advisers. In effect, he became an insider.[9]

Another common denominator in all three elections was the handover of power from one democratically elected president to another, a first in both Brazil and Argentina. The overwhelming rejection of incumbent parties in all three signaled the depth of despair; democracy was not yielding the anticipated results in solving the continent's staggering prob- lems—or even reducing the burdens. So the newly empowered turned to political outsiders who offered a fresh approach to democracy.

The Soviet Union underwent a similar process in the late 1980s. The first five years of Gorbachev's *perestroika*—qualified liberalization and empow- erment—led to higher prices for fewer goods, a housing shortage and more crime. Voters did not reject the concept, but they did begin looking for new faces to implement it. Among them was Boris Yeltsin, who became popular only after he was expelled from the Communist Party's politburo in 1987 and became an outsider. Four years later, Yeltsin was elected president of the Russian republic and, in 1991, he won worldwide acclaim as the leader of the popular resistance to the aborted coup d'état.

The changes are not only at the top, illustrated by the sudden demise and subsequent rise of Oleg Kalugin. A former K.G.B. general, Kalugin was forced to resign in 1990 for publicly criticizing the world's largest security agency as "a state within a state." Stripped of his military rank and the twenty-two medals* he earned during three decades of K.G.B. service, Kalugin suddenly became an outsider—and a political alternative.

After joining the Democratic Platform, a movement of critical social democrats within the Communist Party, he ran for a seat in the national Congress of People's Deputies. "After five years of *perestroika*, we have

---

*One of those medals was earned for running the Walker case, the father-and-son team who stole military secrets for Moscow from the U.S. Navy.

come to a deadlock, politically and economically," Kalugin said on the eve of the election. *"Perestroika* is very good, but it has not profoundly affected society yet. Gorbachev has made an historic move, and Russians will always be grateful to him. . . . However, he has fulfilled this historic task and other people, more energetic, more vigorous, less chained to the old ways, need to come to the fore."[10]

Facing nineteen rivals, including a famed cosmonaut, in the conservative Russian region of Krasnodar, the odds were against him. Local papers refused advertisements for his public appearances. At one campaign rally, two planes sprayed thousands of leaflets promoting an army general on the crowd. But the former chief of K.G.B. counterespionage and a top agent at the Soviet embassy in Washington only became more outspoken about the system he had spent most of his life enforcing. "Socialism looks like a very good idea, summing up all the best aspirations of man," Kalugin said during the campaign. "But through seventy years, wherever we have an experience of socialist construction, be it in the Soviet Union or China, in Albania or Cuba or Cambodia, there has always been bloodshed, always conflict, always misery for the people." The voters apparently agreed. Kalugin survived the first round; in a runoff, he won.

"As long as leaders, the present generation of leaders, cling to the conceptual frameworks they have developed—still looking backwards into the future—they will not only lose," explained Francisco Sagasti, the World Bank's leading strategic planner, "they will open the way for others to take over."

When mixed with frustration and populist fervor, "opening the way" increasingly produced unexpected leaders—like the outsider who emerged in Haiti to challenge 186 years of corrupt and ignominious rule. Father Jean-Bertrand Aristide was one of the last candidates to file, late in the campaign, for the 1990 presidential race. The slight priest had no political experience and, on the surface, little to support his candidacy.

A linguist and a student of psychology, Aristide spent many years during the father-and-son Duvalier dictatorship studying in Canada and Israel. After returning home, his original power base was a small parish church. Not one of Haiti's traditional power centers—the military, the business community and the Catholic church hierarchy—supported him. Indeed, most were alarmed by his candidacy; the Vatican had banned the

clergy from politics. The thirty-seven-year-old priest also had limited fund-
ing. And the coalition that backed him did not even field enough parliamentary candidates to give him a majority, in the unlikely event that
Aristide would win.

But Aristide did have a message. A champion of the poor on an impoverished island, he mesmerized a growing following. His speeches, blending
Creole folklore with Biblical proverbs, were filled with promises of re-
demptive justice and passionate exhortations to rise up. In a book adapted
from his sermons, Aristide wrote, "Haiti is a prison. In that prison, there
are rules you must abide by, or suffer the pain of death. One rule is: Never
ask for more than what the prison warden considers your share. . . .
Another rule is: Remain in your cell. Though it is crowded and stinking
and full of human refuse, remain there, and do not complain. That is your
lot.

"I say: Disobey the rules. Ask for more. Leave your wretchedness
behind. Organize with your brothers and sisters. Never accept the hand
of fate. Keep hope alive. . . . Life in a charnel house is a disgrace, an affront
to humankind."[11] Aristide quickly acquired the aura of a political messiah,
a credible savior from Haiti's misery. His movement was called *Lavalas*,
Creole for "flood" or "landslide." It was also an apt description of Haiti's
first truly free election. In a field of eleven candidates, Aristide won 67
percent of the vote; the runner-up, a former World Bank official, won less
than 15 percent. On February 7, 1991—the fifth anniversary of the
Duvalier dynasty's demise—he was sworn in as Haiti's fortieth president.
The hemisphere's poorest country switched overnight from right-wing
military rule to a leftist civilian government.

For all the public faith in Aristide, the young priest had marginal hopes
of implementing significant change. The army gave him little chance;
Aristide was ousted after only nine months in power. But his election also
exemplified how "opening the way" is dangerous in unstable countries.
Empowerment and pluralism hold the promise of dreams being realized;
but their strength is also their greatest vulnerability. When they fail to
produce, desperate constituents turn even further afield, to "outsiders"
who veer off to extremes—and undermine empowerment.

For twenty months in 1976–77, Antonio Domingo Bussi, a tough-
talking general, was the military governor of Argentina's Tucumán prov-

ince. It was a tumultuous period in the mountainous and impoverished northwest region. Leftist guerrillas of the People's Revolutionary Army had established their main base in Tucumán, and the military dictatorship was determined to wipe them out. Under the general, the government succeeded—but at a cost. At least nine thousand Argentines were killed in the ruthless counterinsurgency campaign, the so-called dirty war that eventually contributed to the demise of military rule in 1983. Like dozens of other ranking military officers, Bussi retired into oblivion.

But by 1989, the brassy general was back. He returned to Tucumán and formed his own party, the Republican Force. Under the new-old slogan, "Let's clean up Tucumán," he ran for a seat in the national congress on a platform glorifying the law-and-order success of his former rule. He won. Then, in elections for the provincial assembly, his followers won half the seats at stake in the lower house and a third of those at stake in the upper house. Almost immediately, Bussi announced that the Republican Force was setting up nationally. He vowed to become Tucumán's governor again—this time by public choice, not by appointment.

Bussi symbolized a distinct extreme of the fringe politician: the charismatic or messianic leader who promised political magic to counter the failure of new democracies and free market economies to provide urgently needed solutions. Like a handful of others who emerged at the turn of the 1990s, Bussi's appeal embodied the frustration, disaffection or rage with the Enlightenment's failure, especially when poor societies cannot afford democracy and break down into lawlessness to survive. The draw of the charismatic and messianic leaders has not meant a rejection of the Enlightment, only a desperate reaction when it was unfulfilled.

Running for governor on a "reform" ticket, Bussi pledged to end corruption, inflation and crime—the by-products of Argentina's latest stab at democracy. Although only on the fringe in the early 1990s, Bussi and others could come in from the outside if empowerment and pluralism do not generate tangible results. Without resources to pay for the transition, new democracies may founder.

Argentina was already in trouble. Menem's economic-recovery plan so backfired that the value of the austral—almost on a par with the U.S. dollar in 1986—plummeted to an exchange rate of six thousand to the dollar in 1990. By 1992, the economy appeared to be recovering—but at the cost of accepting rule by decree from a government tainted by charges of corruption.

In Peru, "Fujishock," as the president's economic-recovery plan was nicknamed, led to a jump in the cost of a gallon of gasoline from thirteen cents to four dollars overnight—in a country with an annual per-capita income of less than a thousand dollars. Unemployment also soared. In 1985, only one out of every two hundred Peruvians could not afford basic foods; by 1991, it was one in six. During Collor's first year in office in Brazil, prices rose 400 percent while the economy shrank by 4.6 percent, the biggest drop since 1947. A million Brazilians lost their jobs during one of the nation's worst recessions in living memory. The first generation of "outsiders" fulfilled virtually none of their promises in all three countries.

Indeed, by 1991, only a few of the new democracies in either Latin America or Eastern Europe made much of a dent in multiple-digit inflation, billion-dollar foreign debts, or enormous budget deficits. Nor did foreign investors show much interest in privatization schemes, the premise of generating new funds for stalled development. Various economic shock therapies also produced only higher unemployment, soaring prices and even greater stagnation.

Despite the widespread commitment to democracy in Argentina and throughout the continent, the end of dictatorships and the introduction of new freedoms also produced soaring new crime waves—in part because survival often depended on stealing. In Lima, visitors were warned in 1990 to keep their hands in their pockets to prevent their wristwatches from being stolen by nimble-fingered street thieves. In Prague, immigration officials warned newcomers not to change money on the street; among the new rackets in free Czechoslovakia was swapping dollars for bundles of worthless paper sandwiched between local koruna notes.

In the process, issues of discipline have begun to challenge the priority of democracy, the desperation of hunger has begun to outweigh concern for human rights. In 1992, few in South America wanted to see the return of military rule, nor, ironically, did most military officials show even remote interest in taking on the unprecedented problems. But many did want the strong leadership symbolized by the former *caudillos*, or charismatic strongmen. This time around, however, they were elected rather than imposed by force after coups.

"Progress in Latin America is under great stress," said Atilio Boron, an Argentine political scientist. "If democracy does not work in Latin America, then the way is open for fundamentalist, messianic leadership that will consider expedience a higher value than democracy. Frankly, the situation is getting ready for a fanatic leader."

At the beginning of the 1990s, Guatemala headed in that direction. For fourteen months in the early 1980s, General José Efrain Rios Montt ruled the nation with a gun in one hand and the Gospel in the other. On weekdays, he fought a counterinsurgency campaign against leftist guerrillas that left thousands dead and hundreds of villages razed. His secret military courts also dispensed stiff and usually summary sentences for civilian crimes. On weekends, as leader of *El Verbo*, or "the Word," an evangelical fundamentalist sect, he preached born-again Christian homilies about moral renewal to a flock of the faithful. His fiery Sunday sermons were televised nationwide.

The rule of Rios Montt, a messianic authoritarian, was one of Guatemala's most violent eras. He did, however, manage to cripple the rebel movement, and he did come close to eliminating major crime. Yet his regime was so brutal that his own military turned against him. He was ousted in a coup d'état in 1983.

In 1990, however, Guatemalans began displaying feelings of nostalgia about Rios Montt. More than four years of democratic rule had coincided with a revival of the bloody guerrilla war and a violent wave of rapes, murders and thefts. As the presidential election neared in November, public surveys on possible candidates showed the growling general ranking at or near the top. When he declared his candidacy in September, supporters flooded the streets of Guatemala City to celebrate. He already had the backing of three rightist parties. "Democracy doesn't mean live and let live," he told reporters. "The challenge is to make people comply with the law."[12]

In the end, Rios Montt was barred from running by a 1985 constitutional ban on candidates connected with earlier coups. But Guatemalans' attraction to authority to alleviate their problems persisted and was reflected both in the field of twelve candidates and in the chief election issues. The political spectrum ranged from right to extreme-right parties. The candidates included two generals, a colonel and two evangelicals. The campaign centered on who would take the toughest measures to restore law and order, to crack down on corruption and to end economic decline.

In January 1991, Jorge Serrano Elias, a right-wing businessman as well as an evangelical protestant, won almost 70 percent of the vote. A former chief of staff to Rios Montt, Serrano was the general's hand-picked successor. Indeed, he had entered the race only in case Rios Montt was disqualified. Just as telling was the turnout: Guatemala's experiment in democracy since 1986 had so disillusioned voters that less than half turned out to exercise their franchise for a watershed event—the first handover from one elected civilian president to another.

In the early 1990s, charismatic and messianic leaders were still a long way from peaking. They are likely, however, to be a sporadic and irritating feature of the decade, threatening the return of authoritarianism in history's most democratic era—reflecting how the demand for accountability could take a toll on troubled democracies as well as on failing totalitarian regimes. But their longevity is doubtful. They may be able to rally short-term trust by restoring law and order and perhaps even by force-feeding economic programs, especially in countries where democracy turns out to be too expensive. But, long term, they will fail in most places since they ignore the now unquenchable demand for empowerment.

The outsiders and the nonpolitical politicians—products of the media age and the political uncertainty that accompanies transition—may be a more persistent feature of the 1990s. But the leadership arising, initially anonymously, from the grass roots may prove to be the most enduring novelty to emerge from the 1990s, leading the world into the twenty-first century.

"What is going to happen is that new ideas, concepts, are going to sit up and permeate and effervesce," said Sagasti, the World Bank strategic planner. "We don't need heroes, saviors or martyrs. That is out. What we need are leaders who can guide with a light touch, who can guide by empowering other people. It has to be an enabling leadership. It has to be something in a different form. But, most of all, it has to be compatible with the ideas that come from below—because that's where the new ideas are."

Broadening Battlefields

"War, my lord, is of eternal use to human kind."
—FRANCIS LORD JEFFREY

On a midsummer day in 1990, while the rest of India scorched, a reflection of the snow-tipped Himalayas shimmered across the serene waters of Lake Dal. Cool pine-scented air breezed through the valley. Once the summer home of Mogul emperors and for decades an idyllic tourist haven, the Vale of Kashmir has been justly extolled in song and verse for centuries as paradise on earth.

But the lake's quaint houseboats, a legacy of British colonists who were never allowed to buy land here, were empty of tourists, and hotels along the shore had been converted into barracks for Indian troops. Both had become part of a new battleground: A few months earlier, rebels had used the filigreed verandah of a houseboat as an artillery platform, firing rocket-propelled grenades into the hotels' upper floors. In Srinagar, the graceful old wooden mosque was permanently draped with black flags of mourning for the more than two thousand killed in violence during the first half of the year. The bazaar, which once sold carpets and curios from distant places on the ancient Silk Road, was shuttered and locked, its labyrinthine alleys guarded by soldiers peering from behind five-foot sandbag berms.

Beautiful Kashmir, India's only state with a Muslim majority, was in the grip of a vicious and deadly civil war. Since January 1990, a long-smoldering separatist movement once limited to extremists had become a full-scale insurrection. And paradise had been converted into hell.

The crisis in Kashmir was more than just another remote insurrection in a continuously unstable corner of the Third World. It also offered a bitter taste of future warfare as the superpowers began drawing down their armies and arsenals from the European theater, the main arena of world tension over the past half century. The Cold War may have ended, the threat of an apocalyptic confrontation between East and West receded, but, as demonstrated in Kashmir, the post–Cold War world will be no less volatile.

Nor will it exempt the major powers. President Bush called his decision to go to war in the Persian Gulf in 1991 "an opportunity to forge for ourselves and for future generations a new world order." But, just as the century's two world wars were designed to end all wars, the promise again proved an illusion. The devastating onslaught of Operation Desert Storm only demonstrated instead that military conflict will be as much a part of the future as it has been of the past—for the United States, the Soviet Union and Europe and, increasingly, the world's smaller nations.

The roles will differ. The Cold War, which was a de facto third world war, pitted the superpowers against each other largely through Third World surrogates. The decades ahead may see the superpowers clashing with smaller powers, such as Iraq, which they have created along the way as well as with other well-equipped aggressors. But the cost and impact will be just as high.

Three factors will make future conflicts even more varied in origins, tactics and goals—and therefore more destabilizing in both their regional and worldwide impact.

The arming of developing countries with high-tech weapons in the 1970s and 1980s marks the most ominous single trend in warfare for the 1990s and beyond. Of the world's top fifteen arms importers in 1990, ten were in the Third World; they included the unstable regimes of Angola, Syria, Afghanistan, Iraq, North Korea and Libya.[1] As demonstrated in Iraq, developing countries are capable of building massive and mighty arsenals that require major force—in Baghdad's case, the armed forces of twenty-eight countries—to counter.

Unlike the United States, Russia and Europe, many of these countries are either beyond the constraints of treaties or unlikely to willingly surrender sophisticated gadgetry perceived as an equalizer in the widening gap between the North and the South. "It is remarkable that in spite of the progress of arms-control negotiations in the East-West framework and the usefulness of such a model for stability and security elsewhere, there is no functioning formal arms-control mechanism in any Third World conflict situation," the Stockholm International Peace Research Institute stated in 1990.[2]

Even more ominous is the proliferation of the three weapons of mass destruction: chemical weapons, ballistic missiles and nuclear capabilities. Unlike the Cold War period, when such weaponry was largely confined to a handful of nations and subject to the discipline of the East and West blocs, the post–Cold War era is already marked by the spread of sophisticated poison gases, nerve agents and diseases encapsulated in warheads as well as intermediate and long-range missiles. All effectively "democratize" the potential for catastrophic conflict.

Even the great powers' nuclear monopoly has been broken. No one has been killed by an atom bomb since the United States dropped "Fat Man" and "Little Boy" on Hiroshima and Nagasaki in 1945. Throughout the Cold War, the use of nuclear weapons was controllable mainly because so few countries had the capability; their use was largely neutralized by a military standoff. But as the nuclear club grows, so do the dangers.

The brutal fighting on the streets of Srinagar was testimony to more than the increasing ability of Kashmiri insurgents to get their hands on ever more powerful weapons. Behind the combatants was an even more sobering reality: The two countries on each side of the vale, India and Pakistan, could go to war over the territory. And this war would be different; both now have nuclear capabilities.

Just as weapons have spread, so, too, has the trend among the newcomers with big-league arsenals to produce daunting weapons systems for themselves; many are increasingly less dependent on purchases from the bigger powers. At the turn of the twentieth century, only a handful of countries had significant arms production capabilities; as it ends, most do. Developing nations such as Brazil, India, Egypt, South Africa, Israel and both Koreas were, by 1990, among the world's top arms producers and/or exporters[3]—all of them larger than Iraq which, whatever its fighting capability, had a world-class arsenal.

In terms of money changing hands, the arms trade was the world's biggest industry between 1988 and 1990.[4] And it is a growth industry as developing nations build a trade among themselves—once again often beyond the constraints of either the major powers or international treaties. Brazil, Argentina and Egypt were among many countries that worked with Baghdad on missile technology and other deadly weapons systems.

But repeated attempts aimed specifically at limiting or banning weapons of mass destruction in the Third World—notably chemical weapons and ballistic missiles—have all failed. By 1990, the Non-Proliferation Treaty on nuclear weapons had been signed by 140 of the world's 170 nations; among the holdouts, however, were at least 4 countries with nuclear capability: India, Pakistan, Israel and South Africa.*

"The most dangerous situation in the world now is the proliferation of weapons," said George Mirski, a leading analyst at the Institute of World Economy and International Relations in Moscow. "What kind of century will it be if a lot of countries now have the potential for having their own nuclear weapons? What will it matter, for instance, if a lot of situations arise around the Third World, in which countries possessing the terrible weapons will be in confrontation? Will the United States and Russia have leverage enough to influence them? It is very doubtful."

In other words, the twenty-first century faces an even greater danger of devastating conflicts among a broader range of countries—most of them probably increasingly intractable as the major powers' political influence and control over the flow of weaponry diminish. The principle of collective security, first attempted in the Persian Gulf, may offer an alternative. Yet unprecedented international unity, embodied in twelve U.N. Security Council resolutions was, in the end, not enough. Because diplomacy failed, Operation Desert Shield became Operation Desert Storm to force Iraq's withdrawal from Kuwait. The U.S.-led coalition's crushing victory, capped with a hundred-hour ground war, may serve as a deterrent, at least temporarily, on other potential regional aggressors. But it is unlikely to affect the chief flashpoints in the 1990s and beyond—the second change in future conflict.

Warfare, traditionally conducted between or among nations over ideol-

*In 1991, South Africa said it would sign the N.P.T., mainly due to fears among the white minority government about what would happen to the weapons after a transfer to majority rule.

ogy, territory or trade, is increasingly centered within societies. "Lebanon-ization"—the process by which nations are torn apart in multifaceted conflicts over issues of identity, resources and a new domestic order—has already grown in countries as disparate as the Soviet Union and South Africa. The enemy is no longer outside; it is within.

"Now that the ideological Cold War is over and now that national liberation movement countries have attained their goals, now each society is getting back to the delayed items on the agenda: how to divide power or to distribute power, to distribute wealth, to distribute prestige. And the quest to do so is not always easily accommodated," explained Saad Eddin Ibrahim, the Egyptian sociologist.

Indeed, ideology will play a far more limited role in future conflicts. The new Lebanons will instead be the natural by-products of the push for empowerment, the redefinition of the nation-state, and the clashing passions of ethnicity, nationality and religion. India and Pakistan not only confront each other over Kashmir; both also have mounting turmoil at home. India faces a Sikh secessionist insurgency in Punjab as well as the ever-escalating showdown between Hindu and Muslim zealots. Pakistan has witnessed the total deterioration of law and order in Karachi as a result of fighting between local Sindhis and Mohajirs, the name for Indian émigrés.

Like several other countries, Yugoslavia faced the further danger of wars within civil wars among rival ethnic groups and republics. In Yugoslavia, dominant Serbia clashed with the republics of Croatia and Slovenia while, within its own autonomous province of Kosovo, fighting ethnic Albanians. Even though republics in Yugoslavia did win independence, many may still face challenges just as volatile from minorities within their new borders. The same is true on a larger and even more complex scale in the former Soviet Union. In just one of dozens of messy internal clashes, the Turkish Christian Gagauz minority has fought for autonomy within the Moldavian republic, which has, in turn, struggled to free itself from Russian domination.

The outside world uncomfortably—and at a cost—absorbed the shocks of Lebanon's fifteen years of sectarian and communal strife—from the breakup of the only Arab democracy to the terrorist extravaganzas plotted and executed in the political anarchy of Beirut. But Lebanon is a thousand square miles smaller than the state of Connecticut. Be it the Russian Federation, Iraq, Pakistan, India, the Philippines, South Africa, Peru or any of dozens of other potential candidates for Lebanonization, the cost to the outside world would be far higher, the rippling effect throughout respective regions more destabilizing.

The increasingly chaotic pattern of conflict reflects the third shift in warfare in the decades ahead. The danger of big wars, fought with sophisticated weapons between rival armies, will be matched, maybe even surpassed, by low-intensity conflicts between militias and gangs using conventional arms, often played out in dense urban settings rather than on sparsely populated rural frontiers. The strife within India has increasingly been played out in cities: Sikh extremists have opened fire on late-night strollers and on children at a birthday party and, in return, Hindus have rampaged through the Sikh quarters of large cities to loot, burn or kill. Terrorism is also likely to surge, both in terms of "spectaculars"— attacks on aircraft, diplomatic and military installations or public facilities—and in attacks on innocent individuals, notably hostage seizures. The targets will not only be Westerners. In Karachi, the abduction of rival Pakistani clans or members of prominent families has virtually become a business.

"Conflict toward the end of the twentieth century has become increasingly unconventional, increasingly indiscriminate. It's not the established militaries of established countries clashing on demarcated battlefields but a succession of dirty power struggles, bloody clashes and endemic conflict throughout the Third World," said Bruce Hoffman, a military analyst at the Rand Corporation, a U.S. defense consulting firm.

Since its emergence in 1968, modern terrorism has become one of the most potent instruments of modern warfare.* Indeed, the 1980s witnessed the most violent period of terrorism in recorded history—a total of almost four thousand incidents worldwide, a 33 percent increase from the 1970s.[5] The number of deaths doubled in the 1980s; incidents killing

---

*Ironically, the Rand Corporation's chronology cites the first incident in 1968 as a parcel bomb sent from the United States to Cuba by a group of anti-Castro exiles called Cuban Power. The bomb exploded in a Havana post office. But, at the time, it was not recognized as the beginning of a worldwide trend, and it is not included in U.S. chronologies.

ten or more people increased by 135 percent.[6] Although Baghdad's boasts of a terrorism spree worldwide during the confrontation in the desert sands turned out to be largely bravado, at least 175 incidents related to the Gulf crisis were recorded on six continents during the forty-two-day war.[7] And, just as Third World countries have managed to go high-tech, so, too, have fears grown about the weaponry accessible to terrorists.

In terms of all aspects of warfare, the twentieth century has marked the bloodiest period in history. Just in its second half, the Cold War era witnessed more than 125 wars and almost twenty-two-million deaths—on an average yearly basis five times more than the nineteenth century and eight times more than the eighteenth. And the 1980s marked one of the most violent decades in the Modern Age. In 1987, almost half a million people were killed in 27 separate wars worldwide, the highest total since 1700.[8]

The twenty-first century promises to be no better. Even if longstanding conflicts—over Kashmir or a Palestinian homeland—are finally resolved, war will be a constant feature of the decades ahead, if in different forms. "The world threats might be less likely than they have been for some time," said Brent Scowcroft, the former U.S. Air Force general who has served as national security adviser to both Presidents Bush and Ford. "They're not [about] 'I've got a vision for the world and I've got to conquer the world to do it'—not like a Hitler or a Stalin.

"There is a real possibility that conflicts will be more local [but] perhaps more dangerous, because there has been a spread of military technology, especially the possibility of horrible things like chemical warfare and biological warfare, not to mention nuclear [capabilities]."

His identity concealed by sunglasses and a kerchief tied bandit-style across his face, Nasruddin ul-Islam, a twenty-two-year-old Kashmiri rebel, bragged of his latest exploits during a clandestine rendezvous at a rebel safe house in Srinagar. "I have attacked Indian soldiers many times. My greatest achievement was the Dalgit attack. We saw Indian policemen bathing in the river, and we surprised them." With cold satisfaction, he smiled and said, "We killed about a hundred." His real identity hidden behind a nom de guerre, the medical student–turned–militant was one of a growing number of Kashmiris who had been joining proliferating opposition groups in the idyllic valley when the full-scale insurgency erupted in January 1990. India's crackdowns had been so repressive that even Kashmir's middle class was backing the rebellion.

Ul-Islam was a member of Hezb-e-Mujahedeen, or the Party of Holy Warriors, one of at least a dozen movements, ranging from secular nationalists to Islamic zealots, that were challenging Hindu domination of the Muslim-populated vale. Their new popularity and daring reflected more, however, than just spreading secessionist passions; the new breed of rebels was a genuine threat. Once largely self-trained and equipped with only odd lots of pistols and vintage single-shot rifles, ul-Islam and his compatriots had gained access to automatic rifles, rocket launchers, grenades and even antitank mines. "We are buying [weaponry] from the Afghans and also [from] inside India," he claimed. The young Kashmiri had also spent a year training with Afghanistan's most radical Mujahedeen faction; among the arms in Kashmiri hands were American weapons intended for the Afghan resistance which had been provided by a new underground arms network. Other Muslim rebels had been newly trained in Pakistan and Iran.

As insurgents obtained potent weapons and professional training, the stubborn little war in Kashmir became ever more difficult to stop—a trend likely to characterize many of the wars in the coming decades. Tension over the disputed border, which dates back to the partition of India and Pakistan, erupted into full-scale war in 1947 and 1965. But a generation after the last war, the fight for Kashmir has qualitatively changed. As Kashmiri secessionists increased the pace and scale of their revolt in 1990 to a steady stream of hit-and-run attacks against Indian troops, an even greater danger emerged: the potential for a cataclysmic conflict within the Third World once thought limited to the East and the West. Unlike the dozens of major and minor brushfire wars that plagued the Third World during the Cold War era, the two nations both claiming rights to Kashmir had access to all three major weapons of mass destruction.

They are not alone; the dangers are not limited to Kashmir. Once restricted to the developed North, the world's deadliest arms—ballistic missiles, chemical and biological weapons and nuclear capabilities—have been quietly but quickly proliferating in the developing South.

At least ten Third World countries have or are working on acquiring nuclear capabilities.* In 1991, Algeria—a country never even suspected of having an interest in nuclear capability—was discovered to have been secretly building a nuclear reactor for more than three years; China had provided the technology. The threat is no longer hypothetical. In 1990, the Third World experienced its first nuclear scare when India and Pakistan went on alert and deployed troops, armor and aircraft close to the frontier. For the first time, two developing countries were openly debating the circumstances under which they might use atomic weapons against each other.

As of 1990, at least twenty developing countries also had or were trying to develop chemical weapons.† And up to twenty-five Third World countries were working on ballistic missile programs;‡ by the turn of the twenty-first century, at least fifteen are expected to be producing their own.[9] Indeed, as the major powers move toward slashing both weapons and manpower—the United States by 25 percent by 1995, the former Soviet Union by at least half as much in the same period—developing countries appear ever more determined to acquire ever more deadly arms.

The menace of all three weapons of mass destruction played out vividly in the Gulf War. Although Iraq was widely believed to be as much as five years away from delivering a sophisticated nuclear weapon, Baghdad did have, or was nearing the ability to construct, a "dirty bomb." Combining fissionable material with conventional explosives, a dirty bomb could spew radioactive material over a vast area.

Because of Baghdad's widespread use of chemical weapons during its

*The ten include Algeria, Argentina, Brazil, India, Iran, Israel, North Korea, Libya, Pakistan and South Africa. An eleventh, Iraq, had its budding capability destroyed during the Gulf War. South Korea and Taiwan have also shown an interest, but they have shelved programs for the time being, according to nuclear-arms-proliferation analyst Leonard Spector of the Carnegie Endowment for International Peace.

†Among the countries that are believed to have or be developing secret chemical arsenals: Afghanistan, Burma, China, Egypt, Ethiopia, France, India, Iran, Iraq, Israel, Laos, Libya, North Korea, Pakistan, South Africa and Syria. Others suspected at some point of an interest in chemical weapons include Argentina, Chile, Cuba, Taiwan and Vietnam.

‡Third World countries that are widely believed either to have acquired or to be developing their own short-, intermediate- or long-range capabilities include: Afghanistan, Algeria, Argentina, Brazil, Cuba, Egypt, Greece, India, Indonesia, Iran, Iraq, Israel, North Korea, South Korea, Kuwait, Libya, Pakistan, the Philippines, Saudi Arabia, South Africa, Syria, Taiwan, Thailand, Turkey and Yemen.

eight-year war with Iran, American troops went into battle with heavy, stifling antichemical suits. Whenever a missile alert went off, Israelis huddled in "safe rooms" sealed with plastic and clutched government-dispensed survival kits; an enterprising Israeli company even marketed gas-proof kennels for pets and special masks for Orthodox Jews with beards and earlocks. Thousands of Saudis fled Riyadh and Dhahran after the first sirens went off, not returning until the war was over.

The precautions were not unwarranted. After the war, Iraq had to hand over a list of weapons remaining in its arsenal to the United Nations. Despite forty-two days of savage air bombardment aimed primarily at weapons' production and storage facilities, Baghdad admitted that it still had nearly ten thousand nerve gas bombs and shells, more than a thousand tons of nerve and mustard gas and almost fifteen hundred chemical bombs and artillery shells.

Of the three weapons of mass destruction, however, Saddam Hussein's Scud missiles—enhanced to travel twice their normal distance—turned out to be the most serious offensive threat. From mobile missile launchers, which were constantly moved around the desert countryside, Iraq fired more than eighty missiles deep into Saudi Arabia, Bahrain and Qatar in the Gulf and as far afield as Tel Aviv on the Mediterranean. The new missiles also had the range to hit deep inside Russia, Turkey or Syria. Again, despite round-the-clock air bombardment, not all of Iraq's missiles or launchers were eliminated during Operation Desert Storm.

For developing countries, ballistic missiles provide an ideal weapon of surprise attack, against which, unlike aircraft, most countries do not have a defense. Indeed, they can serve as an effective alternative to an air force for countries without the financial or human resources to purchase, man and maintain sophisticated bombers. Saddam was willing to dispatch his finest warplanes to safety in Iran, in part because he had another offensive option. The Scuds' impact, both physical and psychological, forced the United States to scramble to deploy Patriot antimissile batteries in both the Gulf and Israel.

Only five major powers—the United States, Russia, Great Britain, France and China—have deployed long-range ballistic missiles capable of reaching thousands of miles beyond base. But developing countries are pushing fast and furiously to join the club. As of 1990, the International

Institute for Strategic Studies concluded, "The spread of ballistic missile systems is a truly global Third World phenomenon."[10] A survey by the U.S. Congressional Research Service added ominously, "Soon, a few of these countries may have missiles capable of striking the United States."[11]

Missile proliferation could also change the complexion of Kashmir's war. *Agni* is the Hindi word for "fire." It is also now the name of a ballistic surface-to-surface missile with a range of fifteen hundred miles. In 1989, India test-fired the *Agni,* which could hit any part of Pakistan as well as many areas of Iran and China. "In the past, regional powers have not been able to threaten the major powers. But at the end of the 1980s, you began to see new possibilities emerging. With India's test of the *Agni,* the possibility it could seriously threaten China with nuclear weapons began to loom on the horizon," said Leonard Spector, a proliferation specialist at the Carnegie Endowment for International Peace. "Before, there was no way India could threaten China. Now it will be able to. Even Beijing will be within range. That will completely change the balance in the region."

India is also working on the *Pritvi,* the Hindi word for "earth." A smaller surface-to-surface ballistic missile with a range of 150 miles, it would be most effective against Pakistan. And, since 1987, Pakistan has in turn test-fired the *Hatf*-1 and *Hatf*-2 (*Hatf* means "from the heavens"). The two ballistic surface-to-surface missiles have a range of between 50 and 180 miles and were designed primarily to target India.

But what makes the ballistic missile even more threatening—in a new war over Kashmir or any other part of the world—is the potential to alter its warhead. Developing countries are learning how to replace conventional explosives with chemical and biological agents or nuclear devices. Although Baghdad did not use chemical weapons in the Gulf War, Iraq had nevertheless secretly developed a capability for the new "doomsday" scenario. Saddam's soldiers test-fired a ballistic missile loaded with chemical agents in 1989.[12] Under terms of the U.N. ceasefire after the war, Baghdad reluctantly disclosed that it had a stockpile of thirty chemical warheads. Syria may also have chemical warheads for some of its missiles.[13]

The impact, however, is not limited to war fronts. Missiles and their various warheads are one of several factors increasingly bringing conflict into urban areas. "These developments portend greater destruction and loss of civilian lives in future regional conflicts as adversaries become more likely to fire missiles, possibly armed with chemical or even nuclear warheads, into the cities of their opponents," the Congressional Research Service study warned.[14] In the most deadly single Iraqi attack during the entire Gulf War, a Scud blasted into a warehouse in a populated sector of Riyadh, the Saudi capital. The warehouse was temporarily serving as a barracks for American reservists; twenty-eight were killed, more than a hundred injured. The Scud's warhead contained only conventional explosives; chemical agents would have killed many more.

Of the three weapons of mass destruction now proliferating in the Third World, chemical weapons are the simplest and cheapest. Production of the two major types—primitive mustard gas that blisters the skin and burns the lungs and complex nerve agents, like sarin and tabun, that destroy the nervous system—is also the most difficult to track, or limit.

Banned by the 1925 Geneva Protocols after the devastating use of mustard gas in World War I, poison gases have since been deployed in isolated cases: by Spain against Morocco in the 1920s; in the 1930s, by Italy in Ethiopia and by both the Soviet Union and Japan against China; and by Egypt in Yemen in the 1960s.

But a threshold was crossed in the 1980s when Iraq made repeated and widespread use of mustard gas and, for the first time anywhere in the world, nerve agents. Its victims were both Iranians and Iraq's own Kurds. In a 1988 attack on the Iraqi village of Halabjah, which lasted only a few hours, as many as five thousand Kurdish women, children and old men died as they ate or slept in their homes, as they walked on the streets and as they worked. By the onset of the Gulf War in 1991, Baghdad had so mastered production that it was manufacturing at least a thousand tons of chemical agents a year—probably the largest ongoing program in the world. More ominously, Iraq had become virtually self-sufficient, no longer reliant on precursors or technical assistance from the outside world.

After the Gulf War, the U.N. ceasefire resolution demanded that Iraq dismantle its plants and destroy its remaining weapons stock; Baghdad was also effectively sanctioned to prevent it from rearming. Neither measure, however, may have been enough. Once developed, chemical-weapons production is almost impossible to curtail without full cooperation; the weapons are simply too easy to hide. And compared with missile or nuclear-arms treaties, chemical-proliferation treaties are far more complex. Many of the chemicals and much of the technology are also basic to the manufacture of everything from prescription drugs and pen inks to textiles and fertilizers. Blocking the sale of chemical precursors could cripple poor countries unable to afford alternative technologies for producing peaceful commodities.

"We don't have chemical weapons and we don't want them," protested Roberto Garcia Moritan, Argentina's ambassador to the forty-nation Conference on Disarmament, which has struggled since 1980 on a new treaty to prohibit manufacture, stockpiling and use of chemical weapons. But, in a position widespread in the developing world, he added, "The proposed treaty's discrimination and restrictions are prohibitive. What we see is that it's going to restrict the effect of all chemical industries in Latin America. A good number of Third World countries will not adhere. They want chemical industries [for everyday uses]."

The dangers of proliferation of all three weapons of mass destruction—as well as other deadly arms—are not, however, limited to potential use. Equally ominous is the growing arms business within the developing world. Since the 1980s, the groundwork has been laid for arms trade—from tanks and artillery to aircraft and missiles—among developing countries' own new consortiums. It is rapidly becoming an alternative network. Although most Third World countries are still dependent on others for the parts, technology or expertise involved in major weaponry, many are increasingly turning to each other—and, in the process, vastly diversifying and expanding the international arms industry. The major powers are, in turn, effectively losing their monopoly not only on production and use but, more important, on control.

Iraq proved the potential. Saddam Hussein came to power in 1979, when Baghdad had virtually no major arms industries of its own. Although the Soviet Union and France were the sources of his most sophisticated armor and aircraft during the 1980s, the Iraqi leader also built the world's fourth-largest army with growing help from other developing states. Distant Brazil and Chile sold armored cars and helicopters. South Africa provided artillery and tiny Taiwan antitank and antipersonnel mines. Egypt sold secondhand tanks and sent arms experts to help Baghdad expand its own industries.

At home, Iraq developed the al-Hussein and al-Abbas missiles—both

enhanced versions of the Soviet-made Scuds that were fired at Israel and
Saudi Arabia during the Gulf War—with the help of allies and mercenary
profiteers. Ironically, among the foreigners "detained" in Baghdad during
the first two months of the Persian Gulf crisis were a retired Brazilian
army general and twenty-one Brazilian scientists who had spent nearly a
year in Iraq secretly developing the Piranha, an air-to-air missile that
Brazil does not even have in its own arsenal. Brazilian specialists worked
with both Iraq and Iran on ballistic-missile projects. Argentine and Egyptian experts also worked with Baghdad on the Condor missile system.

Developing countries on four continents are fueling the new network.
With reported Egyptian assistance, North Korea replicated a Soviet-
designed Scud ballistic missile in the 1980s and expanded its range to hit
any target on the Korean peninsula. Pyongyang is, in turn, a major arms
exporter throughout the Third World. North Korea sold Iran missiles and
also assisted Tehran with its own missile development; it also sold Scuds
to Syria. Besides its own development program, Pakistan bought surface-
to-surface missiles from China—enabling Islamabad to deploy the weapons in the field before India. In 1990, Nicaragua's army, still controlled
by the Sandinistas despite the election of a democratic government,
secretly sold twenty-eight antiaircraft missiles to El Salvador's leftist guerrillas. Two Salvadoran air-force planes were subsequently shot down.

As both India and Pakistan improved weapon capabilities for their own
use, they also created an export potential. "Pakistan is already selling.
India is not selling anything more than spare parts—yet," said a senior
U.S. arms analyst. "They are both now producing for themselves what
they had once been forced to buy. They are now also beginning to
recognize the potential of an arms industry for sales, to pick up on what
countries like Czechoslovakia no longer provide. It could be a major new
source of badly needed foreign exchange."

The trend is now spreading throughout the developing world to unlikely places. Isolated South Africa quietly became a major Third World
producer and exporter in the 1980s.[15] It sold military equipment to more
than two dozen countries on three continents including Chile, Israel, Sri
Lanka, Somalia, Morocco and Iraq. "Anywhere there's a conflict, whether
it's counterinsurgency on the part of the government against terrorists or
guerrilla war or conventional war between two or more states, the South

Africans are on the lookout to sell," said Dr. Simon Baynham, a military specialist at the Africa Institute in Pretoria.

The incentives were reflected in the dilemma of Czechoslovakia's new democratic regime in 1991. After pledging to dismantle more than half of the massive arms industry that thrived under communist rule—and provided the developing world with everything from tanks to explosives— Prague discovered that its good intentions came at a price the country's fragile economy could not afford. Faced with the prospect of laying off eighty thousand munitions workers and no new industries to absorb them, Czechoslovakia announced that it had no choice but to sell three hundred tanks to Syria and another three hundred to Iran.

Sales by most developing countries are based less on political alliances or morality than on the clout and income they generate. Of the fifty countries that supplied military matériel to Iran and Iraq during their devastating eight-year conflict, twenty-eight sold to both sides.[16] "During the 1950s, you used to produce weapons as an indicator of pure national strength. In the 1980s and 1990s particularly, we produce these things to enhance our trade capacity," said Gehad Auda, a military analyst at Cairo's Al Ahram Strategic Studies center. "The way technology advances opens the way for later powers in the world—Korea, Brazil, Israel, Egypt, Argentina—to be weapon suppliers on the international market. Because in the United States, when you get advanced, you start dumping the lower technology. But lower technology is very sophisticated to the Third World," Auda added. "So the Third World, all these little traders in arms, start getting into these little games."

Arms proliferation in the developing world may, in turn, trigger new competition for political and military supremacy within regions. Smaller powers will react to each other's new capabilities in the same way the superpowers did during the Cold War. Ironically, the end of the Cold War could accelerate that process. Individual countries may feel more vulnerable as they lose their superpower ally or shield—and therefore a need to establish regional superiority. The disappearance of a global "order," in which most states were neatly divided into one of two camps, could foster an increasingly unruly international disorder, in which Third World players try to throw their weight around.[17]

Indeed, by the turn of the century, strategists around the world may look back nostalgically on the Cold War era, when "The Threat" was singular and, comparatively, simple—both to understand and to control.

Tiny brick homes gutted. Rejected loot—shoes, kitchen utensils and papers—dumped on scrawny lawns. Rough dirt roads strewn with broken glass, rocks and, often, still-drying bloodstains. In Edendale, South Africa, the debris and death from the last battle had yet to be cleared away before the next one erupted. And it was coming. On an early morning in the black township abutting the Zulu tribal homeland, youth gangs could be seen prowling the impoverished community, their rivals hiding behind the high, wild grass of the surrounding hills, both stalking political prey.

"You can usually tell when there's going to be trouble," explained a young guide pointing up at a ridge. "They start forming in the hills just before dawn. Then they come down in formation, a long line marching side by side, carrying *sjamboks* [whips with steel tips] and *pangas* [machetes]. There's little most people here can do but run."

The black political violence that ripped through South Africa in 1990 killed more than four thousand people, or just over ten a day, according to the South African Institute of Race Relations. The area around Edendale was hit the worst; the rampant violence led survivors to dub it "Death Valley." On the surface, the flashpoint was a power struggle, originally among Zulus, between rival factions: Nelson Mandela's African National Congress (A.N.C.) and Zulu Chief Mangosuthu Buthelezi's Inkatha movement. But the stakes were, in fact, much higher: the future identity of a country undergoing political transformation.

The underlying cause reflected a trend increasing around the world and the flashpoint of pivotal conflicts in the decades ahead: the "Lebanonization" of countries divided among fractious movements vying for control of the new order. Prussian General Karl von Clausewitz's dictum in the eighteenth century—"War is merely a continuation of political intercourse with the addition of other means"—will still apply, but now more as an extension of rising domestic rather than international political tensions.

The countries most vulnerable are crumbling nation-states. In South Africa, the political challenge is not only to create a single nation of both blacks and whites, but a single nation out of nine distinctive African tribes whose rivalry predates by centuries the advent of the first white Dutch settlers. Mandela's A.N.C. offered a new identity that broke ancient ethnic ties and brought all blacks together as equals in a non-apartheid system. Buthelezi's campaign was ultimately based on preserving the powerful Zulu tradition as a separate social—and political—identity in the new order. Tribal resistance and rivalries have spawned worse destruction and more deaths than any confrontation between blacks and whites since apartheid was first instituted in the 1950s. "We're going to see a lot of conflicts in the Third World because the societies there are in a state of flux. You see all these issues of creating nations where a single nation doesn't exist," said Mirski, the Russian international political analyst.

Already threatened by two insurgencies, Peru also faces the threat of full-scale civil war because of the widening distance among its three nations: whites, mestizos and Indians. The standing axiom in the Andean country is that the white-dominated government does not extend above an altitude of a thousand feet—because mestizos and Indians populate the mountainous interior. "Peruvian identity doesn't exist. The Indians in the Andes and the mestizos in Cerro de Pasco and the corporate executives in Lima do not define nationality the same way. They have a different relationship to the state," said Diego Garcia Sayan, a Peruvian human-rights expert and the chairman of the Andean Jurists Commission. "If this country is to have a solution, it must gradually solve this gap between the perception and feeling and needs of the people and what is the state. We also need to finish with racism. It is a minor goal, but for Peru that means a revolution."

Widening economic disparities often exacerbate or accelerate the process—particularly in fragile new democracies. "There is a good reason to fear the Lebanonization of these countries. In the past, democracy worked well when the standard of living of the overwhelming majority was healthy. But the world has never had this experience—of democracy surviving alongside overwhelming poverty—before," said Atilio Boron, an Argentine political scientist. "And it's a prelude to hell when an ethnic or racial component is added to a deteriorating economy."

By the early 1990s, Pakistan had already been Lebanonized. Ripped apart by violence between native Sindhis and Mohajirs, Muslims who fled

India after the 1947 partition and later gained financial and social ascendancy, Karachi had the feel, politically and physically, of prewar Beirut. In 1990, an estimated half million automatic rifles were in the hands of civilians in Pakistan's largest city; security units formed around political parties had taken on the look of private militias.

Lawlessness had become the only order of the day in what was once the country's liveliest city, where parties often went on through the night. As of 1988, few dared go out after dark. And even daylight could be dangerous. In October 1990, eleven-year-old Hasson Saleem was dragged from his schoolbus in Karachi by a gang of kidnappers. The same day, three other boys and a former chairman of the Pakistan National Shipping Corporation were abducted; it was the worst single day in two years of abductions, during which more than a hundred men, women and children were seized off the streets or from their homes. In most cases, wealthy families ended up buying back their loved ones. The flashpoint was not ideology, but the same passions and rivalries that threatened nation-states worldwide.

The potential is not, however, limited to the developing world. Former Soviet President Mikhail Gorbachev used the word "Lebanonization" in 1990 to describe the dangers his country faced under pressure from ethnic and national divisions. Flashpoints for violence or civil war emerged at the turn of the decade in all fifteen Soviet republics, which declared themselves either sovereign or independent of Moscow's control.

Even before their formal independence, most republics witnessed violence: nationalities pitted against Soviet troops, or rival nationalities fighting among themselves, often within borders. As early as 1988, Soviet troops were dispatched to quell nationalist demonstrations in Tbilisi, the Georgian capital; dozens were killed. But that was only a taste of the trouble to come.

By 1991, the former Soviet Union faced disintegration and disturbances at every point on the compass. In the south, a virtual civil war raged between Muslim Azerbaijanis and Christian Armenians in the Transcaucasus. On the southwestern frontier, after the Moldavian republic declared Romanian its official language, the Russian minority declared its own secession from Moldavia—as, then, did the two-hundred-thousand-strong ethnic Gagauz. On the northwestern Baltic coast, Latvia responded to an assault by elite Soviet Black Beret troops on its interior ministry by creating its own "self-defense unit," a synonym for a militia—and a growing trend as new vigilante groups in several republics raided Soviet arsenals to arm themselves. Even resource-rich districts in eastern Siberia, part of the Russian republic, demanded control over the wealth within their borders—independent of fellow Russians.

With more than a hundred separate nationalities in the former Soviet Union, ethnic unrest could make Lebanon's labyrinthine internal strife look simple. The aborted 1991 coup ironically increased the chances of a peaceful devolution of power from the center to the republics. But it did not diminish the danger of nationalist or ethnic strife within republics over minority rights or for political control over pieces of the fragmenting empire.

In just one tiny corner of the world's largest country, a little-noticed civil war affecting almost six million people—twice Lebanon's entire population—raged in 1991. More vicious than the independence struggle in all three Baltic states combined, it pitted Ossetians against Georgians over independence—from each other as well as from the Soviet Union. The republic of Georgia voted overwhelmingly to secede from the Soviet Union, while the autonomous Ossetian enclave within Georgia, in turn, demanded its own independence from Georgia.

Politically and statistically, a war seemed unlikely. Both regions wanted the same thing: self-rule for their nations. And ninety thousand Ossetians could hardly hope to hold out against 5.5 million Georgians. But tension ran as deep as ethnic differences. Ossetians, who have lived in the rugged mountains of the North Caucasus for fourteen centuries, maintained a distinct language and culture. They did not want to be part of an independent Georgia—and separated from the three hundred thousand Ossetians in neighboring Russia. Georgia initially feared Ossetian nationalism would provide a pretext for Moscow to hold on to the entire republic. So Georgia responded by suspending Ossetian autonomy and besieging the enclave. Electricity and water were cut off; food supplies became scarce; tens of thousands were isolated from the outside world.

In early 1991, the politics of separatism disintegrated into civil strife. Georgian militias raided Tskhinvali, the Ossetian capital twelve hundred miles southwest of Moscow, attacking the national theater, smashing monuments and raiding public facilities. Young Ossetian gunmen responded by slipping over the mountains and striking Georgian villages. Within weeks, militias from both sides were engaged in nightly clashes, using automatic rifles, mortars, rockets and grenades; streets and schools became battlegrounds; Tskhinvali, littered with the debris of warfare and divided with barricades, became another Beirut. Yet, with all the other squabbles and clashes then deepening the Soviet internal divide, this one went virtually unnoticed by the outside world well into 1992.[18]

"The Soviet Union is in for a long period of sheer, frightening trauma," predicted Admiral William Crowe, the gravelly voiced but affable former chairman of the U.S. Joint Chiefs of Staff. "Freedom brings a lot of problems. It's taken us two hundred years to get to the point where we are today. All these emerging countries, they don't want to take two hundred years. They want it in three years. [But] these enmities don't disappear in three years. That's just a fact of life. What's the outcome? Trauma . . . probably killing, probably violence. Transitional periods are horrible."

The destruction of societies from within is also the result of empowerment deferred. "What has happened in the late twentieth century—as education has improved, as media and communications have reached down into even the most isolated villages—is that people have become much more aware of themselves as members of political societies and have begun to make increasing demands. For decades—even centuries—weak, fragile, inefficient, corrupt, inept governments could stumble along as long as they only had to satisfy a few elites and a small percentage of the population," explained Augustus Richard Norton, a research fellow at the International Peace Academy who served in Lebanon as a U.N. Observer. "But now, with much broader demands for government action or services, most of these governments are incapable of accommodating the citizens. The necessary result is turmoil, chaos and, all too often, conflict. Lebanon exemplifies precisely this process."

Lebanon's disintegration was no fluke. In the Arab world's only democracy, Beirut erupted over the imbalance of power between politically dominant Christians and embittered Muslims as demographics shifted. As Muslims became the majority, they demanded corresponding representation. In the absence of a resolution, both sides began to arm. As awareness of the right to empowerment spreads elsewhere in the world, so does the danger of Lebanonization in virtually any country that tries to resist. Rather than being an exception, Lebanon's fifteen years of civil strife were instead something of a harbinger.

After the Persian Gulf War, the immediate eruption of rebellions within Iraq by Shi'ite Muslims and non-Arab Kurds posed a greater threat to the longevity of President Saddam Hussein's rule than had a twenty-eight nation military coalition during the Gulf War. Although both uprisings were crushed within a month, the underlying causes that sparked them promised sporadic turmoil and the potential creation of a giant Lebanon. After its liberation, Kuwait was immediately beset with dissension between nationalists who had stayed behind to fight off Iraqi occupiers and were demanding democratization and the religious right who were urging the state to Islamicize. Both carried long-term implications for all the Arabian peninsula's oil-rich sheikhdoms.

Africa has also been plagued with new waves of internal strife produced by the failure to empower—with decisive results. Presidents-for-life have been challenged or overthrown in simultaneous rippling waves from north to south, east to west. In Zambia, bloody rioting and street protests in 1990 left twenty-three dead and triggered a short-lived coup attempt, the most serious threat to the quarter-century rule of President Kenneth Kaunda. The Zambian leader, one of the original fathers of African nationalism, was forced to agree to multi-party elections, which voted Kaunda out of office. President Samuel Doe's decade-old dictatorship in Liberia collapsed in 1990 when he failed to liberalize. A small student uprising in Mali over failed government promises and alleged deaths by torture eventually brought tens of thousands onto the streets of Bamako and Timbuktu in 1991; within three months, the twenty-three-year rule of General Moussa Traore was over.

The series of crises have not, however, been just a continuation of the coups and countercoups that have been a trademark of African politics since the wave of independence began in the 1960s. "Those coups were mainly revolving-door changes of elites, which did not really change the basic structure of the political system. It was musical chairs at the top," explained Pauline Baker, an African specialist at the Carnegie Endowment for International Peace. "What's occurring now in Africa is that there are demands from people from the bottom to open up the political system entirely. It comes from a number of sources, including the economic distress the entire continent has suffered since independence, and it's aimed at the state."

But the ousters were often just the first step; internal strife over what happened next frequently followed. In Somalia, a popular uprising terminated the autocratic twenty-one-year rule of President Mohammed Siad Barre in 1991. The end of repression, however, opened the way for clashes between six guerrilla movements centered around clans—the Isaaks, the Hawiye, the Ogadeni and others—vying for control over their respective fiefdoms. After decades of heavy arms sales to the once strategic country on Africa's eastern horn—first from the Soviet Union, then the United States and finally from Libya—guns had become more prevalent than toothbrushes. Somalia simply broke down.

To a certain degree, violence may be a part of building new nations for the new order, especially where compromise is initially beyond reach. "If you look at the creation of modern nations, they have inevitably been accompanied by a degree of violence," said Yunus Carrim, a sociologist at the University of Natal, near Edendale. Violence is part of the transition process of emerging new societies in which the old order is destroyed by force—and from which a new order arises. Reflecting wistfully on his own nation's problems, José Gonzales, a Peruvian journalist, added, "Europe had two world wars to get real democracy. The United States needed a civil war to establish democracy, then it took a hundred years to work. Japan needed two atomic bombs to see. What we need is a big conflict."

Unlike past wars in developing countries, the world's major powers may have limited ability to defuse the new Lebanons. Although the end of the Cold War opened the way for major power cooperation on regional conflicts, neither the United States nor Russia may be able to stop internal strife. "Until today, the conflict of interest of each country was suppressed by the conflict between the United States and the Soviet Union," reflected General Hiroomi Kurisu, a former chairman of Japan's Joint Chiefs of Staff. But détente has actually eliminated the superpowers' control of strife in which they had no hand in either supporting or arming the factions.

The one up side, however, is that in 1990 Lebanon made yet another stab at ending a generation of war that left more than 120,000 dead. Although the ceasefire remained fragile, the last of the nine major militias pulled out of Beirut by the end of the year. "If Lebanon's problems can be solved, then there's hope for the resolution of virtually any contemporary conflict," said a leading envoy to Beirut. "The problem is the cost along the way."

On March 27, 1990, British Airways flight 0217 from London to Washington was scheduled for a 4:30 p.m. departure. The first hint of a delay was when a Mr. Tajdar was paged and asked to "kindly report to the cabin staff." No one showed. A second page—and still no response. In an apologetic voice, Captain Ian Shephard announced a brief delay. A passenger who had checked in luggage had not boarded the plane; the ground crew was searching the terminal. Several minutes later, the pilot announced that the passenger could not be found; his baggage was to be off-loaded. "His origins are from an area that requires us to take his baggage off," Shephard explained.

What the pilot did not disclose was that Adel Tajdar, the missing passenger, had disembarked from an Iran Air flight from Tehran that morning. Suspicions were first aroused when Tajdar told the security checkers that, before boarding, he was going to buy caviar. Caviar is not available at Heathrow—but it is among the few items for sale at Iran's Mehrabad Airport. Tajdar had been given a number: security passenger 094. Since the 1988 bombing of Pan Am Flight 103, which exploded in midair en route from Heathrow to New York, airline computers in London show where each bag is stored. Tajdar's lone bag, tagged 700075, was in the first bin. Forty-five minutes later, after it was removed, the British Airways jumbo finally took off. "It's become a way of life," responded a cabin steward queried by an anxious passenger. "It's changed the way we do everything."

Since the hijacking of an Israeli El Al plane by radical Palestinians to Algeria in 1968 marked the onset of modern international terrorism,*

*The hijacking ended after Israel released sixteen Arab infiltrators.

sixty-five hundred people on six continents have been killed and tens of thousands injured in more than seven thousand attacks; thousands more have been taken hostage.[19] The annual figures are as erratic and unpredictable as the groups involved, but terrorism is almost certain to increase in the 1990s, and beyond, for one simple reason: it accomplishes many of its goals.

Indeed, the mere psychology of terrorism is an effective weapon. During the Persian Gulf War, economies of countries from the Caribbean to the Far East were affected as both tourists and businessmen cut back on air travel; some airlines almost went under. Cruises and international conferences were canceled. Shops in countries thousands of miles from the frontlines—including one on Madison Avenue in New York—ran out of gas masks due to public panic over chemical terrorism; the reaction was unprecedented since the scramble to build bomb shelters in the 1950s. In the end, however, less than a dozen people died worldwide in terrorist attacks related to the Gulf War.[20]

Yet terrorism, too, is evolving—in flashpoints, tactics and the arena of activities—in tandem with the shifting political spectrum and the issues of the new era. Many leftist groups all but collapsed as Marxism went into decline; hard economic realities and ethnic, nationalist and religious passions replaced populist ideology as the rallying cry. In 1968, the thirteen identifiable terrorist groups were predominantly ideological, with the major exception of Palestinian nationalist groups. In 1990, of the seventy-four known groups, fifty-eight were ethnic separatists or nationalists, and twelve had a strong religious identification; only fifteen were ideologically motivated.[21]

Many of the European groups that made headlines in the 1970s and 1980s, notably France's Action Direct and Italy's Red Brigades, had been virtually eliminated by 1990 as significant threats. Germany's Red Army Faction was weakened by internal rifts and the loss of sanctuary in Eastern Europe's former communist regimes. Even attacks by the Irish Republican Army, the major exception, were down significantly from the 1970s.[22]

The same pattern applied in Latin America, where most of the notorious and predominantly leftist terrorist groups either died out as democracy spread across the continent or were squelched. In Colombia, three of the five leftist rebel armies laid down their arms in 1990 and 1991. M-19 was among the most infamous groups to change its stripes. In 1980, the Marxist group invaded an embassy party and held a houseful of diplomats, including the U.S. ambassador, hostage for two months. In 1985, it seized the national Palace of Justice; an army counterattack left a hundred dead, including eleven supreme court justices. By 1990, however, M-19 had become a legal political party. Its second-in-command, Antonio Navarro Wolff, a British-educated engineering professor and a guerrilla for twelve years, was named Colombia's new minister of health. After twenty-three years, guerrillas of the Popular Liberation Army also laid down their guns and stopped kidnapping landowners in exchange for representation on the assembly drafting a new Colombian constitution.

As terrorists have changed, so have their targets. Although no major power will ever be exempt, the West may no longer be a primary target. An hour before President Bush arrived in Santiago in December 1990 a bomb exploded at a downtown McDonald's; the night before, a small explosive went off in a park near where Bush was to speak. But the countries more likely to be threatened by terrorism are instead those undergoing major transitions, on both the right and the left, or those under debilitating economic pressure. Once again, troubled nation-states are vulnerable to indiscriminate violence.

In South Africa, white right-wing groups with bloodcurdling names such as the Order of Death, the White Liberation Army and the White Wolves launched a series of attacks in 1990 to protest the government's decision to scrap apartheid and introduce majority rule in the continent's last white-ruled nation. White extremists were linked to a spate of assaults—using firearms, grenades and small bombs—on black homes, hotels, offices and even black taxi stands. They also pledged attacks on their own white government.

Equally violent may be the transition at the other end of the political spectrum. Just as Lebanon's civil war disintegrated into terrorism—suicide bombings, assassinations and hostage seizures—so could the ethnic and nationalist clashes in the former Soviet Union and Eastern Europe. Moscow's economic disintegration could invite further outbursts of terrorism. The potential was evident in a rash of hijackings in 1990. In June, seventeen-year-old Dimitri Semyonov, armed with a fake grenade, hijacked an Aeroflot plane to Sweden, where he said he was "fed up" with hardships at home. It was the first of ten attempts by disgruntled young Soviets seeking economic refuge in Europe. The hijackings ended after Moscow lifted restrictions on exit permits.

But economic misery may replace ideological divides as a leading flashpoint for indiscriminate violence in the years ahead. "I think terrorism is going to increase because of frustration," predicted Ahmed Fakhr, a military analyst retired from the Egyptian Army. "Total wars, limited wars, regional wars, are going to decrease. But these little incidents of trying to twist your arm, Soviets or Americans or Germans or Japanese, I think we can expect an increase."

"You would call it terrorism. The poor will call it fighting for their piece of the cake," added Tahseen Basher, the jovial former Egyptian envoy to the United Nations. "That will happen even in advanced countries. The homeless and the poor, whom nobody pays attention to, will resort to violence unless we start coopting them into the mainstream."

Indeed, economic sites rather than military or diplomatic installations were increasingly vulnerable targets. Colombia's National Liberation Army sabotaged the country's largest oil pipeline 125 times, 21 times in 1990 alone, in what was locally referred to as "petro-terrorism." "Eco-terrorism" was blamed for the cyanide contamination of imported Chilean grapes in 1989 which led the United States, Canada, Hong Kong and Japan to temporarily ban all Chilean fruit.* The cost to Chile—an estimated three million dollars a day—was devastating. As countries worldwide face recessions or radical economic overhauls, economic targets may prove increasingly attractive—and effective.

Of even greater future concern in the 1990s, however, will be two trends: hostage seizures and the "terrorism spectaculars," which premiered in the late 1980s with the midair bombings of Pan Am Flight 103 over Scotland and UTA Flight 772 over the West African nation of Niger. Those bombings were only two of the more than 170 hijackings

---

*Both the U.S. and Japanese embassies in Santiago had earlier received warnings that Chilean produce was deliberately being contaminated. The only reported claim, made by a group protesting the Bush Administration's talks with the Palestine Liberation Organization in 1988–89, was not taken seriously.

in the 1980s, but they killed a total of 441.[23] Like every other industry, terrorism has gone high-tech.

Some expert scenarios are electrifying. "Although a new generation of thermal-neutron-analysis devices"—the multimillion-dollar explosives-detection machines in airports—"is coming on line and will make it more difficult to hijack or bomb an aircraft, terrorists are not going to give up trying. The next danger is from the shoulder-fired missile," predicted Bruce Hoffman, the Rand military analyst. "It's axiomatic to say that it won't be long before terrorists start using them. All they have to do is sit on the edge of the airport tarmac and fire at the tailpipe. And there's almost no protection against them." But it was not an outrageous possibility. Egypt, China, Brazil, South Africa and Sweden are beginning to manufacture their own state-of-the-art versions of the U.S.-made Stinger and Blowpipe, portable shoulder-held missiles. Although the marriage of terrorism and chemical or biological warfare has received widespread publicity, other high-tech weaponry is probably more of a threat than poison gases or anthrax and cholera spores.

The most cost-efficient terrorism tactic, however, remains hostage abductions. By 1990, political kidnapping of foreigners had spread to five continents. In Kashmir, a new phase in the escalating conflict was marked when Muslim rebels began seizing hostages in 1991. Among their targets were three Swedish engineers working on a hydroelectric project and, three months later, six Israeli tourists vacationing on a houseboat.* The Janbaz—or "Crusader"—Force claimed responsibility for the Swedes. "We were compelled to take such an extreme step because the world has been a silent spectator to the criminal doings and offenses by Indian security forces," it said in a communiqué. Hostage-taking had become a standard idiom of warfare.

The trend reached an unprecedented peak with a single incident: Iraq's "detention" of more than four thousand foreigners during the Gulf crisis. Baghdad's move reflected a fundamental shift in the tactic. When Charles Elbrick, the U.S. Ambassador to Brazil, became the first modern American hostage in 1969,[24] the demand by his leftist captors was the

---

*The Israelis' ordeal ended when four escaped, one was killed and the sixth freed after U.N. mediation.

release of Brazilian political prisoners, on which the local government conceded.

In the 1980s, however, hostage seizures were increasingly aimed at demands on foreign governments—specifically, the kind of policy shifts or reversals demanded by the various abductors in Lebanon of more than 130 foreigners from twenty-two countries. France, Korea, India, even Switzerland, and others reversed policy decisions on a host of issues to win freedom for their nationals; the Reagan Administration engaged in an arms-for-hostages swap with Iran to free three Americans.

The magnitude of hostage seizures and their impact has grown with each decade, and not only in the Middle East. The Peace Corps withdrew all its volunteers from the Philippines and Liberia in 1990 because of the threat of abductions. The move was too late for twenty-six-year-old Timothy Swanson, who was seized by communist rebels in June 1990. Swanson and a Japanese relief worker were released seven weeks later, in part because the rebels had won their objective: a diminished American presence in the Philippines.

The hostage threat, however, is no longer limited to terrorist groups or insurgents. Hostages are increasingly becoming pawns in drug wars and in economically unstable environments. In 1990, Colombia surpassed Lebanon as the site of the world's most kidnappings; the total doubled to almost thirteen hundred in a single year.[25] The Medellín drug cartel seized dozens, including foreign journalists and the daughter of a former president, to pressure the Bogotá government to grant amnesty to the so-called Extraditables. Others were abducted for ransom by former drug runners put out of business by the U.S.-backed antidrug crackdown; Colombia's economy had not generated alternative jobs. Still others were seized by gangs, again for money, in a country where the per capita income has hovered around a thousand dollars a year since the early 1980s.

In 1990, Medellín alone had some 155 armed gangs vying for territory in which to steal and kidnap; unemployment in the poorest neighborhood, from which most gangs emerge, was as high as 50 percent.[26] In Brazil, various gangs abducted up to a hundred and fifty hostages in 1990; their ransom demands totaled at least sixteen million dollars. The hostages were victims of a crime wave that Latin American economists linked to desperate, and growing, poverty—a pattern unlikely to change in the near future.

In 1991, the kidnappers of Francisco José Coeho Vieira, a Brazilian businessman, demanded a ransom of thirty-two thousand dollars—in food. When twenty tons of meat, sugar, pasta, beans, rice and milk were left near a Rio shantytown, a line of slum dwellers half a mile long battled for the goods. After fifteen minutes, everything was gone; five people were injured in the melee.[27]

The three trends—arms proliferation in the Third World, a wave of internal conflicts, and the growth of terrorism—represent an irony as the Cold War ends. "One can see the paradox of the world becoming both a less and more dangerous place," reflected Iqbal Akhund, national security adviser to Pakistan's–then Prime Minister Benazir Bhutto, in 1990. "The greatest powers today have learned that no profit is to be gained from war and that war is no longer a usable instrument of policy." At the same time, he added, "The world may be faced by an increase in wars"— of a different variety.

The Human Wave

*"A great multitude, which no man could number, of all nations,
and kindreds, and people, and tongues."*
—REVELATION OF ST. JOHN THE DIVINE, 7:9

With huge bundles balanced on their heads and a dozen tiny children in tow, three women wearily navigated the weather-gutted dirt roads toward Phoenix Settlement. They were the third group of new arrivals, and the day was still young. In search of better jobs, better homes—just about anything better—the black families had trekked for days from South African rural areas to reach the shantytown outside Durban. Phoenix Settlement, established on a fertile knoll for a dozen families at the turn of the century by a then-unknown young Indian lawyer named Mohandas Gandhi, had by 1990 become a putrid maze of ten thousand squatters— all on the same quest. Crammed around a free clinic, a legacy of Gandhi's twenty-one years of exile in South Africa, was a labyrinth of homemade shacks built off of or on top of each other from mud, cardboard and plastic sheeting. Crates marked "Toyota spare parts" were favored building materials; their thickness better protected barefoot children from rain and biting winter winds.

North across the equator, the pace was more frenzied, often even panicked. Hundreds of Albanians braved gunfire from army troops trying to prevent them from tearing on foot across land borders to Greece or Yugoslavia from Europe's poorest country; thousands more comman-

deered ships to flee across the Adriatic to Italy, virtually stripping the
Albanian ports of Durres and Viora of seaworthy vessels. At Tel Aviv's
modern Ben Gurion International Airport, planeload after planeload dis-
gorged Soviet Jews seeking refuge at the rate of at least two thousand a
day. In Tehran, the crush to get on Iran Air flights to Tokyo—cynically
nicknamed the "flight to happiness and economic success"—was so overwhelming that airline officials devised a lottery to pick who would be
allowed to fly; for a single flight, the turnout at a Tehran soccer stadium
was seventy thousand.[1]

Like a global game of musical chairs, the world is witnessing the uproot-
ing of tens of millions in the biggest human migration in history. The
Modern Age is the first to be synonomous with mass movement on a
global scale: the dispersal of mankind to settle or colonize "new" continents; the shipment of slaves from Africa and indentured labor from Asia
to build the white man's dream; the flights from the pestilence of famine
or plague; the lure of the Industrial Revolution's opportunities; and dis-
placements during and resettlements after the two world wars. But the
new migrations are expected to surpass the sum total of them all, even
proportionately.[2]

The tidal wave of mankind on the move is surging in two directions.
First, an "urban revolution" within countries is leading millions to abandon rural areas for cities, sapping the strength of the countryside and
overwhelming already-burdened cities in at least 120 of the world's 170
countries. The Phoenix Settlement squatters were, comparatively, a drop
in the bucket of a trend long coming.

In 1800, only 3 percent of the world's population lived in cities. By
1900, the proportion had risen to 10 percent. Since 1950, the world's
cities have been flooded with unprecedented numbers—leading on average to a doubling of city sizes in developed countries and a quadrupling
in developing regions. By the year 2010, for the first time in history, at
least half the world will be urbanized.[3] "This is the century of the great
urban explosion," concluded a 1990 U.N. report on human development.
"This growth has been far beyond anything imagined only a few decades
ago—and at a pace that is without historic precedent."[4]

But the trend is more than just a numbers game. Once centers of
wealth, cities are increasingly centers of poverty. Traditionally centers of

human and societal progress, cities are increasingly stagnating and even imploding. Squatters' camps are not the only by-products. The urban revolution also portends serious economic and political upheavals.

A now irreversible flooding of cities, almost all unprepared or outright unable to cope with the deluge, has begun to drain national economies and strain nations' social fabric. Phoenix Settlement is not unique in South Africa. In 1980, a tiny plot on the edge of Soweto was an overgrown three-hole golf course; a decade later, it had been renamed Mshenguville and converted into a squalid camp by fifty thousand squatters. And it was only one of five unsightly camps in Johannesburg's sprawling black township. South Africa's Urban Foundation predicted that the population of all the country's major cities would double by the year 2000. Up to seven million were already squatters around South Africa's major cities in 1990, creating a housing crisis that would take the construction of eight hundred homes a day for the next ten years to resolve—before taking the projected increase into account.

New megacities have begun to consume old city centers, their suburbs and growing exterior rings of slums or shantytowns heightening the potential for explosive urban strife as the burgeoning fringe vies for limited resources. By 1990, India alone had six cities with populations of between four and thirteen million. Among the largest megacities by the year 2000 will be Mexico City at twenty-six million, São Paulo at twenty million, Bombay and Calcutta at sixteen million each, and Shanghai, Seoul, Rio de Janeiro, Jakarta, Tehran and Delhi, each at thirteen million.[5] In 1990, not one had the capacity to accommodate its current numbers, much less millions more.

Finally, faced with destitution, city migrants and squatters have begun to form unregulated "informal" sectors to create their own solutions to problems involving housing, employment and social services outside the control of the state; in turn, they are creating de facto states-within-states. In greater Lima, crammed with more than seven million of Peru's twenty-two million people in 1990, up to 80 percent of all markets and bus transport and 40 percent of the capital's overall economic activity were controlled by informals beyond the control of the state.

The long-term result of overcrowding and unregulated growth may well be a redefinition of cities—and their role in human life. "Throughout history, dating back to Greek times, cities have been seen as places where people become 'urbane' and have access to the benefits of progress," reflected Francisco Sagasti, the World Bank's leading strategic planner. "But at the close of the twentieth century, the historic role of cities is now being compromised. On the one hand, they still offer the main means for upward mobility and modernization. But, simultaneously, they now include all the negative aspects of excessive overcrowding and violence. The problem is that cities are becoming massive ghettos of people confined in small spaces with very little interaction with the rest of the city except through violence or illegal activities. The danger is that these ghettos will be institutionalized."

The second surge is playing out on an even larger scale. An international exodus is leading millions more to flee across borders, even leapfrog across continents, altering the profile of both countries abandoned and adopted. Virtually every country will be affected either by the exodus or the influx. Vietnamese are fleeing to Hong Kong, and Hong Kong Chinese to Australia, Bolivia, Canada, Belize, Costa Rica, New Zealand or Singapore; Moroccans, Tunisians and Algerians to France, Spain and Italy; Burmese to Thailand; Mozambicans to Malawi and Zimbabwe; Russian and Ethiopia's Falasha Jews to Israel; Lebanese to Latin America or West Africa; Argentines to Spain, Italy, Ireland, even Uruguay; Afghans to Pakistan and Iran; Eastern Europeans to Western Europe; Filipinos and Gypsies to any place that will take them. And the migrations are only beginning.

"By their very numbers, today's refugees are something of a political force in their own right . . . complicating the prospects of regional stability," concluded the International Institute of Strategic Studies in 1990. "The prospect of a potential flood of refugees has become a major consideration in the security affairs of all states."[6]

The United States is not exempt from the flood. Although only a tiny percentage of the vast numbers who want to immigrate to the United States make it, the total is enough to change the complexion of the American population. In the twenty-first century, white descendants of European settlers will, for the first time, be in the minority—due to both immigration and a higher birth rate among blacks, Hispanics and other minorities. By 1990, New Mexico was already only half non-Hispanic white, California only 57 percent white.[7] For the first time in history, the largest ethnic group in the freshman class at the University of California at Los Angeles in 1990 was not white, but Asian.[8]

Unlike urbanization, international migrations are impossible to measure accurately; they depend on intangibles, such as political instability, civil or regional strife, and economic decline. Millions of immigrants are also illegal and therefore uncounted, while the 1990 tally of fifteen million refugees shifts constantly. The 1991 Gulf crisis alone unleashed another two million when Kurds began fleeing Iraq; it was the biggest human migration in the shortest period of time in history. But migration appears to be growing exponentially. During the 1980s, the pool of people seeking access to other countries doubled—at least.[9] The figure is expected to double again by the end of the century, especially with a growing number of political and economic wild cards.

The pace promises to alter the world's shape—economically and politically—as much as, perhaps even more than, urbanization. Since émigrés tend to be younger and more skilled, the countries they leave behind because of limited opportunities will become ever more destitute. As unemployment in the eastern sector of newly unified Germany rose to 25 percent in early 1991, at least five hundred former East Germans, mainly young, fled to the West each week. With unemployment expected to rise to 50 percent by the end of the year, the better part of a generation may forsake a once-vital part of Europe, leaving it to the aging and inactive who have no hope of rebuilding it.

Politically, unprecedented cross-border migration is already a divisive and destabilizing issue, fueling racism or "nativism" among right-wing movements domestically, and a sharper North–South divide internationally. In France, where immigrants accounted for 7 percent of the population in 1990, Jean-Marie Le Pen's rightist National Front became a credible political force on the lone issue of rigidly limiting immigration. Rioting and street fights between young North Africans and French police became an increasingly regular feature of life in ghettos, where most immigrants live.

The crises represented a tragic irony. Unprecedented freedoms at the end of the twentieth century have allowed unprecedented movement. But unlike the last mass international migration at the end of the nineteenth and the beginning of the twentieth century, when cheap foreign labor was welcome to fuel industrialization, doors are closing in the 1990s. "For all the free flow of information, the tremendous flow of capital, the great mobility because of cheap transportation, borders are more impenetrable than they've ever been for *people,*" explained Doris Meissner, former commissioner of U.S. Immigration and Naturalization. "It's a paradox— between the rigidity of the state in physical terms and a world where everything else is opening up." The result is not, however, a halt of the flow, only an increase in illegal immigrants.

The common denominator in both the internal and international migrations is not political oppression or war, as in the past; this time around, the primary motive is economic misery. And fueling both is a third factor: an increasingly uneven pattern of demographic growth. From the birth of Christ, it took seventeen centuries for the globe's inhabitants to double. As of 1990, the world's population of more than five billion is expected to double in less than four decades. Barring a major reversal, the ten-billionth human being will be born before the year 2030.

As dramatic as the growth rate, however, is its imbalance; while birth rates are plunging in the industrialized world, the numbers in developing communities are surging. As of 1990, more than 90 percent of population growth was in the developing world; the populations of India and China alone accounted for almost 40 percent of the world total. The figures are so staggering that, when accompanied by poverty, they are literally squeezing people out of wretchedly poor rural areas to cities in places like South Africa, Peru, Iran, Mexico and Indonesia, or out of poor and over-populated countries like Egypt, Bangladesh, India and the Philippines altogether.

The human dimensions of the current historic transition are among its most visible changes. The imagery of the teeming influx in Third World cities, of the rush to escape Eastern Europe for opportunity in the West, of destitute and homeless children in even the developed world became potent, even unavoidable, by 1990. They have, however, also been among the most ignored. Yet all three factors shaping the new human wave will be powerful components reconfiguring countries and alliances, politics, economics and social movements worldwide in the 1990s and beyond— particularly because there is now no place for the spillover.

In the fifth century, hordes of Goths moved across the Rhine to accommodate their numbers. One-fifth of Europe's population explosion in the nineteenth century was absorbed by North America or Australia. But unlike the population surges and migratory swells of the past, these are occuring in a world that will run out of inhabitable frontiers in the twenty-first century. "Space is the future, not because the world is going to blow itself up but because it's going to be very unroomy," lamented Ezer Weizman, a member of Israel's Knesset and former defense minister. But even migration into space may not be the answer.

"Do you know how long it would take to occupy all the planets if they were all completely as inhabitable as earth? About two hundred years at current growth rates. Then every planet would be as full," said American biologist Paul Ehrlich, coauthor of *The Population Explosion*. "Mars buys you only about thirty years."

Demographics will also play a key role in determining whether fragile new democracies survive and whether traditional powers can sustain economic superiority, now the preeminent criteria of power, in the twenty-first century. Third World societies are producing more people than they can accommodate in housing, education, health care or employment. Soaring numbers will increasingly strain the limited resources of countries experimenting with liberal democracy.

In 1990, Mozambique began the transformation from a one-party Marxist state to a multiparty democracy—only to find that the costs may be prohibitive. The population of Maputo, the capital, was already 1.4 million and was expected to reach almost 2 million by 1995—in a city with an infrastructure built for a hundred thousand. Underemployment and unemployment were estimated at 40 percent; thousands of children were without schools. "The burden represented by a high birth rate is going to be unbearable if we are to relaunch our economy," conceded Luis Bernardo Honwana, Mozambique's culture minister.

The developed world faces the reverse dilemma. In 1990, successful birth-control policies in Japan and key Western countries were already creating aging societies and a shortage in the younger labor force—and threatening a future of sluggish economic growth and heavy taxation to support the elderly. A further decline in birth rates may jeopardize the manpower requisite to any economy's growth. "The strength of European democracies, of Western Europe, is tremendously overestimated because of the coming demographic decline, which is going to be much worse than anywhere in the world," explained Emmanuel Todd, a French social historian at the National Institute of Demographic Studies during an interview in Paris.

The 1990s, which will witness greater population growth than any decade in history, "will decide the shape of the twenty-first century," concluded a 1990 report by the U.N. Fund for Population Activities. "They may decide the future of the earth as a habitation for humans."[10]

Looking out across the rippling Turkish hills, the adviser to the mayor of Sultanbeyli beamed. "There wasn't much here until three years ago. It was mostly fields or running wild. Today, we have twenty-eight thousand buildings. There's no sewerage yet. And, technically, we're not yet a legal district. But we're growing so fast that one day," he paused, nodding his head with certainty, "one day, we'll be our own province."

Sultanbeyli is a *gecekondu,* or "built-by-night" suburb, one of hundreds that have been spawned throughout Turkey since the end of military rule in 1983 and the subsequent economic reforms. Dismantling political and economic barriers triggered an unprecedented boom—and a rush to the cities to be part of it. In 1990, the *gecekondu* on the outskirts of Istanbul had the distinction of being the fastest-growing area in Turkey. Home to fewer than four thousand in 1985, it was crammed with more than 180,000 by 1990. The mayor's adviser estimated Sultanbeyli would hold three hundred thousand by 1992.

"It's an unbelievably rapid pace," reflected Emil Kongar, a Turkish political analyst and pollster. "At this pace, by the year 2000, somewhere between 65 and 70 percent of the Turkish population will be living in cities. It was only around 10 percent in the beginning of the republic in the 1920s. Just think what that means. The problem is that more than half the population of our large cities live in these *gecekondu* mushroom areas. That's more than ten million people!"

The urban revolution at the end of the twentieth century represents the largest and fastest growth of cities in human history. Only one city in ancient times—Ch'ang-an, the imperial capital of the T'ang dynasty in China—had more than a million inhabitants. Mass movement from rural areas to cities did not really take off until the Industrial Revolution. In the middle of the nineteenth century, London was the first industrialized city to exceed a million. The pace of the urban wave—and where it is happening—is underscored by two figures: London took 130 years to reach eight million in 1990. Mexico City's population, which did not reach one million until 1940, had soared to twenty million by 1990.[11]

Yet never in history have cities—old or young, in the developed as well as the developing world—been so ill-prepared to accommodate the growth. Istanbul, founded in the seventh century B.C. by Greek traders who called it Byzantium, surpassed 7.5 million in 1990—and began spinning off more and more *gecekondus*. Karachi, a well-planned city for four hundred thousand built after Pakistan's partition from India in 1947, held more than nine million in 1990, the majority in *katchi abadis*, Urdu for "unfinished settlements."[12] Cairo became so crowded that at least 750,000 occupied a downtown cemetery where entire families converted tiny mausoleums into homes; Egyptians referred to it as "the City of the Dead."

Even China, which has the world's largest rural population and officially discourages urban migration, is feeling the squeeze. At least two hundred million Chinese—equivalent to more than two-thirds of the U.S. population—are expected to move from the countryside to the cities in the last decade of the century. Forty-six Chinese cities already have more than a million inhabitants.

Yet the urban revolution is only beginning. In the Third World alone, a billion people are expected to move from the land to megacities and the new "hypercities" of fifteen million or more between 1990 and 2020,[13] despite a host of local and international efforts to slow or block the mass migrations. By 1990, six hypercities—two in Japan and one each in the United States, Brazil, Mexico and South Korea—had already "reached a size off the scale of human experience," concluded a report by the Population Crisis Committee. "Their management takes us into uncharted territory."[14]

As stunning as the growth, however, is its imbalance. The human wave is most dense in the developing world. By the year 2000, the pace of urbanization in Third World nations will be almost twice as fast as in the developed world. By 2025, Africa's urban population is expected to be three times larger than North America's.[15] "Governments are discovering the impossibility of reversing urbanization—or even of slowing it down," concluded the U.N. report.[16]

The developed world is not exempt. Los Angeles, New York, London and Moscow are all expected to have populations of more than ten million, while Tokyo-Yokohama could have up to thirty million by the turn of the twenty-first century.[17] In the United States, the rural population declined by almost half between 1950 and 1990 to 23 percent. In the former Soviet Union, the disintegration of the empire is expected to lead millions of ethnic Russians to flee the fourteen non-Russian republics— mainly for the cities.

Besides political intangibles, Kongar said, "People are moving for two reasons. One is that rural production really forces people to move out because of the mechanization of the culture." Farming has become a subsistence form of existence in vast parts of the Third World, not a means of making progress. In countries such as Peru and Bolivia, few small farmers can survive beyond subsistence on coffee, cotton, potatoes, sugar or corn crops. Thousands who have opted to live with the land have turned instead to coca, the source of cocaine.

"The second reason is that the government has not furnished enough services in the rural areas. Thus the city means electricity, modern life and all kinds of facilities clearly lacking in the rural areas," added the Turkish pollster. Since development has centered in cities, moving forward means moving to urban areas.

Each trend, however, has a rippling side effect that, in turn, is reshaping the economic and social patterns of existence. First, abandoning the countryside saps agricultural production, a vital sector for developing regions that can barely afford food imports for their current populations, much less the numbers expected in the years ahead. "All the expected growth in Latin America is going to be in urban settings. That means a decreasing percentage responsible for feeding this growing urban population. It's an extraordinary reality," explained Eric Rodenburg, the research director at the World Resources Institute in Washington.

Second, because of sheer numbers and limited resources to absorb urban immigrants, the traditional pattern of progress threatens to work in reverse in the 1990s. In many cities, notably in the Middle East, it already has. "People just went to the cities and formed slums. These people brought in with them their village values and they dragged us down, they took us back to the village. It wasn't the urban sectors taking these people forward with them," explained Mustafa Hamarneh, a bearded and intense young political scientist at the University of Jordan. Long term, many cities may become giant slums, with development restricted to tiny enclaves of the wealthy. "None of the cities in the developing world can afford the infrastructure of developed megacities," the U.N. report concluded.

The same problems face dozens of countries—and the megacities that now dominate the demographic landscape—in the Middle East, the Asian subcontinent, the Far East and virtually all of Africa and Latin America. Lima is among the most chronic cases; at last count, it had eight hundred "illegal" slums or slumlets ringing the capital, whose population had increased from one million, in 1940, to seven million, in 1990. Among them is San Juan de Miraflores, a labyrinth of mud-brick or reed-thatch hovels, bleached colorless by the sun, built along dirt alleys strewn with garbage on the Peruvian capital's arid outskirts. In 1990, the extent of government services was a single phone for a population in the thousands growing so fast that no one had an accurate count.

Peru's debt-ridden government has no hope of accommodating the numbers anytime in the near future. "Lima grows at 5 to 6 percent a year," explained Felipe Ortiz de Zevallos, a Peruvian economist, with quiet urgency. "That means Lima will double in twelve to fourteen years. Therefore we'll have to double our institutions and services and schools and health facilities and job opportunities in only twelve to fourteen years." His palms opening upward to signal helplessness, Ortiz shrugged, "The way things are now, it can't be done."

The urban revolution has, however, generated alternatives growing more visible—and powerful—on every continent. Destitute and all but officially abandoned, Peru's squatters started mobilizing themselves. Although always alive with street vendors, Lima became a giant open-air market. On the tatty main roads, hawkers walked among speeding cars or meandered near stoplights to flog hardware, magazines, flyswatters, cake covers, motor oil or whatever else had been produced or imported lately. On the sidewalks around Plaza de Armas, Lima's main square and the site of its ornate seventeenth-century city hall, hundreds of street merchants offered fruit, underwear, T-shirts, watches and toys, each "business" neatly laid out on plastic or newspaper on a tiny corner of the pavement. They shouted their prices to the accompaniment of a child tapping out tunes on empty Coke bottles.

Once referred to as the subsistence sector, the ignored or illegal elements of society that fend for themselves in systems either unable or unwilling to absorb them have become known as the "informals." A label describing individuals, communities or professions, the informals in Lima and elsewhere around the world do more than just flog oddities on street corners. They have built homes and jobs from scratch; they have created a flourishing network of wholesalers, suppliers and service industries; they have established alternative infrastructures with bus lines, small industrial cooperatives and police brigades, which dispense "informal" justice in their neighborhoods. All of San Juan de Miraflores is informal—its residents, its little businesses and food cooperatives, even its clinic and cemetery.

"Many planners see the informal sector as probably the greatest source of new urban jobs in the next few decades and as an important safety valve to fill the gap created by inadequate city services," the World Resources Institute reported in 1990.[18] Because of their enormous, and still-growing, numbers, the informals will be among the most dynamic—and the most volatile—elements in society well into the twenty-first century. In Lima, they already account for almost half of the capital's economic activity— figures mirrored throughout the developing world and in nations undergoing political or economic transitions.

After the wave of 1989 revolutions ousting communist rule, informal open-air markets sprang up throughout eastern Europe. On weekends, street corners and parking lots of Yugoslav cities were awash with Poles, Romanians and Hungarians who flooded across the borders to sell everything from vegetables and textiles to camping accessories. Working out of homes and garages a continent away in Mozambique, informal businesses made shoes, clothes, spare car parts not available because of the lack of foreign exchange. "Our markets are now 50 percent informals. They began to develop in 1983–84. They were doing a significant part of the nation's business by 1986," said Firminio Mucavele, an agro-economist in Maputo, in 1990. "Now they are the most resilient part of our economy."

In comparatively prosperous neighboring South Africa, the roads between Johannesburg and its black suburbs bustled with four thousand

Toyota or Nissan minibuses, the most popular transportation link in 1990. All were run by informals. Downtown, informal street merchants who had come in on the informal minibuses sold fruit and vegetables, jewelry and jeans, shopping bags and wrapping paper, on sidewalks outside boutiques and department stores. Informals even extended into the arms industry. Among the homemade guns in South Africa were the *qwasha,* a handgun named for the sound it makes, and a rifle that used standard-issue military ammunition.

Informals in transportation, taverns, indoor and open-air shops and other informal businesses accounted for up to 25 percent of South Africa's GNP in 1990.[19] Informals were the biggest buyers of bananas from the Banana Board and the second largest fuel purchasers. "In the informal sector, there is a great deal of dynamism, because usually the informal sector can really generate entrepreneurs and things that can really later on feed the formal sector even—and better than the formal sector," said Egyptian economist Essam Montasser, the former director of the U.N.'s Africa Institute.

The volume of informal sectors in several countries, however, has converted them into de facto states-within-states, each illegal or unrecognized, but most so powerful that they rival the state for local authority and control. Excluded from the formal empowerment process, the informals are increasingly empowering themselves. Long term, they represent a challenge to the Modern Age's emphasis on order—in organizing the form of human settlements, in regulating the norms and conduct of human life, in providing standards for commerce, education, development or political intercourse.

"You can't tax them. You can't ensure their standards in health," said Jonathan Moyo, a University of Zimbabwe political scientist. Nor does informal construction conform to building codes, or schooling—if it exists—to basic curricula, or businesses to safety, sanitation or environmental standards. And homemade guns are not registered. "The fact that they're growing usually is a commentary on the failure of the overall system," Moyo added.

Not all informal suburbs are chaotic. Turkey's Sultanbeyli still had dirt roads in 1990, but most of the *gecekondu's* twenty-eight thousand buildings were neat brick shops and small apartment blocks, a welcome relief from the decaying and polluted center of Istanbul. Sultanbeyli was starkly different from South Africa's Phoenix Settlement, Cairo's City of the Dead and Karachi's *katchi abadis* because it had a central force mobilizing its new residents: Islam. The majority of the urban immigrants were attracted by the application of Islamic principles—in local administration, in schools, in sports groups and in politics; the mayor won on an Islamic ticket. Religion provided a framework for establishing local order. But Sultanbeyli was an exception, even in Turkey.

Whatever the hopeful side of homemade solutions, informals accentuate the widening gap within societies—and the problems ahead. "This situation is going to produce a social disaster, increasing the level of illiteracy, downgrading public health, converting cities to slums and creating a social structure with a deep cleavage and a large percentage of marginalized people," warned Atilio Boron, an Argentine political economist.

The causes of cleavage were already visible in 1990. In Manila's slums, infant mortality was three times higher and tuberculosis nine times higher than in the rest of the Philippines capital, according to the U.N. survey of cities. In Bombay, the prevalence of leprosy was three times higher in one slum surveyed than in the city proper. And the dangers grew as the *gecekondus, katchi abadis* and Latin America's *callampas*—or "mushrooms"—were no longer limited to the fringe of society. In 1990, slums accounted for up to half or more of the population in a growing number of cities: in Casablanca, 70 percent; in Calcutta, 67 percent; in Bogotá and Kinshasa, 60 percent; in Mexico City, 42 percent.[20]

The increasing imbalance in development also threatens to heighten social tensions within the new megacities and hypercities. By 1990, many squatters' camps and "built-by-night" suburbs worldwide were riddled with drug traffic, crime and prostitution. "You have a belt of village immigrants who are unable to be absorbed in the city, who are living on the periphery and who don't get either the benefits or the advantages that the city can offer. [Because of] their frustration . . . they constitute clusters that can be dragged into any chaos. They have nothing to lose," explained Mona Ebeid, an Egyptian sociologist and politician, as she looked out her apartment window at overcrowded Cairo.

.   .   .

An even greater danger, however, is that, left on the fringe, the informals' alienation and isolation will turn to open hostility—and conflict. "Urbanization usually means housing problems, job problems, overcrowding, disease, social conflict," commented Dr. Simon Baynham of Pretoria's Africa Institute. "As more and more impoverished people come in from the rural areas, they come into areas that are already limited in terms of the amount of land available. So you've got fighting over land, fighting over housing, fighting over influence in these areas." And the cleavage has been further accentuated by the fact that informals often come from racial or ethnic lower classes—such as blacks in South Africa or mestizos and Indians in Peru. San Juan de Miraflores and its counterparts around Lima were ripe recruiting grounds in 1990 for Peru's Shining Path guerrillas, South America's last major insurgents.

Comparatively small-scale violence connected with the growing urban crunch is already a part of daily life in illegal slums and informal suburbs from Argentina to Zimbabwe—and including Gandhi's beloved Phoenix Settlement. The day before the three exhausted women and their children reached the shantytown, two young boys were killed. The violence has not, however, been limited to the developing world. The first major outbreak of violence in Berlin after German reunification erupted in 1990 when police, using tear gas, water cannons and bulldozers, tried to evict hundreds of squatters who had taken over thirteen apartment buildings in former East Berlin.

"To maintain law and order is going to be terrible because you have all these thousands of people coming to urban areas without houses or without health system, without jobs, with no conditions at all," said Honwana, the Mozambique culture minister. "Cities are no more safe places to live. You're risking your life."

Turning people back to the countryside is no longer an option, however. Indeed, informals have become such a disproportionate part of the social equation in cities worldwide that the formal sectors of society may no longer be in control of their fates. "Although the process will play differently in different cities on different continents," said Sagasti, "it's clear that the future of cities around the world will be determined more by the overwhelming numbers coming in at the bottom than by the people who now run them at the top."

Ahmed Fakhr, a career military officer who risked his life for Egypt in three wars, sat back in his chair and paused. The words were clearly difficult. "Fifteen years ago, I used to tell my two boys, 'If you leave this country and go work abroad, you are betraying your national cause. Stay here. Develop Egypt. The government paid for your health care, for your education.'

"Stay *here*," he repeated with urgency.

"Today," Fakhr sighed, then shrugged, "I am preparing my two boys to emigrate. It's a question of the resources available and the population." In a country impossibly tasked to accommodate a million new mouths every nine months on a tiny strip of arable land running alongside the Nile, leaving has long been the response to an economy that cannot keep up with changing demographics. The desperation, however, has reached new lows. By 1990, a full 15 percent of Egypt's active labor force had gone abroad as migrant labor, a fivefold increase since 1975.[21] And the trend was not limited to Egypt.

Argentina witnessed the first transfer of power from one democratically elected president to another in 1990; ironically, the new chief-of-state was the son of Syrian immigrants. Yet economic deterioration was so chronic that, instead of celebrating, tens of thousands applied for passports from the European countries their grandparents and great-grandparents had abandoned to settle in Latin America.

Peru inaugurated its third democratically elected president, the son of Japanese immigrants, in 1990. Yet efforts to leave were higher than ever because of a desperate sense that not even democracy would solve Peru's myriad problems. Applications for passports jumped sevenfold; informal surveys showed that up to 65 percent of Lima's residents would get out if they could.[22]

With the odds against imminent relief for the common economic plight of dozens of countries, people migrated in ever greater numbers. In 1990, up to five million on six continents migrated legally or illegally.* Patience for delays in the implicit promises of democracy and free markets

---

*This figure does not include the world's fifteen million refugees, such as the hundreds of thousands who fled Gulf countries after Iraq's invasion of Kuwait, or untold millions of tempo-

ran out; in countries where problems persisted, the obvious course of action in the age of the jumbo jet was to get up, en masse, and go in search of solutions. Despite the collapse of communist rule in Albania, Eastern Europe's last holdout, at least eighty thousand fled.

In 1990, the strains of a failing economy and fears of the empire's formal collapse unleashed the biggest Soviet migration since World War II: The easing of exit permits allowed a half-million to leave. A million more applied to migrate to the United States alone—more than the total that left for all countries during the entire Cold War.

What lies ahead may be the biggest migration in Russian history: Officially, another seven million are expected to roll across Europe in the last decade of the century. Unofficially, as many as twenty million may depart, spurred in no small part by the shift to a market economy which is expected to cost between thirty and forty million jobs by 1994.[23]

Also pleading poverty, not persecution, another ten to fifteen million want to flee Eastern Europe. Staying home, their plight can only get worse. The transformation to market economies is expected to cost another fourteen million jobs in Eastern Europe by 1994.[24] Tens of thousands abandoned Poland, the first to experiment with economic shock therapy, in 1990 as inflation hit 240 percent and 1.3 million lost jobs. "That's why people are leaving, that's why university professors are trying to send their kids abroad," explained Manfried Goertemaker, an historian at the Free University of Berlin. "It's not that these people don't like Poland; they would of course prefer to stay. But they don't see any hope, and they don't want to wait another generation." The same crisis faces fledgling new democracies throughout Africa, Asia and Latin America.

The drain will change more than just numbers. Entire countries will be transformed, economies and cultures challenged and even political changes undermined by the losses. In each country, those most eligible for migration elsewhere have universal skills—in medicine, science and technology, business, academics or the arts. The countries they leave behind will face sudden shortages in exactly the fields they need most to make the leap to strong pluralistic societies.

---

rary migrants, such as the fifty to a hundred thousand Iranians who sought illegal temporary work in Japan.

"Migrations will overhaul nations," said Sagasti. "Some countries are simply going to lose their elites, while the lower-educated will be the ones to stay. That will leave these nations mediocre and flat economically. They will lose those best able to spur development. For some, it will be a disaster."

Indeed, migrations may increasingly shape the futures of various countries. The exodus of Jews and other well-educated ethnic groups could contribute to the decline of Russia and other former Soviet republics into Third World status. Moscow will be less able to compete in fields ranging from computer technology to space exploration. Other countries will, conversely, be transformed by the gains. For Israel, the expected infusion of a million well-educated Soviet Jews over the next few years—a whopping 20 percent increase in its Jewish population—may not only revive a stagnant economy but also eventually elevate the tiny state to First World status. Indeed, initially, thousands of Soviet immigrants were educated beyond the means of Israel's economy to employ them all. Professionals, ranging from neuropathologists to professors, stooped to waiting tables and street-sweeping just to get a job.

Politically, the impact could be just as stunning. Those leaving the former Soviet Union have also generally been among the most outspoken in demanding democratic openings; those staying behind are among the most dependent on the socialist net and the least able to fend for themselves in a competitive free-market climate. With patience already wearing thin in 1992, the prospect of a prolonged and costly transition could, long term, provoke a backlash undermining liberalization.

The political balance in Israel will also be transformed. By 1992, the electorate is expected to increase by 30 percent—in a country where only 2 or 3 percent have determined whether past coalitions would veer to the right or the left.[25] Most Soviet Jews are nonobservant, thereby potentially weakening the disproportionate power of Israel's religious parties. But disillusioned with communism, many may also be turned off by the Labor Party's socialist platform. And less ideological and somewhat disgruntled by the government's mismanagement of the absorption process, the majority may also not be drawn to the ruling conservative Likud coalition. Indeed, Soviet Jews may end up forming their own bloc capable of reshaping Israel's deeply fragmented and polarized political spectrum—potentially capable of determining Israel's future.

Dual migrations will also reshape South Africa. Thousands of English-speaking whites, proportionately the most highly skilled of the country's many white nationalities, responded to the end of apartheid by applying for citizenship in the nation of their ancestors who settled the tip of the continent a century or more ago. A million whites—or more than one in five—qualified for British citizenship. In 1990, the British embassy in Pretoria was issuing an average of two thousand new passports each month.[26] Hundreds of other Europeans—Portuguese, Belgians, Germans and French—who fled to the last bastion of white rule following decolonization in other parts of Africa also applied to go "home." Although many were liberal or moderate by South African standards, they will be a conservative force in any of the countries to which they move.

The prospect of majority rule also opened the way for the return of tens of thousands of blacks who went into exile during the four decades of apartheid. Vast numbers, however, worked as guerrillas or in the political underground; most do not have the education or skills to replace the fleeing whites. The most industrialized and wealthy of Africa's fifty countries could take a generation, and probably more, just to stabilize the production level achieved in South Africa during the apartheid era.

Soviet Jews and South Africa's migrating whites are among a fortunate few. Their skills are marketable commodities; they have legitimate claims in other lands; their passage will be peaceful. At the end of the twentieth century, however, most migrants were either unwanted or could not meet ever-tightening criteria. Even Australia and Canada, traditionally two of the world's most open countries, began to limit refugees and unskilled labor, particularly from Southeast Asia.

Political asylum, once fairly freely offered those living under authoritarian or totalitarian rule, has also diminished as an option as ideologies, like communism and apartheid, disappear. Nicaraguans who fled the right-wing Somoza dictatorship in the 1970s or the leftist Sandinista rule in the 1980s usually won refuge. But in 1990, those who wanted a way out of the economic problems inherited—and still unsolved—by Managua's new democracy were turned away. New regional blocs, notably the European Community, virtually slammed their doors for fear of becoming a dumping ground for the unemployed of North Africa and Eastern Europe. "United Europe does not seem to be a new United States," said Tahseen Basher, a former Egyptian envoy to the United Nations. "It has dangerous lines of becoming fortress Europe, which rejects non-European, non-white, poorer people."

Tension over immigration played out even between East and West; tolerance for despair has been limited in the two halves of Europe as the ideological divide has disappeared. Once an escape route for East bloc refugees, Austria in 1990 deployed army patrols along the border because of domestic reaction against Romanians seeking escape—at a rate of up to 180 a day—from economic hardship. Mass cases of homelessness led Vienna to reintroduce visa requirements for Eastern Europeans—and to send thousands of Romanians packing. A major flap erupted in unified Germany in 1990 when state and federal governments proposed an immigration ceiling of only a thousand Soviet Jews. Despite emotional debates over guilt for the Holocaust, Bonn repeatedly pledged that Germany was not a country for immigrants.[27]

Indeed, the backlash has bordered on xenophobia; immigrants worldwide have felt the pressures. Vietnamese in Czechoslovakia complained publicly and in letters to local papers about increasing assaults and racial insults. In Hong Kong, street protests erupted against the government's policy of offering Vietnamese boat people "first asylum," even though they were restricted to detention camps.

More ominous has been the swelling violence. Hundreds of North Africans in France went on a rampage outside Lyon, France's second-largest city, to protest police harassment of immigrants in 1990. After five nights of urban warfare, French President François Mitterrand warned that racial tension could flare in hundreds of bleak tenements and ghettos where immigrants were packed. "We are facing an underlying problem which will weigh on our society in the years to come," he told a somber cabinet session.

By 1991, strife had soared in dozens of European cities, from Birmingham to Frankfurt and Marseille, where immigrants were concentrated. Even sedate Belgium, home to 135,000 Moroccan and 80,000 Turkish immigrants, was stunned by a series of clashes in Brussels between young immigrants and the police. Throughout Europe, new parties—Italy's Lombard League, Austria's Freedom Party and Germany's neo-Nazi National Alternative—stimulated new waves of xenophobic nativism in anti-immigration campaigns, in turn heightening racial tension and threatening future friction.

Controversy and confrontation over the human wave—those who have already migrated and those who are still trying—will be a major flashpoint in the 1990s and beyond. "The spillover of the demographic explosion is no longer going to be confined to the cantons and the bush," said Saad Eddin Ibrahim. "The spillover will go north [to the developed world] and will begin to create tension and probably the emergence or reemergence of racism and all kinds of chauvinisms in the world." Since survival is at stake, many of those turned away will only try again illegally, and those harassed will fight back even harder.

The new nativism is ironic because major political and economic powers are facing unprecedented population declines and will soon need new labor. Before reunification, West Germany's fertility rate was only 1.4—way below the 2.1 average that sustains a population without growth. Italy's rate is only 1.2, the lowest in the world. The economic might of several European countries and Japan may, long term, be undermined by birth rates so low that they are unable to sustain economic superiority.

"The characteristic feature of these demographic processes is that they are very slow and nonreversible," explained Todd, the French social historian. "In the first period of decline, the demographic contraction is [a] positive aspect on the economic situation. People don't produce children. So with all their time, economies are getting more and more productive. That's the Italian miracle. That's part of German might in the economic field. Then one generation after that, you will have a contraction of the active population, and you've got the beginning of the decrease. [Then] it's too late, and you can't do anything."

Germany, he predicted, "is going to be very old. Even an increase in the birth rate would not change anything. The low birthrate in Germany has been produced for fifteen or twenty years, so the retraction in the base of the German population is done." As a result, he said, "We're about to experience a dramatic decrease in German economic power. If you think in military terms, well you might conceive [of] a disintegration."

Japan faces the same crisis. In 1990, it had one of the world's lowest fertility rates, down from 3.1 after World War II to under 1.6. But Japan also has the longest life expectancy, meaning it faces a decreasing labor force to support increasing numbers of pensioners.

In general, the developed world—including both halves of Europe, North America and Japan—accounted for 23 percent of the world population in 1990. By the year 2000, it will account for only 6 percent of the world increase. Africa, at the other extreme, represented 12 percent of the world-population mass but is expected to provide 23 percent of the increase by the beginning of the next century.[28] Africa's growth is so rapid that even the AIDS epidemic, which will devastate some countries, may yet make only a small dent in the continent's overall population increase.

But the two trends are unlikely to neatly cancel each other out. Indeed, the gap between the gathering elite in the developed North and the masses of poor in the developing South threatens only to widen in the 1990s and beyond—and to create a plethora of flashpoints for social, economic and political tensions. "The line of tension will be without a doubt a line of North–South tension. It is there already," predicted Valéry Giscard d'Estaing, the former French president. "Now it's a line of tension between the weak and the strong. At this point, the strong don't worry much about the weak. But with demography and with the general liberalization of life in the world, you will have problems of immigration and problems of competition, new kinds of pressures."

During the postwar era, many developed countries encouraged immigration, temporary or permanent, to provide a labor force for jobs the locals no longer wanted or needed. But by 1990, most of the developed world was refusing even to consider balancing its population or labor shortfalls with new permanent immigrants. Whatever the need, the costs of integrating alien cultures, religions, customs and higher birthrates—which, individually or together, could erode the long-dominant social fabric—was not deemed worth the benefits.

"The United States, Canada and Australia were built on immigration. But other societies don't have an immigrant tradition embedded in their national psyche," said Meissner, the former U.S. immigration official. "They could use immigration as a solution. But from a social and political point of view, it's unlikely that they will because of the controversy that surrounds the admission of large numbers of people who are seen as foreigners—and all that entails."

Indeed, rather than take more immigrants, France increased welfare benefits and tax incentives to encourage families to have more children. Italy tried to lure its emigrants back from Latin America. Japan began offering financial baby "bonuses" for each additional child—while at the same time neighboring China was again enforcing its single-child policy, necessitated by overpopulation. Yet Tokyo shunned the prospect of Chinese immigrants. "If China gets poorer, then I think the refugees, huge numbers of refugees will come out of China," said Naohiro Amaya, a former deputy vice-minister of the ministry of international trade and industry. "Of course they will come to Japan in the millions. This causes terrible problems for us."

In the absence of some legal means of evening the world's population imbalance, the impact may run even deeper. The vast numbers stuck in unviable nations may even undermine the trend toward pluralism. Reflected George Mitchell, the U.S. Senate majority leader, "Over 90 percent of [the world population] increase will occur in less developed and underdeveloped countries, where the pressure to feed, clothe, house, educate and employ the new billions will place the governments of those nations in a situation where rapid industrialization will be required of the sort that the Western democracies went through in the previous century, but in a much condensed time frame"—a virtually impossible task. The alternative, however, is migration or implosion—or both.

In other words, too many people can endanger democracy. "Democracy seems to be breaking out all over. Whether these fragile new democratic institutions survive or not will depend partly on the intensity of population pressures and the strains they add to the problems of governance," said Dr. Sharon Camp, vice-president of the Population Crisis Committee.

A Population Crisis Committee survey of the world in 1989 offered a taste of the future. "For many countries the stability of new democratic institutions depends not only on the wisdom of leaders and on the support they receive from abroad but on their ability to slow the continuing buildup of population pressures. . . . Only a handful of countries with serious demographic pressures managed to maintain stable constitutional governments with good records on civil and political rights." The survey's conclusion was sobering: "In an increasingly interdependent world, the ill effects of population pressures anywhere have adverse consequences everywhere."[29]

Global Plagues

"What ills from beauty spring."

—SAMUEL JOHNSON

The Moscow dusk was summer-soft, with a welcome breeze that swept away the polluted-city smells of truck exhaust and cigarettes. In the old days, before Gorbachev's reforms, Sergei Ivanov and his friends might have stayed outside to enjoy a stroll in the late northern light. But leisurely strolls, Ivanov lamented, were becoming a thing of the past; now, people wanted to get off the streets before the muggers came out.

"Punks," he warned under his breath, nodding across the street at a clutch of teenagers dressed in torn denim. The youths swaggered toward him with deliberate menace and passed with raucous laughter, their point of intimidation made. "Moscow was a safe city when I was growing up, but it isn't anymore," Ivanov, a screenwriter, complained. "There are thieves on the street these days, all kinds of criminals."

That evening in 1990, around Ivanov's kitchen table, a half-dozen young Russians exchanged tales of lurid crime: the taxi driver who abducted young women passengers, the knife-wielding thieves who hid in unlit courtyards, the "night market" of prostitutes and drug peddlers. "This country is going to the dogs," declared a would-be film director named Sasha.

Russia's heady new freedom has brought unwelcome side effects to the streets of Moscow and other cities: crime, incivility and fear. In a country that acknowledged almost no crime a decade ago, the discovery that Moscow's streets had turned into a jungle—"like Chicago or New York," Ivanov exclaimed—came as a major shock. Crime became a major political issue; Communist Party conservatives blamed reformers for unleashing chaos. The hard-liners who launched an aborted coup d'état against Gorbachev in 1991 cited the rising crime rate as one of the reasons they decided to act. "We are determined without further delay to restore law and order . . . and to wage relentless war on the criminal underworld," promised Gennady Yanayev, one of the coup's leaders. "We will rid our cities of crime."[1] The people of Moscow rejected that solution and defeated the coup; but for most ordinary Russians, the soaring crime rate still ranked as a major issue, every bit as threatening as the collapse of the economy or the disintegration of the Soviet Union.

The paradox faced by the Russian people was felt in even more tragic forms in other parts of the world, from North America and Western Europe to impoverished Africa and Latin America. A wave of frightening social disorders and ills, from crime and drug abuse to AIDS and other epidemics, swept the entire world at the turn of the 1990s, destroying millions of lives and diminishing the quality of the lives of millions more, even as democracy spread and economies boomed.

In the United States, a society that often considered itself the most successful in history, more than twenty-three thousand people were victims of murder in 1990, a record. The number of prisoners incarcerated for serious crimes rose above half a million, another record. The U.S. government estimated that almost 13 million of its citizens used illegal drugs—and celebrated, for that was a drop from 14.5 million two years earlier. More than sixteen thousand Americans died of AIDS in 1990, and more than forty-three thousand new cases of the disease were reported. Even in America, old epidemics were returning to take lives as well: cases of tuberculosis, measles and cholera were all recorded in their greatest numbers in a generation.

In the developing world, entire cities reverted to lawless camps after dark, from Nairobi, once an urban model for black Africa, to Rio de Janeiro, where criminal gangs murdered street children. Asia and Latin America battled not only drug addiction but the growing wealth and power of drug traffickers, who fielded private armies in Burma, Colombia and Peru. In Africa, the most pitiless of epidemics was wiping out much of a generation; by the year 2000, Africa may count sixteen million AIDS orphans, more than the population of Illinois. The disease was altering the demographics, the economy and even the balance of military power of a continent. It would be remembered as Africa's great calamity, the central fact of the continent's history in the 1990s. But in another sense, Africa was not alone: At the end of the century, every society was haunted by a fear of multiplying ills—and the fear of regression.

The health of a society can be measured by its illnesses; progress can be gauged by problems solved and problems unmet. In the last years of the twentieth century, many of mankind's social illnesses were not merely recurring, they were increasing. Some of the structures of society that modern citizens took for granted, like protection from epidemic disease, were slowly disintegrating. Like rust on a bridge, the signs of decay had been ignored for years—until the bolts began to fail. Crime, drug addiction and disease were all symptoms of societies whose underpinnings had been neglected. For a time, elites comforted themselves with the belief that these ills were largely limited to their societies' marginal citizens, the poor and the weak. But while the marginal were indeed most vulnerable and most victimized, the modern epidemics rapidly seeped into the better neighborhoods as well.

As the Russians noticed, these plagues had a paradoxical side: in some ways they were the unanticipated dark half of the world's "globalization," unwelcome social by-products of political, economic and technological progress. Politically, the new freedoms enjoyed by millions in the world's young democracies also provided openings for criminals to exploit. Virtually every country that liberalized found that social problems became more visible, if not necessarily more acute. In Russia, half-hearted economic reforms created just enough freedom to allow racketeers to flourish, but not enough for legitimate free enterprise to take root. The collapse of the Iron Curtain allowed Russian organized-crime bosses to travel to the West and seek out their counterparts abroad, from Italian mafiosi to American drug dealers, for collaborative projects—a form of multinational enterprise noticed by both the American F.B.I. and its Russian counterpart, the M.V.D.

The massive expansion and diversification of the narcotics trade mirrored the world economy's globalization almost precisely. Since the 1960s, drug abuse has spread to unprecedented numbers on an unprecedented geographic scale. A United Nations survey of crime from 1976 to 1986 found a far higher increase in the rate of drug-related crimes than in any other category.[2] The advent of mass marketing in the world of illegal drugs—some varieties of heroin and crack have their own brand names, like "China White" and "Golden Lion"—has opened gigantic profit opportunities for canny drug dealers. The giant underworld organizations that control drug supplies—cocaine from the Andes, heroin from Southeast Asia and the Middle East—have become swift and sophisticated at seeking out new markets in America, Europe and Asia and in developing new products, just like any other up-to-date global business.

Just as faster, cheaper transportation made the global drug trade possible, so it also contributed to the rapid spread of AIDS, a disease that researchers believe lay dormant in central Africa for years before it suddenly went international. Not until air travel between the farthest corners of the world became widely available did the human immunodeficiency virus (HIV) spread rapidly beyond Africa to every continent, beginning with the United States, the most open of countries. A handful of governments attempted to close their borders to the disease, but in an era of expanding international contact it was a quixotic gesture at best.

Epidemics have marked all of history, but few have spread across as wide an area as AIDS. The Black Death of 1348 killed as many as forty million Europeans, a quarter of the continent's population; but the wealthy were able to escape the disease simply by fleeing the cities. Spanish soldiers brought smallpox to Mexico in 1519, but the effect—while devastating—was local. AIDS can be avoided by a change in behavior, but not by moving; by 1991, even authoritarian China and isolated Albania had recorded their first cases.

Crime has also been a constant presence in history; Thucydides described Greece five centuries before Christ as being plagued by pirates and brigands, and Dickens' nineteenth-century London was rich in colorful cutthroats. Narcotics trafficking, too, has a long past, including the period when the British government operated an official drug cartel in China, ultimately touching off the Opium War. But instead of declining in the face of economic and political progress, crime has kept pace and even increased.

These painful social failings have had far-reaching political effects. In Russia, rapidly spreading panic over crime provoked popular demands for authoritarian rule to restore law and order. Elsewhere, the enormous profits of narcotics trafficking enabled drug lords to buy, or attempt to buy, national and provincial governments in Panama, Colombia, Bolivia, the Bahamas, Pakistan and Burma. In Colombia, the cocaine kings of the Medellín cartel negotiated as sovereign powers with the national government, ran political candidates and finally lost power only after fighting a virtual civil war. In Southeast Asia, opium lord Khun Sa reigned over much of Burma's northeast.

AIDS, too, has had an unexpected impact on world affairs, imposing a grisly new polarization between prosperous Northern countries, which can contain the disease, and poor Southern countries, which cannot. AIDS is not the only epidemic to ravage the developing world in this scientific age. In 1991 alone, cholera swept through South America, killing more than thirteen hundred people; measles killed more than five hundred in Zaire and more than one hundred in the United States.

The defeat of epidemic disease has been one of the grand conceits of the twentieth century. Instead, AIDS has shown that nature can still humble us; no unknown new disease was ever charted and identified so rapidly, only to remain beyond medicine's power to cure. Much of human history has been a struggle toward the perfecting of mankind and his institutions. The persistence of crime and drug addiction give each generation fresh evidence of human weakness and the existence of evil; the appearance of AIDS suggested that the quest for perfection was as impossible as the labor of Sisyphus. Nature, like man, seems to invent new imperfections all the time.

Colonel Alexander Gurov of the M.V.D., chief of the Soviet Union's first organized-crime strike force, had studied his country's underworld as a policeman and an academic for more than two decades. He had investigated rackets in Moscow, gunrunning in Azerbaijan and official corruption in Uzbekistan. But in 1990, Gurov said even he was shocked by the brutal crimes that gripped Moscow after the advent of *perestroika*.

"Everybody remembers Al Capone, but he only killed seven people," the scholarly-looking colonel said, drumming his fingers for emphasis on his glass-topped desk at the modern headquarters of the Soviet interior ministry. "Our own godfather, Osmanov, killed ten people a few months ago—and the eleventh victim was a dog."

Thugs from one Russian gang burst into one of Moscow's new, privately owned restaurants in 1989, opened fire with handguns, and beat several customers with clubs—apparently because the restaurateur had failed to pay protection money. Russian newspapers and television newscasts trumpeted lurid stories of a genre already all too familiar in the West: a woman stabbed to death by an acquaintance who wanted to steal her videocassette recorder; a woman shot by two men after she rebuffed the advances of one of them; a nine-year-old girl kidnapped, raped and killed, her body found near the Moscow River.

With a kind of grim national pride, Gurov asserted that crime in the Soviet Union was as bad as anywhere on earth. "We are going through a criminal shock," the investigator said. "It is something that comes when you move toward a market economy." Was *perestroika* part of the problem? "I am in favor of *perestroika*," Gurov said, "but there is no question that it is making our job much harder. Respect for the law has not replaced fear, so we have a vacuum of legitimate authority."

The shock of crime affected the lives of ordinary Russian citizens in large ways and small. Muscovites who were lucky enough to own automobiles routinely removed the windshield wipers and put them inside the car, lest thieves steal the blades to sell. Passengers on trains and airplanes watched their carry-on luggage warily, lest it exit in someone else's hands. Prices on merchandise in privately owned stores were hiked up to include the cost of "protection" from local gangsters; more than one shop was burned out after its owners neglected their payoffs. Taxi drivers in Moscow offered to change dollars to rubles, in a city where dealing in foreign currency was almost unheard of a decade ago. Gasoline, meat and other commodities were traded openly for dollars, German marks or American cigarettes.

The most immediate effect of the crime wave was to convince many Russians that they had tumbled from a world of order and authority into the kind of anarchy they had once thought of as a hallmark of the decadent West. A 1990 poll found that Soviet citizens listed crime even ahead of food shortages as a pressing national issue. Another survey that year found that 33 percent of all Muscovites said they were afraid to go out at night because of crime—a level of fear surpassed only by New Yorkers, at 38 percent, according to the weekly *Moskovski Novosti* [*Moscow News*].[3] "This city is no place to bring up children," complained Andrei Ostroukh, a translator and father of a four-year-old boy. "Little kids are being kidnapped from playgrounds—from the hallways of apartment buildings! This is another reason I want to emigrate. I'm sure it can't be this bad in the West."

In fact, the crime rate in Russia was still notably low by Western standards. In 1989, the interior ministry estimated that an average of 20 violent crimes were committed in Moscow every day. In Los Angeles, with a population less than half of Moscow's, the number was 207—or more than ten times as many.[4] But what mattered to the Russian citizen—and the Russian policeman—was the staggering rate of increase. The interior ministry's official crime statistics showed a 32 percent increase nationwide in 1989 and a 13 percent increase in 1990. The impact in Moscow was even greater—an astonishing 81 percent increase in violent crime in 1989.

But then, according to a United Nations survey, crime has increased almost everywhere in the world. Between 1976 and 1986, the U.N. study reported, murder increased globally by 30 percent, theft by 22 percent and drug crimes by 120 percent. Crime, it seemed, was an inescapable companion to modernization, urbanization and the other processes that arrive under the general heading of progress.[5]

In Poland, as in Russia, an end to authoritarian rule unexpectedly made life easier for criminals; one gang of impecunious thieves robbed a string of Catholic churches of their unguarded wealth. In the eastern half of Berlin, the increase in crime was more modest after the reunification of Germany—but only, police said, because the most gifted criminals headed to the more lucrative western side. Still, Mayor Eberhard Diepgen warned in 1991, the fact that Germany's borders had been opened to Poles and other Eastern Europeans meant that crime would soon rise in his wealthy city too.

In Brazil and Colombia, gangs of criminal boys roamed the streets of major cities, looking for easy prey to rob; sunbathers at Rio's famed Ipanema and Leblon beaches dared not wear expensive watches or sunglasses. In Argentina and Peru, as in Russia, exploding crime rates pro-voked a wave of nostalgia for the days of dictatorial rule, when few dared to step out of line.

In South Korea, economic prosperity brought a wave of murders and robberies. Even in orderly Japan, robberies, kidnappings and murders took an alarming upswing. The crime rate in 1990 was only one-fourth that of the United States, but the newspapers began to notice an upsurge in grisly crimes of a sort most Japanese once believed could happen only elsewhere, like the kidnapping and murder of three kindergarten-age girls. Japan's once-orderly criminal gangs, the Yakuza, expanded their operations beyond traditional gambling and prostitution to attacks on ordinary citi-zens. A 1990 government survey found that the mob had attempted to extort money from one out of every six leading companies; 30 percent of the firms admitted that they paid protection money.[6]

In short, freedom's unhappy side effects have come more easily than its benefits. The trend has been most visible in the sudden blossoming of minor vices, from prostitution to pornography, through the once-prudish and tightly controlled capitals of Eastern Europe.

In Moscow's best hotels, hard-currency prostitutes brazenly knocked on the doors of rooms and asked to come in; their chutzpah was priced at a hundred dollars per visit, in foreign currency only. The hookers' elegant clothes and easy access to dollars—popularized by a hit film, *Interdev-uschka*, about a fictional prostitute who marries a Swedish client and moves to the West—made them, improbably enough, role models to alienated Russian teenagers: In a poll conducted by a youth magazine, high-school girls listed "hard currency prostitute" as one of the professions they found most attractive. (The others were modeling, film acting and "marrying a professor.") So serious was the problem that the education ministry issued a special decree warning high-school girls against falling into a life of vice.

Pornography, too, has swept through the one-time homelands of com-munist virtue. At Moscow subway stations, young men hawked sex manuals and pornographic drawings, often grainy photocopies that offered little prurient detail but still drew crowds of sensation-starved Russians. Conservatives in the Supreme Soviet called for a crackdown for the sake of "social order," but their case was weakened by a news-paper report that Communist Party leaders had long enjoyed the privilege of borrowing pornographic videotapes from the state film company—with the most explicit tapes available only to the most senior communists.[7]

In Prague, the elegant city of Jan Hus and Franz Kafka, one of the longest lines in the first year of freedom was in front of the theater showing the soft-core porn film *Emmanuelle*, which opened in Czechoslovakia some twenty years late. Nightclubs offered amateurish but graphic stripteases. Newspapers carried candid personal advertisements—"Seeking playmate for erotic games." The state-owned television even presented a topless beauty contest, dubbed "Miss Monokini."

Czech journalist Iva Drapalova called the phenomenon, wryly, "our sex explosion. Suddenly we have a Czech version of *Playboy*, we have striptease, we had Miss Monokini. . . . Every newspaper thinks they have to print at least one nude. We were so puritanical before.

"Striptease—there was even a striptease right down on Wenceslas Square [in the center of Prague]. The police had to be called in to take [the strippers] out. After so many years of puritanism, it is sort of an explosion."

Even if the new Czechoslovak government had wanted to, there was virtually no way to stop the tide. The massive circulation of once-forbidden smut was, in its own way, just another successful challenge to the authority of the state.

Pornography in Prague was only the most harmless tip of a larger and more dangerous iceberg. Just as businesses in every other industry have sought to operate on a global scale, so has organized crime steadily expanded its range to seek new opportunities for profit.

Beginning in the 1980s, F.B.I. officials said, crime syndicates on five continents stepped up both their cooperation with and competition in cross-border rackets. In the United States, the old-fashioned, home-grown Mafia has ceded pieces of its monopoly to an exotic new assortment of ethnic crime organizations, from the Sicilian Mafia and the Calabrian N'Drangheta to Colombian cocaine traffickers, Jamaican drug posses, Japanese Yakuza and a variety of Chinese gangs. The new groups operated both in the United States and abroad, moving members in and out of the country as it suited them. Most worrisome for police, some of the multinational crime groups have begun to cooperate with each other.

"We have seen some integration of organized-crime groups, and we expect to see more," said Jim Moody, the F.B.I.'s chief organized-crime investigator, in 1991. Already, he said, the Sicilian Mafia operated in more than a dozen countries, shipping drugs from the Middle East through Turkey and the Balkans to Europe. "In 1992, there will be no borders in Europe; people can move around freely," he noted. "That will be a great convenience for organized crime."

Even Russia and the other republics of the former Soviet Union were being brought into the international crime market. "Our Mafia is beginning to establish transnational contacts, since foreign criminals regard our country as a real Klondike," said Gurov of the Soviet interior ministry. "Our criminals are learning from your organized crime," he added. "In Tashkent, we confiscated a video film on how the police fight drug trafficking. It was being passed around in Mafia circles there—it was like a training manual for them. It showed a drug trafficker landing an airplane on a closed highway. I don't think they had thought of that before."

International crime has not been confined to sophisticated cross-border smuggling operations or exotic money-laundering schemes. Simple automobile theft has become an international affair, with thousands of cars in the United States stolen for transshipment to buyers in Latin America, and luxury cars from Europe turning up in the Middle East. After Iraq's invasion of Kuwait, the flow briefly turned around, with Kuwaiti automobiles popping up in European used-car lots. In 1990, five countries, including the United States, formed an international league of theft bureaus to begin combating the global car thieves on an equally global scale.

But the most important field of global crime remained drug trafficking. As sales of cocaine and its cheap, cruder derivative, crack, surged in the 1980s, thousands of lives in the United States were lost or destroyed—some through addiction, others in shootouts between drug dealers. In the Third World countries that produced the drugs, however, the impact was even greater: drug traffickers amassed so much power that they threatened not only the health of their customers but the viability of national and local governments.

During the 1970s and 1980s, wealthy narcotics barons became powers unto themselves in a half-dozen countries. Colombia's two cocaine cartels, from the cities of Medellín and Cali, were only the best known. Similar organizations also existed in Burma, Thailand and Laos, where the world's largest opium crop was grown, and in Afghanistan and Pakistan, where much of the heroin that reached the United States and Europe was manufactured.

"The drug traffickers have armies and bases and governments, and they have caused more deaths by gunfire in the United States than any single cause since the Civil War," noted Richard Fisher, a Texas banker who helped organize a civic antidrug campaign in Dallas.

In Pakistan, narcotics authorities estimated in 1990 that as many as a hundred heroin laboratories operated in the country's tribal areas—semi-wild lands where the central government's police have no authority. In the smuggler's market town of Dara Adem Khel, shops marked by a goat's fleece over the door openly displayed hashish in their windows; heroin was kept more discreetly under lock and key. "The government has asked us to clean up the town," explained Habib ur-Rahman, a young gun dealer. "So we've stopped [people from] selling heroin and stolen cars and we've stopped the kidnapping." But the government did little to stop the more lucrative international heroin trade, which some officials estimated was controlled by no more than twenty well-known—and well-connected—kingpins. Much of the opium they used as raw material came from fields in Afghanistan that were controlled by anticommunist rebels who had been financed and armed by the C.I.A. since 1980.[8] American diplomats feared that drug money could make both Afghanistan and Pakistan ungovernable; "This could be the next Lebanon, in spades," said one.

In Burma, the power that drug money offered was exercised even more openly by feuding opium lords who governed large parts of the country, largely tolerated by the central government. The most famous lord was Khun Sa, a half-Chinese, half-Shan tribesman whose Mong Tai Army fielded an estimated six thousand well-equipped troops. Khun Sa was indicted in an American court in 1989 for masterminding a shipment of 2,389 pounds of heroin, the largest single heroin cargo ever seized. Yet he lived openly and received reporters at his headquarters at Homong, in northeastern Burma. He once offered to sell Burma's entire opium crop to the United States government—if Washington would offer a reasonable price.

In 1991, Khun Sa was at war, but not with the government of Burma.

Instead, his men were locked in battle with the rival Wa Army, led by
Ie Shio Sue, a former militant in the Burmese Communist Party. At the
same time, the two drug armies were under attack by the armed forces
of neighboring Thailand, which decided that the opium lords had become
a national security threat. "This is a tourist area," explained Lieutenant
General Pairoj Chanurai, commander of Thailand's Third Army. "If they
want to fight deeper inside Burma, that is one thing. But they won't be
allowed to disturb our people."[9]

The drug traffickers' threat to national sovereignty was what finally
impelled governments like Colombia's and Bolivia's to cooperate with
U.S. crop-eradication efforts, in which U.S. troops flew into the South
American jungle to destroy coca crops and cocaine laboratories. Yet even
when cartels were tamed, as Colombia's government succeeded in doing
in Medellín in 1990, the effect on the world narcotics market was unclear.
Use of drugs in the United States has declined since the early 1980s, a
decline due partly to a shrinking pool of young people and partly to tireless
public campaigns. One survey found that 15 percent of college students
in 1990 said they had used drugs, a significant decline from 38 percent
in 1980. The federal government estimated that the number of drug users
in the United States declined from twenty-three million in 1983—more
than a tenth of the population—to thirteen million in 1990. And U.S.
officials claimed a major victory in 1990 in forcing the wholesale price of
cocaine from twelve thousand dollars a kilogram to eighteen thousand
dollars, an increase that apparently reflected scarcer supplies. But by the
same measure, supplies were still abundant—for in 1983, a kilogram of
cocaine had commanded fifty-five thousand dollars.

Law enforcement struggled to keep up with the ability of narcotics
entrepreneurs to innovate and adapt. Throughout the 1980s, drug syndicates developed new products, sought new markets, and found new ways
to move their merchandise as adeptly as any global corporation. The great
innovation of the late 1980s was the introduction of crack, which opened
the markets of the poverty-stricken ghetto to cocaine dealers because of
its low price. Drug investigators said new, cheaper forms of heroin and
methamphetamines began turning up at the beginning of the 1990s,
seeking to emulate crack's success. The one certainty, criminologists
James Q. Wilson and John De Iulio noted, was that "some chemist

[would] discover a drug that is even cheaper and more euphoria-inducing than crack."[10] The realities of the marketplace limited the ability of governments to act in the drug market as much as in the bond market.

As traffickers broadened their horizons, they were able to compensate for the decline in drug use in the United States by a gradual increase in consumption overseas. In Japan, police arrested more than twenty thousand people in 1988 for selling or using "ice," a potent methamphetamine. Japan's organized-crime gangs, the Yakuza, derived roughly half their income from illegal drug deals, Japanese experts estimated. "Japan is an ideal market for drugs. We have enough money, and the younger generation is sick and tired of peace and happiness," worried Atsuyuki Sassa, a former national security adviser to Japan's prime minister. "I am afraid we will follow your route on that."

In Europe, investigators said that South American traffickers were flooding cities with cocaine in a concerted effort to push prices down and attract new customers. In Argentina, the price of cocaine dropped to only five thousand dollars per kilogram, well below the U.S. price, because of lax enforcement of smuggling laws. Poor countries became a target as well; India estimated 800,000 heroin addicts in 1990. China, which once boasted of having eradicated opium addiction, discovered a new population of addicts in southern Yunnan Province, where Burmese traders dumped much of their surplus production. Even Egypt reported an alarming rise in heroin use among young urban professionals, a side-effect of increased prosperity.

The effects of this epidemic were similar in every society: increased crime, lost productivity, broken lives—and demands on governments to act. So alarmed were Americans by the plague of crack in 1989 that President Bush proclaimed the drug epidemic a national-security problem and ordered the armed forces to help choke off the inflow. "If you look at the polls, 90 percent of the American people believe that drugs are the number one national security problem in America," noted General Maxwell Thurman, then commander of U.S. forces in Latin America. "If that's the case, then the American public has a right to say, 'If you're spending $300 billion annually on the Defense Department, what role are you playing in the Number One national security problem?'"

The result was a series of hurried and sometimes reluctant military initiatives, from air patrols along the Atlantic coast to radar balloons over the once-unguarded Caribbean. In the California desert, an elite unit of desert scouts—soldiers who had once probed the borders of Iraq—was put to work watching for drug traffickers from Mexico. The mission was just as arduous as war; it merely lacked the satisfaction of winning a battle. Only thirty miles away, in booming San Diego, a seemingly endless supply of drugs was still being sold openly on downtown street corners, and drug-related robberies and murders remained at near-record levels.

Police officials in the world's most advanced society said they were powerless to halt the drug trafficking and the violence in their streets. "People probably get tired of the same explanation, but it's the ready availability of guns," said Norman Stamper, an assistant police chief in San Diego. "This is just a more violent society."[11] The tools available to the U.S. government, from high-tech surveillance and superbly trained troops to well-funded police forces, simply were not enough.

The Zimbabwean doctor spoke softly and sadly as he recounted a session in his Harare office. "When the mother brought the child in, she said he'd had a skin problem. It looked like eczema. But he was also clearly suffering from something more serious. So I decided to give him some blood tests.

"Sure enough, he was HIV-positive. So then I asked the parents to have blood tests. Of course, they were HIV-positive, too. It was one of the hardest things I've ever had to do. I asked the family to come in, and I tried, very gently, to explain their situation." He paused. "Then the mother asked for some ointment for the eczema. And they left.

"I was dumbstruck." He shook his head. "I finally realized that they either didn't understand or they didn't believe me."

Of all the ills shaping the world's societies in the next century, AIDS may have the most tragic impact. The saga of the disease that stunned the world in the 1980s only began to approach its ghastly climax in the 1990s. The next two generations, at least, will be traumatized by its devastating toll.

The impact will not be limited to the deaths of African families, Southeast Asian prostitutes, or European and American homosexuals and drug users. Indeed, the loss of millions of lives is only the beginning. Even if a miracle cure were to prevent the further spread of AIDS, the crippling side effects of those who already have it incubating in their bodies will shape the future of many nations as much as political and economic events—in some cases, even more.

Since AIDS has been most widespread among those aged twenty to forty-five, the most productive strata of societies will be ravaged in the 1990s and beyond. Soldiers are among the first to be infected, meaning that the ability of even well-equipped countries to defend themselves will be endangered because of loss of troops to AIDS. In Zimbabwe, the disease was decimating the armed forces as effectively as missiles or artillery. As many as 50 percent of Zimbabwe's forty-six thousand troops carried the HIV virus in 1990, and some estimates ran even higher. The readiness of combat units to fight depended not so much on their training as on their illness rate. The stark result: "In a few years' time, you have no army," said Dr. MacLeod Chitiyo, chairman of Zimbabwe's National AIDS Council. The casualties went far beyond the army. "With the most productive—the professional, the skilled, the educated people—going, the economy will be shattered," Chitiyo said wistfully.

Since the dormancy period between becoming HIV-positive and developing AIDS is eight to ten years, hundreds of thousands of infected mothers in developing countries, either unaware of their disease or ignorant about its consequences, continue to bear children. About 30 percent of those children will also develop AIDS and die, according to international research estimates. But that leaves behind an even bigger problem: the 70 percent who will be orphaned—creating an enormous welfare strain and a gaping hole in terms of a generation's development. Since the cost of adequately treating AIDS patients is prohibitive in even wealthy nations, any serious effort to take care of them in the world's poorer corners would drain national economies and set back development in regions already unable to keep up with the twentieth century.

The dimensions of the future problem are often difficult to fathom because the numbers have, already, been blindingly high. In 1990, up to ten million people were estimated to be infected worldwide. Until 1991, the World Health Organization (W.H.O.) had estimated that the number would rise to thirty million at the turn of the century—but then, faced with a flood of newly reported cases, it adjusted the projection upward to forty million. Even then, the worst is still to come. A W.H.O. survey concluded, "It is very unlikely that the global prevalence of HIV infections will stabilize or level off for at least several decades."

Amid the flamboyant festivity of floats and costumes, bands and balls, Rio de Janeiro's famed annual carnival had a new touch in 1991. Along with confetti strewn in the streets were thousands of leaflets. Revelers who "play around," they warned, should "play safely." Circulated by a private group, the leaflets reflected the fact that Brazil ranked second only to the United States in the number of officially reported cases in 1990. Although the country registered only fifteen thousand confirmed cases, specialists estimated that the number of Brazilians already infected totaled at least half a million, and possibly 1.5 million.

Unlike the world's earlier plagues, AIDS has left no continent untouched, no individual invulnerable. Identified largely with Africa, North America and Europe in its initial stages, the deadly disease had, by the beginning of the 1990s, hit every corner on earth—from remote Iceland to isolated Albania, from the city-state of Singapore to the island-state of Sri Lanka. The most shocking revelation after Romania's anticommunist revolution was not the sorry state of the nation's political health but the epidemic proportions of AIDS among its babies, thousands of whom were infected by blood transfusions shortly after birth.

Disappearing barriers around the world only hastened the spread. In the 1980s, South Africa was largely insulated from the initial outbreak of the disease because it was cut off from most normal trade and travel with its neighbors. Most of the first cases were among white homosexuals who had traveled abroad—earning AIDS a reputation among blacks as a "white man's disease," despite its prevalence elsewhere in Africa. But since political liberalization in South Africa has opened the borders to more travel, the incidence of AIDS among blacks has begun to spread rapidly. Worst-case projections in the South African press have suggested that up to 40 percent could be affected by 1998, potentially halting the growth of the black population.

As the dimensions of the disease widened, so, too, did the implications. The main problem will no longer just be diagnosing and treating the stricken. Just as deeply affected will be those who survive AIDS, especially, but not exclusively, in the developing world.

Zimbabwe is a microcosm. An unpublished analysis by Harare's Central Statistical Office estimated in the late 1980s that the country's population will eventually be halved by the epidemic. Given its high birthrate, the southern African nation's population should, by rights, reach eighteen million by the year 2017; instead, AIDS may reduce it to eight million—a million less than in 1990. And Zimbabwe was by no means Africa's worst case. For the poorest and most undeveloped of the world's six populated continents, the implications of the modern-day plague are already almost insurmountable.

AIDS has taken a toll on even the political elite. In Harare, at least one cabinet minister and two of the hundred members of parliament are widely believed to have died of AIDS. In neighboring Zambia, the son of President Kenneth Kaunda died of AIDS in 1989. Throughout Africa, soldiers, migrant labor and transport workers, because of their mobility, have been among the groups with the highest infection rates. The Zimbabwe cabinet minister who died was minister of state for defense. A former guerrilla during the thirteen-year civil war, he was based in Mozambique, where Zimbabwean doctors believe he was infected.

The effects of AIDS will, in turn, create an unparalleled crisis for the next generation. In its first study of AIDS among children, W.H.O. projected in 1990 that ten million children worldwide would be infected with HIV by the year 2000—and that "the vast majority" of them would in fact be dead by then. In Zimbabwe, one of four confirmed AIDS cases was among children under the age of five. Behind the figures was the implication that the effects of the disease will linger long past the time either a cure is found or AIDS begins to ebb. Among them is the fate of children left behind. Michael Merson, W.H.O.'s AIDS director, predicted Africa would have ten million orphans by the year 2000 because of AIDS. Zimbabwe's share, he estimated, could number more than a million.

"It's got serious repercussions for society," said Dr. Chitiyo. "Who's going to look after them? The resources of the state are going to be stretched fully." Throughout Africa, the extended family has historically absorbed orphaned offspring of relatives, however distant. But the vast numbers will challenge even this centuries-old tradition.

The loss of half the older generation and the resultant side effects will

create a new generation that actually sets back society rather than contrib-
utes to badly needed development. "Many of them are going to reach the
end of school without parents. Many of them are going to reach the end
of school without the number of teachers they should have and without
the number of elders in rural settings," said John Robertson, a Scots-born
white Zimbabwean economist who tracks AIDS trends. "They will possibly be a deprived group of children. At the same time, they are the
country's only hope." The cumulative impact means that many parts of
Africa, already struggling to keep up with the twentieth century, may be
decades or more away from being able to enter the twenty-first.

"Going into the twenty-first century . . . about half the [local] adult
population will die of AIDS," predicted Robertson. "That's going to leave
a very severe gap in our work force, in our management structure, and in
the customers for the products and services that our businesses and industries produce." Because of AIDS, he predicted, farmers will face severe
labor shortages soon in the next century. Agriculture is Zimbabwe's chief
employer, accounting for one out of every three workers. Before independence in 1980, the white-minority government of Rhodesia was able to
survive more than a decade of civil war, political isolation and U.N.
economic sanctions—in part because the nation could feed itself. In the
1990s AIDS was threatening to wreak more havoc than the combination
of military, political and economic pressures did in the 1970s. For the first
time, one of the most fertile countries on the continent may not be able
to feed itself.

What can nations so gravely threatened do? For the poorest countries,
both prevention and care for AIDS patients is too expensive. In 1990, the
cost of a single condom at local pharmacies in Harare, the Zimbabwean
capital, was thirteen cents—in a country with a per capita income of less
than three hundred dollars a year. But even for those countries with funds,
the supply is not endless. Condoms and most other medical supplies had
to be imported, draining foreign exchange needed for updating industrial
and agricultural equipment for development.

In effect, African countries were trapped in a no-win dilemma. If they
used limited resources to treat people already condemned to die, they
would have less for education and development, which is vital to both
slowing the growth of AIDS and enabling countries to enter the twenty-
first century.

In Zimbabwe, the care of a patient once AIDS sets in was estimated between fifteen and twenty thousand dollars—well below the fifty-thousand-dollar cost in the United States. But only a few could sustain those costs. Zimbabwe's medical facilities could not even afford to treat the secondary diseases—cancer, tuberculosis, pneumonia, skin diseases and other ailments—that develop in most AIDS victims. As a result, most patients went home to villages to be cared for by families—not the safest practice among people uninitiated in how the disease can spread.

Throughout the 1980s, Zimbabwe was not among the countries that felt threatened by AIDS; in 1987, only 119 cases had been reported. Self-delusion played a role as well: the minister of health claimed that the HIV infection did not necessarily lead to AIDS and that the strain in Zimbabwe was nonlethal. By 1990, however, confirmed cases reached 9,000; another 12,500 were reported to be HIV-positive. Only then, when the crisis could no longer be denied, did the health minister lose his job.

AIDS was in many ways unique, but it was only one of several virulent epidemics scarring the century's final decade like unwelcome ghosts from the premodern past.

In the spring of 1991, Brazil's vast Amazon basin was gripped by panic: Cholera, which had already ravaged Peru's Andean highlands, was moving down the vast network of rivers. A disease of the nineteenth century had returned to attack some of the world's least defended, the Amazon Indians—descendants of tribes that had never before been exposed to the disease because civilization had never carried it to their homes.

Cholera, along with diseases like malaria and tuberculosis, had never been eradicated from the countries of the South. But by 1990, some of the old illnesses were spreading more widely and more quickly than before for two reasons: the new reach of modern transportation and the Achilles' heel of collapsing social infrastructures.

The 1991 cholera epidemic began in Peru, where the ancient Incas had once built sewage systems, but their modern successors had failed to do the same. Rapid, unplanned urbanization had made it impossible to install proper sanitation facilities—and once the barrios were in place, the government did little after the fact either. Forty percent of Lima's seven million residents had no access to drinkable piped water. Within three months, thirteen hundred Peruvians had died from the disease, and the toll was still rising.

South America's great fear in the early 1990s was that cholera would spill like a deadly tide into the Amazon basin—and then spread to Brazil's giant cities, São Paulo, Rio de Janeiro and Salvador, where millions who lived in squalid *favelas*, or shantytowns, would be at risk. Forty percent of Brazil's 150 million people lived without sewers. Physicians began using the frightening word "pandemic," an epidemic of many epidemics; some predicted that once cholera spread across the continent it would persist as long as fifteen years.

"Cholera has been established here, and it will be endemic for a generation," warned Dr. Walter Velázquez, a specialist at the Dos de Mayo hospital in the Andean mountain market town of Cajamarca. "It has died down for the moment . . . but it will be back, raging in summer and receding in winter." The most painful aspect, he pointed out, was that the epidemic could have been prevented relatively easily, if only basic services had been in place. Indeed, the cities and towns of North America and Europe were virtually immune from cholera precisely because they had installed water and sewer systems in the nineteenth century after bouts with similar epidemics.

"It is no good asking a Peruvian to wash his hands," Velázquez observed, "when there is no water to wash with."[12]

Like AIDS and other infectious diseases, the cholera epidemic of 1991 seemed a cruel vestige of an earlier era. But these human problems were more than mere throwbacks to an earlier age; they were gaining unexpected new life from the very forces that were shaping the next century. Political liberalization, economic globalization, migration, communications—even the prosperity that enabled the youth of Egypt, India and China to buy drugs—made the new epidemics nearly as frightening as the plagues of premodern times. These newly global diseases would shape the transition to a new era just as sharply as the political, economic and military transformations that were the focus of high strategy.

In the early days of the twentieth century, optimists grandly declared that man would soon succeed in eradicating poverty, crime and disease. No longer. In the 1990s, from Africa to the Andes—and America's city streets—millions of people still faced a destiny ravaged by one plague after another. As Peru's Dr. Velázquez pointed out, solutions were already at hand: sanitation for cholera, education and condoms for AIDS, education and treatment for drug abuse. But fragmented, individual responses would not be enough; in a globalized world, no individual country could solve its problems in isolation. In the 1990s, even stable, insular Japan was worried about crime, drugs and AIDS arriving from abroad.

Trouble in one part of the world quickly created echoes elsewhere. The same economic despair that prompted emigration from Latin America and Asia drove Andean and Laotian farmers into the drug trade; the same poverty that allowed epidemics to spread unchecked across Africa and the Amazon ultimately endangered Europe and North America. Our destinies were linked—for good or ill.

Conclusion: Diversity and Order

"There is nothing more difficult to take in hand, more perilous to conduct, or more uncertain in its success, than to take the lead in the introduction of a new order of things."

—MACHIAVELLI

In March 1991, George Bush stood triumphant before a special joint session of Congress as the victorious commander of a global alliance. America's armed forces, supported by troops from twenty-seven other countries, had scored a swift and overwhelming victory over the army of Iraq. Yet even more important than the feat of arms, Bush pronounced, was the turning point that the war marked in the history of nations. "Until now, the world we've known has been a world divided—a world of barbed wire and concrete blocks, conflict and Cold War," the President said that night. "Now we can see a new world coming into view, a world in which there is the very real prospect of a new world order . . . a world in which freedom and respect for human rights find a home among all nations. The Gulf War put this new world to its first test," Bush declared. "We passed that test."

Waving small American flags, congressmen and senators cheered loudly; the nation reveled in a victory that did as much for the American psyche as for Kuwaiti sovereignty. But the spree of self-congratulation was short-lived. Barely a month after Bush announced the withdrawal of U.S. forces from the Gulf, he was forced to reverse course and send more than ten thousand troops into northern Iraq; an abortive Kurdish insurrection had unleashed as many as two million refugees on neighboring countries—and a new regional crisis. In Kuwait, the emir's hapless regime also appealed to Washington to leave U.S. troops behind to protect against outside attack as well as internal disorder.

The real lessons of the Gulf War were far more sobering than Bush's hopeful prediction. Despite the proclamations of a "new world order," the hallmark of the early 1990s was not harmony, but burgeoning disorder. For every problem solved, a new and equally pressing crisis unfolded. After two years of tumultuous change, the world was trapped in a troubled transition that was proving bloodier, costlier and more confusing than anyone had anticipated.

"The old order does not want to die," wrote the eminent Egyptian journalist Mohammed Heikal, "and the future is refusing to be born."[1] The Gulf War may have been the first crisis of the historic transition, but it did nothing to solve any of the world's broader problems. Indeed, it only illuminated the issues that will challenge and reshape the world during the turbulent passage to a new era.

First, the war revealed how broadly—and quickly—power had diffused in the post–Cold War world, and how "collective security" had become not just a desirable ideal but a necessity. Despite the unprecedented breadth of the coalition against Iraq, the defeat of Saddam Hussein required arduous international diplomacy, more than a dozen U.N. resolutions, worldwide economic sanctions, 750,000 troops, and seven months from start to finish—a far cry from the time, little more than a century earlier, when a single day of shelling from British warships could compel the surrender of a sultan.*

Second, the war defined the new global threat in the post–Cold War era. Modern arms, especially weapons of mass destruction, were capable of converting small countries into major military threats; the lifting of restraints imposed by the Cold War enabled former surrogates to become adversaries. Worldwide, the spread of unconventional weapons made civilian populations far from the frontlines more vulnerable to large-scale attack than ever before.

---

*The British attack in 1896 was against Sultan Khalid, who had seized the throne in Zanzibar, at the time a British protectorate.

Third, the war demonstrated that the democratic revolution unleashed in the 1980s was still painfully far from complete in many corners of the globe. Although the traumatic conflict unleashed new demands for empowerment and accountability in the world's least democratic region, the Middle East was still dominated by one-man, one-party or one-family rule; the political spectrum was still defined by socialist dictatorships on one end and right-wing monarchies on the other. Both forms of governance appeared increasingly unstable. In both socialist Iraq and the sheikhdom of Kuwait, the war exposed the incompetence of old leaders and emboldened growing numbers of citizens to challenge their right to rule—but with limited initial success.

Fourth, the war's complex by-products—the plight of refugees and migrant labor from dozens of countries, hostage traumas for dozens more, and the global economic overspill—revealed the depth of the world's interdependence and its vulnerability as well. From Poland to Peru, the war was felt everywhere, and not only because of the surging price of oil. So was the conflict's messy aftermath, from the environmental disasters to the explosive pressures on multinational or multireligious states, like Iraq and Kuwait. The bottom line was that regional crises could no longer be isolated—or ignored.

In the end, the allied triumph produced not peace but, rather, new variants of political, economic and social pressures. And with their emergence, the President's description of a bright new era lost its utopian gloss; his promise of universal freedom and human rights gave way to a narrower goal of simply averting new disasters. "The Cold War's end didn't deliver us into an era of perpetual peace," Bush acknowledged in a speech to U.S. military officers five weeks after his victory address. "As old threats recede, new threats emerge. The quest for the new world order is in part a challenge to keep the danger of disorder at bay."

From then on, Bush became far more circumspect about using the phrase he had once triumphantly introduced to describe global changes. Indeed, he even stopped referring to "the new world order" in foreign policy speeches.

. . .

The dawn of the nuclear age in the 1940s, Albert Einstein reflected, "changed everything save our modes of thinking." The 1990s, too, demand a fundamental change in thinking to understand the possibilities, the promise and the peril of a new era.

The international debate over a "new world order" has been confusing and inconclusive, in part because it has focused on the wrong part of the slogan—its "newness." In its most expansive versions, the "new world order" has been employed to mean not only a new balance of power to establish a new peace but also, implicitly, new democracies, new free-market economies, new freedoms of speech and worship, and new development, technology and progress.

The proclamation of a "new world order" has been seized on by different people to mean different things, according to their disparate problems and priorities. In Third World countries, the poor have widely viewed new economic freedoms as promising almost instant and automatic new prosperity. In many multiethnic states, restive minorities have interpreted new political rights as justification for breaking away. In the United States and the West, foreign policy strategists proclaimed the new balance of power a foundation for unilateral American leadership or some form of shared domination by the industrial democracies.

Most of the principles underlying the idea of a new world order, however, were not all that new. Most, in fact, were merely extensions of what the Modern Age was all about: the precepts of the Enlightenment. What was new, however, was the unprecedented proposition of applying those Enlightenment ideas universally—and the resulting challenge of redefining the very concept of "order."

For most of history, the task of imposing order on an unruly world was left to a few dominant powers, from Sargon of Mesopotamia in the twenty-fourth century B.C., through the empires of Asia and Europe, to the Cold War powers forty-three centuries later. For all that time, the idea of order was traditionally hierarchical and usually absolute. In the Middle Ages, the "world order" was a natural ladder in which men and women knew (or were supposed to know) their places before God and king. In the Modern Age, the idea of order became secular, rational and scientific—but remained hierarchical and largely absolute. The world's course was directed by European colonial powers and then the superpowers—in politics and alliances, in economics and development, in social trends and culture, and in war.

But on the eve of the twentieth-first century, a new idea of order is evolving. In an era of diffused and devolving power, its cornerstone is not dominance but global pluralism. Its major aims are empowerment and accountability—both within and among societies.

The new structure of order is less and less hierarchical; it recognizes the legitimacy and rights of both individuals and nations at the bottom as well as the top of the ladder. As a result, the power to direct the world's course is no longer dominated by a few; it is gradually being dispersed among the world's many players. In a sense, the new idea of order is the extension of democratic pluralism on a global scale.

And far from being absolute, the new concept of order instead opens the way for diversity. It no longer views all societies as heading toward a single, universal model—whether the "American way" or a communist ideal or any other—but toward a new profusion of different models. It embraces the Modern Age's ideals of empowerment, reason and progress, but it also adapts them to vastly different cultures.

The shifting concept of order represents the logical fruition of the Enlightenment; in principle, it promises opportunity for all. Some of its changes have already revolutionized aspects of life: men sharing everything from the vote and housework to equal employment with women; regimes of both the left and the right voluntarily ceding rule to elected civilians; whites acknowledging power has to be shared with minorities. And the new order is only beginning to take root.

Yet, while its themes are hardly unfamiliar, the transition to a new era has also already proven to be disorienting, even disquieting. Many traditional mechanisms of control are disappearing, creating uncertainty and the climate of a Darwinian free-for-all. Divergent courses among the newly empowered have created new tensions, rather than a new peace. And while expectations have reached an unprecedented high, finite resources almost surely mean many will be disappointed—and may turn against the new order.

One of the paradoxes of democracy is that it requires societies to accept a measure of instability and uncertainty—uncertainty as to who will lead, for how long, and with what policies—in exchange for a promise of stability in the long run. Just as democracy means uncertainty, any "order" that works in a world of global pluralism will also include a measure of seeming disorder. The challenge will be adapting, locally and globally, to the diversity and paradoxes of a different order.

"We have to learn how to disagree," advised Egypt's Tahseen Basher, "and yet make that disagreement creative—make the disagreement a precursor of working together."

"We need a strategic concept, and we aren't hearing one," complained Paul H. Nitze in the fall of 1990. The white-haired octogenarian, a foreign-affairs mandarin who helped draft the Truman Administration's strategies for the Cold War, echoed a complaint voiced by many thinkers as they surveyed the opening of the new era.

"We are looking for something new—organization, structure, concept," puzzled Valéry Giscard d'Estaing. "What is strange is that, at the moment, there is no thinker who is suggesting a possible course." Reflected Egypt's Basher, "There is a missing element in the Western world today—leadership. But it's not only the Western world. . . . We face a global challenge of uncertainty, and every society—rich and poor, Christian, Jewish, Buddhist, Muslim—is failing to provide an answer."

So far, the world's most powerful countries have failed to draw up anything resembling a global agenda. The United States stepped in quickly to assume leadership after Iraq's invasion of Kuwait, and other countries rallied to the fight. But Washington subsequently assumed no dynamic role in designing a new global security structure or addressing the economic and social crises of the developing world and the new democracies. Nor have the United States, the European Community and Japan worked together effectively on any of the new flashpoints. Most of their actions were reactive to crises, not proactive in shaping a new world.

After two years of tumultuous change, however, the issues requiring decisive action were clearly visible by 1991. Among them:

POWER. Without the East-West balance imposed by the Cold War, the world's powers, large and small, will need to devise new structures to stabilize an unsettled international system. If collective security is the answer, then the United States and its allies must decide whether to cede real power to the United Nations or try to impose a new world order with old-world power.

The experience during the Gulf crisis was inconclusive. The allies used the U.N. Security Council only when it suited their purposes. During the war, they made their own calls; after the war, they did little to strengthen the authority of the U.N. Security Council or other potential mechanisms of collective security. Whether in rescuing Kurdish refugees or in mediating a civil war in Ethiopia, they instead usually acted unilaterally or sought U.N. approval only afterwards.

The United States, especially, must define its role—whether to seek a position of unilateral leadership, support a more genuinely collective security structure or retreat toward isolationism. Each course carries a cost. Unilateral leadership would require Americans to continue bearing a disproportionate burden in the defense of others. Collective security would require giving up autonomy in decision making. And isolationism could mean no consideration of U.S. interests in the outcome.

NATIONS. As ethnic and national passions threaten to divide existing states or redraw their borders, the world community must decide whether to defend countries against disintegration or to support separatist movements. Either choice will have a major impact on the roster of nations: Backing separatists could spawn dozens of small new countries and set precedents for other states made up of multiple nations. But defending the territorial integrity of troubled nation-states could produce a plethora of nasty new civil wars.

So far, the United States and its allies have generally defended existing borders—notwithstanding their rhetorical commitment to the self-determination of nations. The West supported the territorial integrity of Iraq despite Kurdish demands for autonomy and of Yugoslavia despite moves toward division. Even in the case of the three Baltic States, which the United States formally recognized as independent, the Bush Administration endorsed Gorbachev's initial go-slow policy in 1990 and 1991.

DEMOCRACY. After decades of lip service to the idea that the West should promote democracy abroad, Americans and their allies will have to struggle with a costlier and more complicated problem: helping new democracies succeed, or even just survive. The developed world, however, does not have the resources to float every aspiring democracy indefinitely.

The choices will be difficult throughout the 1990s, as demonstrated by the West's debate over aid for Russia after Moscow's democratic revolution of 1991. The first problem is convincing taxpayers in wealthy countries to underwrite fledgling democracies—particularly U.S. taxpayers, who pay less for foreign aid than the citizens of any other major industrial country.[2] The second is devising standards to determine which new democracies should receive help: those with the best records of political reform, those most devoted to free-market capitalism, or those with the greatest sentimental appeal. Some U.S. officials argued in 1991 that Russia was too big to help, others that it was too big to ignore. The worst alternative would be to perpetuate the status quo, in which small amounts of aid barely provide new democracies enough money to pay off their debts and leave little to help convert their failed economies into productive systems.

Developed countries will also need to decide whether their support should extend to unfamiliar forms of democracy as they develop in Africa, the Arab world and Asia. And at home, several Western democracies face a further crisis of confidence; many Americans and western Europeans view their own governments as less and less responsive. The political systems of some of the oldest democracies are in dire need of renewal.

WARFARE. As developing nations acquire ever more deadly arsenals, the world will have to deal with the growing threat of local wars that have a destructive potential once limited to the superpowers. Agreement among the "great powers" will no longer suffice to prevent wars with global repercussions.

But halting or reversing the course of arms proliferation will again mean difficult decisions—whether to push both developed and developing nations, allies and rivals, to surrender weapons and give up arms development programs, or to continue unbridled arms exports. Each course carries a cost. For the developed world, new treaties limiting or prohibiting sales could mean abandoning major domestic industries and eliminating hundreds of thousands of jobs. For the developing world, limiting arms purchases or production would create stark vulnerabilities, tempting some countries to cheat. Even if all governments signed comprehensive new arms-control treaties, implementation and verification would be more difficult and costly than for any bilateral accord.

So far, the international community has been inconsistent. The Gulf War represented the first time the superpowers jointly took on a Third World country that was equipped with weapons of mass destruction; they sealed their victory by formally prohibiting Iraq from rearming. Yet the United States and its allies were slow to even discuss treaties to disarm other Middle East nations with missiles, chemical weapons or budding nuclear capabilities. Instead, Washington moved immediately to sell up to eighteen billion dollars worth of sophisticated weaponry to five countries in the Middle East.

DEMOGRAPHY AND EPIDEMICS. As demographic imbalances and mass migrations alter the size and location of the world's population centers, the developed North will be increasingly taxed by the maladies of the developing South—its burgeoning numbers, its economic morass, and its "informal" or unregulated patterns of growth. Unemployment, disease, malnutrition and crime are already threatening to undo much of the twentieth century's progress. The problem is no longer simply how to close the gap between the North and the South but whether it will ever even be possible. Yet the old strategy of social isolationism—hiding behind the fences of visa restrictions and quarantines—cannot be sustained as economic and communications barriers come falling down.

To help the South, by giving it sufficient aid to reverse the cycles of overpopulation, poverty, famine or disease, the North would have to virtually give away billions of dollars in aid, technology and development matériel, as well as provide expertise; each would at least temporarily strain the North's own advancement. Not to help significantly, however, almost ensures that major parts of the world will be consigned to high death tolls, economic failure, preindustrial or even primitive lifestyles— and bitterness that could, in turn, threaten parts or all of the North.

The new world order will not take shape immediately. The transition from the Middle Ages to the Modern Era, a period of dazzling achievement and terrible wars which became known as the Renaissance, lasted more than two centuries. The next major transition was the age of revolutions, which began in 1776 and lasted three-quarters of a century; it produced modern democracy, the first wave of industrial development and another spate of wars. History is clearly speeding up, but the current transition could last well into the twenty-first century.

The new world will not take shape by accident. Navigating the transition will require not only deliberate direction but leadership of a high order. The policy decisions and steps taken to diffuse these flashpoints will be the beginning. How quickly and decisively they are made may well determine how long the transition lasts—and how soon the world settles into a new era.

Acknowledgments

Rarely have two people owed so much to so many. Hundreds of people on six continents generously shared their time and experience to help us understand the dimensions of change in the transition to a new era. Some were prominent, others unknown. They spanned the spectrum—from communists to neo-Nazis, from Islamists to environmentalists. Among them were chiefs of state, cabinet ministers, members of parliaments and members of political opposition groups; military commanders, militia chieftains and intelligence analysts; philosophers, political theorists and historians; economists, agronomists and ecologists; sociologists, psychologists and clergymen; academics and writers; physicians, human-rights activists and pollsters; city planners and strategic thinkers; street people and squatters. With both enthusiasm and thoughtful deliberation, all worked with us to identify the issues and trends that will shape our common future. This book echoes their reflections, knowledge and wisdom. Although we were able to quote only a few, all have our deepest appreciation.

Several specialists served as advisers throughout, from the embryonic ideas through our travels to the book's conclusion, and deserve very special note. We particularly thank Francisco Sagasti, the World Bank strategic planner, who was our constant guide to the future and who steered us in the right direction whenever we went astray. Augustus Richard Norton of the International Peace Academy generously shared his broad perspective on world trends and combed through the manuscript for us. From the *Los Angeles Times* Washington bureau, Richard T. Cooper, our professional shoulder and sounding board, anguished with us at every turn and helped bring focus to sprawling thoughts and diverse trends. We also owe special thanks to Brent Scowcroft, whose reflections set us off on the road for a year.

Several others read through parts or all of the manuscript and shared their expertise. From the Carnegie Endowment for International Peace, James Clad, Geoffrey Kemp and Pauline Baker offered us overviews on Asia, the Middle East and Africa and helped extrapolate the wider common denominators from regional trends; Leonard Spector guided us on arms proliferation; Doris Meissner counseled us on trends in world migrations. At the Population Crisis Committee, Sally Ethelston was instrumental in helping us understand the dimensions of "the human wave." John Broder of the *Los Angeles Times* offered valuable editorial advice. We are grateful to each for the time and energy they shared.

Robin Wright also owes an enormous debt to the John D. and Catherine T. MacArthur Foundation for its longstanding encouragement and financial support of her independent research. Ruth Adams, George Lopez and Kate Early have been constantly supportive and helpful in guiding her toward broader horizons.

Our greatest debt is to the editors of the *Los Angeles Times.* Editor Shelby Coffey III encouraged us to travel the world during a pivotal year to explore the depth and breadth of global changes; his vision and direction were instrumental throughout the process. Managing editor George Cotliar, national editor Norman C. Miller and Washington bureau chief Jack Nelson enthusiastically urged us on and offered assistance and advice as the project took shape. We relied heavily on the research skills of intern Fabienne Furminieux and librarians Aleta Embrey, Caleb Gessesse and Pat Welch; they collected an avalanche of facts, from obscure historical detail to sweeping statistics, and responded cheerfully to the oddest of requests.

We also owe special thanks to our agents, Esther Newberg and Rafe Sagalyn, and to editor Vicky Wilson at Alfred A. Knopf for believing in the product of our adventures.

We could not have done any of it, however, without the tolerance, love and encouragement of our families. Phyllis Wright and Paula Copeland McManus were constant sources of support and inspiration. Johanna, Rosemary and Rachelle McManus accepted a year of fatherless weekends with understanding beyond their years. They all deserve more thanks than we can ever return.

Among others who helped:

In Argentina: President Raul Alfonsin, Roberto Garcia Moritan, Domingo Cavallo, Mario Brodersohn, Oscar Landi, Dante Caputo, Atilio Boron, Armando Cavalieri, Estebal Lijalad, Arturo O'Connell, Raul Carignano, Martin Granovsky and Jim Smith.

In Czechoslovakia: Daniel Kroupa, Jan Klacek, Michal Illner, Jaroslav Jirasek, Slavo Moric, Jiri Amort, Alojz Neustadt, Adolf Suk, Peter Zajac, Pavol Fric, Marianna Oracova, Lubica Habova, Frantisek Novosad, Tana Sedova, Alexander Varga, Pavel Smutny and Iva Drapalova.

In Egypt: Saad Eddin Ibrahim, Maamoun Hodeibi, Mona Makram Ebeid, Essam Montasser, Mustafa Mahmoud, Tahseen Basher, Gehad Auda, Hussein Mameesh, Ahmed Fakhr, Mohammed Shaalan, Salah Eddin Hafez, Caryle Murphy and Kim Murphy.

In France: President Valéry Giscard d'Estaing, Rone Tempest, Emmanuel Todd and Sarah White.

In Germany: Baerbel Bohley, Hans Peter Drueger, Helga Koenigsdorf, Luise Schramm, Manfried Goertemaker, Helmut Wagner, Hans Joachim Rockstroh, Vera Wollenberger, Hans Zimmerman, Hans-Joachim Willerding, Juri Culjat, Gottfried Kuessel, Tyler Marshall and Jeff Hurd.

In India: Lae Krishan Advani, G. Q. Allaqaband, P. R. Chari, George Fernandez, Mark Fineman, S. Gopal, Abdul Ahad Guru, Nasruddin ul-Islam, Ashis Nandy, K. Subrahmanyam and Bhabani Sen Gupta.

In Israel and the occupied territories: Shimon Peres, Teddy Kollek, Ezer Weizman, Eliyakum Haetzni, Ehud Sprinzak, Rav Abraham Ravitz, Avier Ravitzky, Shulamit Aloni, Yair Tzaban, David Hartman, Dore Gold, Anat Kurz, Israel Stockman, Meron Benvenisti, Nota Schiller, Gershon Solomon, Ze'ev Schiff, Rachel Klein, Martin Kramer, Said Abu Ghazali, Mahdi Abdul Hadi, Ziad Abu Amr, Saleh Amera, Daoud Kuttab and Daniel Williams.

In Japan: Naohiro Amaya, Michael H. Armacost, Shusaku Endo, Yukio Honda, Sam Jameson, Hajime Karatsu, Hideaki Kase, Kanji Kawasaki, Masao Kunihiro, Hiroomi Kurisu, Yasuhiro Nakasone, Thomas Rohlen, Atsuyuki Sassa, Yoshio Satoh, Karl Schoenberger, Motoo Shiina, Josen Takahashi, Tadashi Yamamoto and Maseru Yoshitomi.

In Jordan: Adnan Abu Odeh, Marwan al Kazim, Assad Abdul Rahman, Jamal Al Shaer, Mustafa Hamarneḥ, Omar Nabulsi, Sari Nasser, Elias Salameh, Salah Abu Zaid, Munir Hamarneh, Laila Sharaf, Kamal Abu Jaber, Ibrahim Izzeddin, Jawad Al Anani, Laith Shubeilat, Ziad Abu Ghaneimeh, Taher Masri and Fahed al Fanek.

In Korea: Chi Jung Nam, Chung Jin Hong, Donald P. Gregg, Han Sung Joo, Hyun Hong Choo, Kim Ki Hwan, Kim Kyung Won, Kim Woo Choong, Lee Hong Koo, Lee Kwan, Park Yong Ji and Horace Underwood.

In Mozambique: Luis Bernardo Honwana, Firmino Mucavele, Carlos Cardoso and José Luis Macamo.

In Nepal: Daman Dhungane and Bob Drogin.

In Pakistan: Zahoor ul Haq, Iqbal Akhund, Mumtaz Bashghali, Hussain Haqqani, Mirshahid Hussain, Sahabzada Yacoub Khan, Robert B. Oakley and Riaz Ullah.

In Peru: Gustavo Gutierrez, Max Hernandez, Gustavo Gorriti, Felipe Ortiz de Zevallos, Chuck Loveridge, Luis Pasara, Miguel Vega Alvear, Enrique Zileri, Ricardo Belmont, Enrique Bernales, Sinesio Jarama, Guido Pennano, Luis Bustamante, Hernando De Soto, Diego Garcia Sayan, Veronica Bavestrello and José Gonzales.

In South Africa: Helen Suzman, Simon Baynham, Mike Hough, Tertius Myburgh, Nthatho Motlana, Jan Visser, Ronnie Bethlehem, John Dugard, Sonny Tarr, Christo Nel, Harry Oppenheimer, Hank Slack, Fatima Meer, Paul Zulu, Alex Irwin, Wilkie Kambule, Yunus Carrim, Harry Gwala, John Aitchison, Charles Talbot, Erica and John Platter, Scott Kraft, Mono Badela, Peter, Lucienne and Roland Hunter, Naas Steenkamp and Peter Magubane.

In the Soviet Union: Alexander Chubaryan, John-Thor Dahlburg, Leonid Dobrokhotov, Andrei Grachev, Alexander Gurov, Dadakhan Hassanov, Sergei Ivanov, Sergei Karaganov, Stanislas Kondrashev, Andrei Kortunov, Alexander A. Lebedev, Anatoly V. Malykhin, George Mirski, Andrei Ostroukh, Alexei Pankin, Michael Parks, Nikolai Popov, Abdul Rahim Pulatov, Sergei Roshal, Mohammed Salikh, Abdul Rashid Sharipov, Yuri Shchekochikhin, Vyacheslav N. Shostakovsky, Andrei Shumaikhin, Vladimir Tikhonov, Valeri Tishkov, Nikolai Travkin, Alexei Yablokov, Leonid Zagalsky.

In Turkey: President Turgut Ozal, Eric Rouleau, Emre Kongar, Atilla Uras, John Ong, Emile Sandalci, Fatma Girik, Murat Belge, Erol Kazanci, Ismat Ozel, Binnaz Toprak, Kaya Toperi, Hugh Pope and Erol Kazanci.

In the United States: Ivo Banac, Prince Bandar bin Sultan, Barry P. Bosworth, Seth Carus, Anthony Cordesman, Harvey Cox, Gary Crocker, William J. Crowe, Douglas Engelbart, Paul Ehrlich, Mark Falcoff, Gary Foster, Francis Fukuyama, Rachid Ghannouchi, Paul Goble, Richard Haass, Elisa Harris, Bruce Hoffman, Abid Hussain, Douglas Jehl, Brian Jenkins, Andrzej Kapiszewski, Firuz Kazemzadeh, Robert M. Kimmitt, Mark Lowenthal, Harald Malmgren, Michael Mandelbaum, Phebe Marr, Joseph A. Massey, Robert E. McGinn, Michael Merson, George Mitchell, Jim Moody, Paul H. Nitze, Ronald Ostrow, William B. Quandt, Condoleezza Rice, Eric Rodenberg, Dennis B. Ross, Justin Rudelson, Jeffrey Sachs, Gary Samore, George P. Shultz, Helmut Sonnenfeldt, Robert C. Toth, Michael Vlahos, Alan Zezatarsky, Hania Zlotnick, and Robert B. Zoellick.

In Yugoslavia: President Franjo Tudjman, Vladimir Seks, Aleksandar Prlja, Ibrahim Rugova, Veton Surroi, Vjekoslav Krsnik, Davor Ivankovic, Bozo Kovacevic, Zvonko Letrovic, Mladen Plese, Predrag Simic, Slaven Letica, Zvone Dragan, Bozo Mardendic, Tomislav Popovic, Svetozar Stojanovic, Bozivar Franges, Milovan Djilas, Slaven Letica and Milovan Sibl.

In Zimbabwe: Hasu Patel, Jonathan Moyo, John Robertson, Tony Taberer, MacLeod Chitiyo, Ariston Chambati, Mike Bourdillon, Karin Prendergast and Ian Mills.

Notes

Prologue

1. "After 45/85: A Look at the Future," *ABC News* "Nightline," September 18, 1985.

Reshaping World Power

1. Central Intelligence Agency, Report to Joint Economic Committee, U.S. Congress, May 16, 1991.
2. As quoted in Bernard Brodie, *War and Politics* (New York: Macmillan, 1973), p. 377. John Lewis Gaddis pointed out that the diffusion of power produced a diffusion of threats; see his "Toward the Post–Cold War World," *Foreign Affairs*, Spring 1991, pp. 102–22.
3. John Mueller, *Retreat from Doomsday: The Obsolescence of Major War* (New York: Basic Books, 1990), and Bruce M. Russett, "The Real Decline in Nuclear Hegemony," in Ernst-Otto Czempiel and James N. Rosenau, eds., *Global Changes and Theoretical Challenges: Approaches to World Politics for the 1990s* (Lexington, Mass.: Lexington Books, 1989).
4. International Institute for Strategic Studies, *The Military Balance 1990–1991* (London: Brassey's, 1990).
5. Investor Responsibility Research Center, *The Impact of Sanctions on South Africa* (Washington, 1990), executive summary, p. 3. See also Steven Mufson, "South Africa," *Foreign Affairs*, America and the World 1990/91, p. 123.
6. Robert B. Reich, *The Work of Nations* (New York: Alfred A. Knopf, 1991), p. 138; Kenichi Ohmae, *The Borderless World* (New York: Harper Business, 1990), p. 157.
7. The phenomenon of economic vulnerability was not new in American history. British capital funded much of the industrial development of the United States

in the nineteenth century. But the new foreign capital included an increasing proportion of direct investment. For a counterargument that interdependence is being overrated, see Janice E. Thomson and Stephen D. Krasner, "Global Transactions and the Consolidation of Sovereignty," in Ernst-Otto Czempiel and James N. Rosenau, eds., *Global Changes and Theoretical Challenges* (Lexington, Mass.: Lexington Books, 1990).

8. Mitterrand television interview, March 25, 1990.

9. *Statesman's Yearbook*, 1981–82 and 1990–91. In 1978, the U.S. GDP per capita was $9,700 and Mexico's was $1,290. In 1988, the U.S. GDP per capita was $19,780 and Mexico's was $1,820. (Figures in current dollars.)

10. United Nations, "Global Outlook 2000," p. 11. Figures are in constant 1980 dollars.

11. *The Economist*, March 9, 1991, p. 15.

12. *Los Angeles Times*, March 3, 1991.

13. "U.S. Policy Toward South Asia," speech to the Asia Society, Washington, D.C., January 11, 1990.

14. Japan was a significant regional power from at least 1905, but lacked the global reach she boasts today.

15. Interview with U.S. trade official, November 1990. The problem was that Japanese regulations allowed Tokyo firms to copy any foreign recording made before 1978 without paying royalties. U.S. officials said Yeutter would have pressed for a new Japanese copyright regulation, even without the request from Sony, to benefit all U.S. copyright holders. The Japanese government agreed to change the law in 1991. Ironically, Sony quickly lost interest in the issue because its lawyers discovered that its American copyrights would be protected as soon as CBS formally licensed them to Sony. In other words, once Sony discovered that it no longer needed U.S. government help, it reverted to its original identity as a Japanese firm.

16. Czempiel and Rosenau, p. 251, citing Steven Greenhouse, "Chip Maker without a Country," *The New York Times*, August 1, 1988.

17. Louis Uchitelle, "U.S. Businesses Loosen Link to Mother Country," *The New York Times*, May 21, 1989.

18. See Daniel Yergin, *The Prize* (New York: Simon & Schuster, 1991), p. 718. 1990 production figures are from U.S. Department of Energy, *Monthly Energy Review*, March 1991. The 1990 figure includes Soviet production, now on the world market.

19. Akio Morita, Speech to the Trilateral Commission, Washington, D.C., April 17, 1990.

20. Lee Iacocca, "O.K., O.K., Call Me a Protectionist," *The New York Times*, February 10, 1991.

21. Michael Vlahos, "Thinking About World Change" (Department of State, Center for the Study of Foreign Affairs, 1990), p. 100.

22. Evelyn Richards and T. R. Reid, "U.S. Protests Japan's Overtures to Computer Researchers," *The Washington Post*, May 21, 1991.

23. Sumiko Iwao, "Recent Changes in Japanese Attitudes," in Alan D. Romberg and Tadashi Yamamoto, eds., *Same Bed, Different Dreams: America and Japan—Societies in Transition* (New York: Council on Foreign Relations, 1990), p. 62.

24. See, for example, Michael Oreskes, "Poll Detects Erosion of Positive Attitudes Toward Japan," *The New York Times*, February 6, 1990.

25. Fred Hiatt, "Marine General: U.S. Troops Must Stay in Japan," *Washington Post*, March 27, 1990.

26. Jim Mann, "Testing Limits of New Global Federalism," *Los Angeles Times*, November 25, 1990. Animur Rahman Shams-ud-Doha is quoted in Barbara Crossette, "Shocks from Kuwait hit the Third World," *The New York Times*, September 9, 1990.

The Rise of Nations

1. Peter F. Drucker, *The New Realities* (New York: Harper and Row, 1989), pp. 10–17.

2. Mary Battiata, "Separatist Slovaks Becoming More Vocal in 'Family Feud' with Czechs," *The Washington Post*, March 19, 1991; John Tagliabue, "Slovak Roots: Here, There, and All Over," *The New York Times*, March 19, 1991.

3. "Rally for Rama," *The Economist*, April 13, 1991, p. 36.

Democracy and Its Discontents

1. Elizabeth Shogren, "Hated KGB Symbol Torn Down by Crowd," *Los Angeles Times*, August 23, 1991; Celestine Bohlen, "Moscow Crowds Vent Anger on Communists," *The New York Times*, August 23, 1991; Associated Press, August 24, 1991; John-Thor Dahlburg, "Yeltsin's Warnings Grow Dire," *Los Angelos Times*, February 7, 1992.

2. Václav Havel, "New Year's Message," *The New York Review of Books*, March 7, 1991.

3. On the global crisis of legitimacy, see James N. Rosenau, *Turbulence in World Politics* (Princeton, N.J.: Princeton University Press, 1990), especially pp. 333–415, and Augustus R. Norton, "The Security Legacy of the 1980s in the Third World," in Thomas G. Weiss and Meryl A. Kessler, eds., *Third World Security in the Post–Cold War Era* (Boulder, Colo.: Lynne Rienner Publishers, 1991).

4. Drawn principally from Freedom House, *Freedom around the World, 1992* (New York: Freedom House, 1992).

5. As cited in Joshua Muravchik, "New Dominoes for Democracy," *The American Enterprise,* January/February 1991, p. 72.

6. In 1991, Freedom House counted sixty-five free countries, fifty "partly free," and fifty "not free." Freedom House, *Freedom Around the World, 1992.*

7. Francis Fukuyama, "The End of History?" *The National Interest,* Summer 1989, pp. 3–18.

8. Bob Drogin, "Democracy Takes Hold in Himalayan Kingdom," *Los Angeles Times,* August 5, 1990.

9. Stephen Engelberg, "Old Political Rifts Emerge in Poland Now That the Communists Are Out," *The New York Times,* June 30, 1990.

10. Gallup Poll, Associated Press, January 28, 1992.

11. Li Xianglu, "Regional Pluralism: China's Only Hope," *New Perspectives Quarterly,* Spring 1990, pp. 34–5.

12. "Pakistan: Sharif's sharia," *The Economist,* April 20, 1991, p. 33.

13. National Public Radio, May 5, 1991.

14. David Lamb, "Raising the Blood Stakes in a Dangerous Neighborhood," *Los Angeles Times,* November 25, 1990.

15. Times Mirror poll cited in Robert C. Toth, "Desire for Strong Leader Clashes with Support for Democracy," *Los Angeles Times,* August 20, 1991.

16. Alexander I. Solzhenitsyn, "Excerpts from Solzhenitsyn Article," *The New York Times,* September 19, 1990.

17. Rudolf Bahro, "Theology Not Ecology," *New Perspectives Quarterly,* Spring 1989, p. 38.

18. On the roots of political extremism in Europe, see Emmanuel Todd, *L'Invention de l'Europe* (Paris: Seuil, 1990), pp. 483–91.

19. Allan Bloom, "Response to Fukuyama," *The National Interest,* Summer 1989, pp. 19–21.

20. Times Mirror Center for People and the Press, "The People, the Press and Politics, 1990," Washington, D.C., September 19, 1990.

21. Gianni de Michelis, "From Eurosclerosis to Europhoria," *New Perspectives Quarterly,* Spring 1990, pp. 12–14.

22. "What Chernobyl Did: Not Just a Nuclear Explosion," *The Economist,* April 27, 1991, p. 20 A. Soviet poll cited in *The Economist,* June 23, 1990, pp. 41–2, found that people named issues of major concern in the following percentages: pollution 75, crime 72, food supplies 69.

23. Kevin Phillips, *The Politics of Rich and Poor* (New York: Random House, 1990), p. 221.

24. E. J. Dionne, Jr., *Why Americans Hate Politics* (New York: Simon & Schuster, 1991), p. 344.

25. William Claiborne, "Socialist Democrats Installed in Ontario," *The Washington Post,* October 2, 1990.

Empowering the People

1. Vijay Joshi of the Associated Press, "Actors, Kings, A Prostitute: Exotic Candidate List," May 18, 1991.
2. Peter F. Drucker, *The New Realities* (New York: Harper and Row, 1989), pp. 76–80, 99–105.
3. Steve Coll, "The Mothers Who Won't Disappear: In Sri Lanka, a Maternal Cry Against the Death Squads," *The Washington Post,* March 3, 1991.
4. James Brooke, "For Everyone to See, Governors' Dirty Laundry," *The New York Times,* March 15, 1991.
5. Reuters, "Peasant Militia in Peru Kills 8 Leftist Rebels," *The New York Times,* February 15, 1990.
6. Blaine Harden, "Bulgarian Activists in Tent City of the Streets Demonstrate Power," *The Washington Post,* July 21, 1990; "Bulgarian Opposition Leader Elected President; Political Impasse Ends," Facts on File, August 3, 1990; Associated Press, "Bulgarian President Appeals to Political Parties," August 5, 1990.
7. David Remnick, "Coal Strikes Are Class War Marx Did Not Foresee," *The Washington Post.* July 27, 1989.
8. James F. Smith, "Outsiders: New Latin Leaders," *Los Angeles Times,* May 25, 1990.
9. Tina Rosenberg, "Anti-Politics in the Andes," *The Washington Post,* "Outlook" section, April 22, 1990.
10. Michael Parks, "Ex-Agent Leads Fight Against Powerful KGB," *Los Angeles Times,* July 23, 1990.
11. Jean-Bertrand Aristide, "Disobey the Rules" *The New York Times,* December 12, 1990.
12. Lee Hockstader, "Restless Guatemalans Lured by Strongman," *The Washington Post,* July 23, 1990.

Broadening Battlefields

1. Stockholm International Peace Research Institute (SIPRI), *Yearbook 1990* (New York: Oxford University Press, 1990), p. 229.
2. Ibid., p. 212.
3. Ibid., pp. 220–1; and interviews.
4. John Laffin, *The World in Conflict* (New York: Pergamon Press, 1989), p. viii.
5. From the Rand Corporation's terrorism data base collated by researcher Karen Gardela.
6. Ibid.
7. Ibid.
8. Ruth Leger Sivard, *World Military and Social Expenditures 1989* (Washington, D.C.: World Priorities, 1989), pp. 22–3.

9. SIPRI, *Yearbook*, p. 371.

10. International Institute for Strategic Studies, *Strategic Survey, 1989–90* (London: Brassey's, 1990).

11. Congressional Research Service, "Missile Proliferation Survey of Emerging Missile Forces," February 9, 1989.

12. Interviews with U.S. intelligence and chemical weapons experts, ranking Gulf officials and Israeli military analysts, September 1989 to October 1990.

13. Congressional Research Service.

14. Ibid.

15. Interview with Dr. Simon Baynham, military specialist at the Africa Institute in Pretoria, March 1990.

16. James Adams, "Arms and the Salesman" *The Washington Post* "Outlook" section, January 27, 1991.

17. Augustus Richard Norton, "The Security Legacy of the 1980s in the Third World," in Weiss and Kessler, eds., *Third World Security in the Post–Cold War Era* (Boulder, Colo.: Lynne Rienner Publishers, 1991).

18. Francis X. Clines, "Strife in Georgia Republic Reveals Danger in New Soviet Separatism," *The New York Times*, March 24, 1991; Michael Dobbs, "Nationalists, Minority Battle in Soviet Georgia," *The Washington Post*, March 21, 1991.

19. Rand Data Base.

20. Ibid.

21. Interview with Bruce Hoffman, Rand Corporation, October, 1990.

22. Ibid.

23. Rand Data Base.

24. Ibid.

25. James Brooke, "Colombia's Tortured City: Now It's Kidnappings," *The New York Times*, January 9, 1991.

26. "Colombia Roiled by Gang Battles," *The New York Times*, March 19, 1991.

27. Reuters, "Hungry Rio Slum Dwellers Fight over Ransom Paid in Food," March 25, 1991.

The Human Wave

1. Sharif Imam-Jomeh, "Iranians Cram Stadium for Seats on 'Flight to Happiness,'" Reuters, March 26, 1991.

2. Interview with Doris Meissner, former commissioner of U.S. Immigration and Naturalization, now a senior associate at the Carnegie Endowment for International Peace, March 26, 1991.

3. Sharon L. Camp, *Cities: Life in the World's 100 Largest Metropolitan Areas* (Washington, D.C.: Population Crisis Committee, 1990).

4. United Nations, "Urbanisation and Human Development," in *Human Development Report 1989–90* (New York: United Nations Development Programme, 1990), p. 85.

5. World Resources Institute, *World Resources 1990–91*, (Washington, D.C., 1990).

6. International Institute for Strategic Studies, *Stategic Survey, 1989–90* (London: Brassey's, 1990), p. 216.

7. 1990 United States Census.

8. Jay Mathews, "UCLA Freshman Class Reflects New Ethnic Mix: Students of Asian Descent Outnumber Whites," *The Washington Post*, March 5, 1991.

9. Interview with David Simcox, director of the Center for Immigration Studies in Washington, October 1990.

10. United Nations, "Choices for the New Century" in *The State of the World Population 1990* (New York: United Nations Fund for Population Activities, 1990), p. 1.

11. Camp.

12. Emma Robson, "The Perils of Poverty in Urban Pakistan," in *The Urban Challenge 1990* (New York: United Nations Development Programme, 1990).

13. "Immigration Waiting for the Next Wave," *The Economist*, March 16, 1991, p. 42.

14. Camp, *Cities*.

15. Ibid.

16. United Nations, *Human Development Report*.

17. World Resources Institute, *World Resources 1990–91*, and Camp *Cities*.

18. Robert Livernash, "Human Settlements," in *World Resources 1990–91*, p. 74.

19. Interview with Sonny Tarr of Johannesburg's Small Business Development Corporation, March 1990.

20. Camp, *Cities*.

21. Estimate from the U.S. Department of State.

22. Interviews with American and European envoys in Lima, February 1990.

23. Paul Lewis, "As Soviet Borders Open, the West Braces for an Economic Exodus," *The New York Times*, February 10, 1991.

24. Ibid.

25. Ehud Sprinzak, "Can Israel Survive Another Century?" Lecture at Georgetown University, April 2, 1991.

26. Robin Wright, "Black Scars, White Fears," *Los Angeles Times Magazine*, August 19, 1990.

27. Marc Fisher, "Bonn May Limit Immigration to 1,000 Soviet Jews," *The Washington Post*, December 15, 1990.

28. United Nations, *The State of the World Population 1990*.

29. Sharon L. Camp, ed., "Population Pressures: Threat to Democracy" (New York: Population Crisis Committee, 1990), cover page.

Global Plagues

1. Reuters, "Excerpts from the New Leader's Remarks: 'Law and Order,'" *The New York Times*, August 20, 1991.
2. United Nations, "Crime Prevention and Criminal Justice in the Context of Development: Third United Nations Survey of Crime Trends, Operations of Criminal Justice Systems and Crime Prevention Strategies," July 27, 1990.
3. Soviet Institute of Sociology Poll, June 1990, Izvestia, cited in Jamestown Foundation *Report* (Winter 1990–91). Moscow News poll: Francis X. Clines, "There's a Crime Wave, or a Perception Wave, in the Soviet Union," *The New York Times*, September 17, 1989.
4. Masha Hamilton, "Crime in the Era of Glasnost," *Los Angeles Times*, October 13, 1989.
5. United Nations, "Crime Prevention and Criminal Justice."
6. Reuters, November 22, 1990.
7. Reuters, October 11, 1990.
8. U.S. Department of State, *International Narcotics Control Strategy Report*, March 1, 1990, p. 203.
9. UPI, March 29, 1990.
10. James Q. Wilson and John J. De Iulio Jr., "Crackdown," *The New Republic*, July 10, 1989, pp. 21–5.
11. Mark Platte, "City Avoids Record Year for Homicides," *Los Angeles Times*, San Diego County edition, January 2, 1991.
12. Hugh O'Shaughnessy, "Peru's Cholera Epidemic Begins to Spread," *The Observer* (London), May 5, 1991.

Conclusion

1. David Lamb, "Raising the Blood Stakes in a Dangerous Neighborhood," *Los Angeles Times*, November 25, 1990.
2. Organization of Economic Cooperation and Development estimates cited in Shafiqul Islam, ed., *Yen for Development* (New York: Council on Foreign Relations, 1991), p. 45. According to the OECD, in 1989 the United States devoted 0.15 percent of its gross national product to foreign aid, less than half the share contributed by Japan (0.32 percent) or West Germany (0.41 percent) and one-fifth that of France (0.78 percent).

Index

About the Authors

Robin Wright and Doyle McManus have reported from more than seventy countries for major newspapers, and between them they have covered fourteen wars. Wright has been nominated for five Pulitzer Prizes, and received the 1989 National Magazine Award for her reportage on Iran for *The New Yorker* and the 1976 Overseas Press Club Award. She has written two books on the Middle East: *Sacred Rage: The Wrath of Militant Islam* and *In the Name of God: The Khomeini Decade.*

McManus has won several awards for his writing on foreign policy and was part of a team nominated for the Pulitzer Prize in 1980. He is the author with Jane Mayer of the bestseller *Landslide: The Unmaking of the President, 1984–1988.*